IDEOLOGY & FICTION

RESISTING
NOVELS

LENNARD J. DAVIS

Resisting Novels

Resisting
Novels

———

IDEOLOGY AND FICTION

Lennard J. Davis

METHUEN
New York and London

First published in 1987 by
Methuen, Inc.
29 West 35th Street, New York NY 10001

Published in Great Britain by
Methuen & Co. Ltd.
11 New Fetter Lane, London EC4P 4EE

© 1987 Lennard J. Davis
Photoset by Rowland Phototypesetting Ltd
Bury St Edmunds, Suffolk
Printed in Great Britain
by Richard Clay Ltd,
Bungay, Suffolk

Library of Congress Cataloging in Publication Data

Davis, Lennard J., 1949—
Resisting novels.

Bibliography: p.
Includes index.
1. Fiction. I. Title.
PN3353.D38   1987   809.3   86-23547
ISBN 0-416-37820-X
ISBN 0-416-37830-7 (pbk.)

British Library Cataloguing in Publication Data

Davis, Lennard J.
Resisting novels: ideology and fiction.
1. Fiction
I. Title
808.3   PN3331

ISBN 0-416-37820-X
ISBN 0-416-37830-7

*This book is dedicated to my late
parents – Eva and Morris Davis – who
inadvertently through their
deafness created in me the
interpreter of signs.*

Contents

Acknowledgments

_____

Many people have made this book possible. A grant from the American Council of Learned Societies enabled me to finish the project. My students at Brandeis and Columbia in both lecture classes and senior seminars are the real inspirers of this book – since it was they who provided the occasion for many of my thoughts. One particularly wonderful seminar on ideology and the novel taught at Columbia during 1983 instructed itself and made me a willing participant in many of the arguments I may simply be rehearsing here. Many other scholars fed into my arguments by talking things over with me or else asking vexatious and trenchant questions at lectures and conferences. I include in that list Natalie Zemon Davis, Richard McCoy, Paul Korshin, Fred Keener, Michael Gilmore, Leland Warren, James Thompson, Ronald Paulson, Carol Houlihan Flynn, Manny Schonhorn, Barbara Hernnstein Smith, William Epstein, Terry Eagleton, Edward Said, Susan Staves and Steven Marcus, and the anonymous reader for Methuen, among others. I want to thank Janice Price for a kind of courage and determination rare among publishers of academic books for her faith in this book from its earliest stage. Further thanks are due to Peter Mirabella, who improved the material conditions under which I wrote this book by building the physical structure that holds my computer. With a sense of technological wonder, I would like to acknowledge my debt to my computer – an Osborne 01 – whose electrical life I snatched from its manufacturers' demise and which has more than repaid its debt to me. My wife Bella Mirabella encouraged me with support, affection, and discussion. And my children Carlo and Francesca helped me by entering the world of books slowly enough for me to observe their infatuation and inevitable seduction.

1

Resisting the novel

The dutiful child of modern civilization is possessed by a fear of departing from the facts which, in the very act of perception, the dominant conventions of science, commerce, and politics – cliché-like – have already molded; his anxiety is none other than the fear of social deviation. The same conventions define the notion of linguistic and conceptual clarity which the art, literature and philosophy of the present have to satisfy.

Theodor Adorno and Max Horkheimer, *The Dialectic of Enlightenment*

As for the novelist, he is usually a dribbling liar.

D. H. Lawrence, *Reflections on the Death of a Porcupine*

I

Like many others, I am one who is enamored of fiction. My very sense of myself comes out of the pages of novels as much as it comes out of the working-class apartment in the Bronx where I attained consciousness. In that sense I am a partisan of and a fellow traveller with this literary form. My fantasies are novel fantasies. My conversations are shaped from dialogues in novels. My notions of beauty, truth, and reality peel off the pages of these works. I am the perfect prisoner of the novel. That is why I wrote this book.

I am attempting to explain and explore what novels do and have done to novel readers. Altough I am a partisan, I am also attempting to be an enemy to the pleasure of reading. Like the Greek or homeopathic concept of medicine, I want to be at once the poison and the cure.

What I am saying is that as much as we like reading novels, novels themselves have entered and changed our culture in ways that in fact may not be salutory. It is customary in university literature courses to talk about novels as triumphs of human achievement, as capsules of moral value, as the best and brightest that our society has to offer in the way of commentary on itself.

That may be. But I believe the time is approaching when we may also be allowed to detach ourselves from this rhetoric that protects literary forms and to see them as things that help the culture, or significant parts of the culture, to get by, to cope, to operate. In seeking resistance to the novel, I will be developing the idea that the novel is to culture as defenses are to individuals. Defenses make us who we are, they define us, and they are largely invisible to us – but if too powerful they also limit us, limit our freedom, and (in the extreme) make us neurotic. Novels have created or helped develop a mass neurosis. Look any day and in any place and you will see its victims, though they do not perhaps at first glance appear to be victims. Solitary people, often in the midst of hordes of strangers, sitting passive, silent, hunched almost fetally over a small, actually in ridiculously small, pack of papers. Most often their lips are still, their faces expressionless, their eyes fixed on some invisible moving point. In order to remain in this state, they must block outside stimuli, become virtually autistic – and what is it that they are doing? They are visualizing, analyzing, experiencing a fantasy not their own but which, in this autistic state, they believe in some provisional way to be true – true enough to draw conclusions, form moral opinions, and even shape their own lives to fit.

While I am clearly being facetious, I would ask you to imagine what anyone from another age who did not read novels might think of this phenomenon. Even someone as recently arrived as a Shakespearean contemporary might find such literary devotions strange and unusual. Novel reading is a relatively new phenomenon – as recently as 200 years ago some moralists and religious leaders were complaining about this developing habit. It is true that people of Shakespeare's time might well enjoy the communal experience of attending the theater or listening to a ballad singer, but only the eccentric would spend several hours a day in reading. However, now when you ride on a subway in New York City, for example, the shocking thing is that so many people are lost in fiction. When we look at that activity with new eyes, the whole idea seems rather strange. I remember sitting with my 4-year old son Carlo in a local campus cafe opposite a woman who was reading a novel by Kurt Vonnegut, I believe. Now, recall that any child of a professor of English would surely have begun to realize quite early on that people read stories. After all, I had read him quite a few to satisfy his insistent demands. After a while, Carlo asked me 'What is that lady doing?' I said that she was reading a book. In surprise Carlo came back with 'But why isn't she moving her lips?' What struck me immediately was that for the last four years my son had watched me engaged quite frequently in what must have been to him the mystic and bizarre behavior of silently contemplating an object for hours at a time and occasionally turning its pages. But between that activity and reading a story was a gap as great as that between an oral and a print culture. For my son the only reality of a story was one in which a human being spoke out loud. The social or asocial activity of novel-reading was so clearly a violation of all kinds of 'natural' behavior to him. Without placing greater emphasis on this anecdote than it deserves, I think that what frequently has been neglected in discussions of the novel as a form is the very context of reading as an historical and social phenomenon.

After all, the novel, as the first wave in the sweep of mass media and the entertainment industry, stands as an example of how large, controlled, cultural forms came to be used by large numbers of people who wished or were taught to have a different relation to reality than those who preceded them. As the first powerful, broad, and hegemonic literary form, the novel served to blur, in a way never before experienced, the distinction between illusion and reality, between fact and fiction, between symbol and what is represented.

In effect, the novel began a trend that culminated in the world described by Christopher Lasch in *The Culture of Narcissism* and *The Minimal Self* in which the self is so diminished as to make its highest priority survival. In the latter book, Lasch sees our contemporary period as one in which the goal is to get by on the bare bones of self-identity – as a 'minimal self' merely surviving. Lasch points to child-rearing practices in which parents are increasingly absent figures unable to 'protect them from the devastating impact of the adult world' (190). What results is narcissism – a condition in which people fail to make the distinction between the inner world and the outer world. This failure to distinguish between inner and outer, self and other, fact and fantasy is characteristic of our age, according to Lasch. While the novel did not bring about these conditions, Lasch does indict the rise of the mass media as a significant factor in this degeneration. Since novels are a strange combination of commodity and cognitive experience, they occupy a special role in the development of our culture. What Lasch says about commodities in general can also apply to the novel as a commodity. Noting Winnicott's observation that culture 'mediates between the inner world and the outer world', Lasch says that 'it is the intermediate realm of man-made objects, then, that threatens to disappear in societies based on mass production and mass consumption'. The novel is a particularly amphibious form, since it is both a human-made object and at the same time an object for mass consumption. It is Janus-faced in that sense, since it holds onto an earlier form related to craft and cottage industry for its creation, but it is reliant on technology and merchandizing for its distribution and effect. The effect of this Janus-like quality is that the home-made presence of the novel disguises the newer technology necessary to bring this form of homespun yarn to the reader. It is thus a duplicitous object. As Lasch continues:

> We live surrounded by man-made objects, to be sure, but they no longer serve very effectively to mediate between the inner world and the outer world . . . the world of commodities takes the form of a dream world, a fabricated environment that appeals directly to our inner fantasies but seldom reassures us that we ourselves have had a hand in its creation . . . the commodity world stands as something completely separate from the self; yet it simultaneously takes on the appearance of a mirror of the self, a dazzling array of images in which we can see anything we wish to see. (195–6)

Looking at the novel as the first rearing of the mass media's head, we can begin to understand how in the eighteenth century ideology in conjunction with human defenses began to operate. The novel presents itself as a mediator between the self and the world. As such it

4

acts in defensive ways, as I will stress later. The argument can be made that novel reading began when the authority of religion began to wane. Where religion mediated between the self and the world, now the novel took up that role. But in substituting a traditional form for one that is based on the marketplace – on merchandizing and its 'dream world' or 'fabricated environment' – the distinction between fact and fiction, self and other, inner and outer began to collapse in an entirely new way and with significant consequences. As Lasch points out:

> Reality itself is no longer real in the sense of arising from a people's shared understanding, from a shared past, and from shared values. More and more, our impressions of the world derive not from the observations we make both as individuals and as members of a wider community but from elaborate systems of communication, which spew out information, much of it unbelievable, about events of which we seldom have any direct knowledge. (133)

Again, Lasch is speaking of the fully developed media of our own time, but the incipient news/novels discourse of the late seventeenth and early eighteenth century with its pull in the direction of rapid information dispersal – whether in journalism or in fiction – was the beginning of this process. Of course, one could argue that an unmediated view of the world is impossible, so what difference would it make if we get that view from the novel or the newspaper or hearsay? This objection begs the question because the issue is precisely that different organizations of information carry with them different forms of meaning. Fictional narrative is defined by the fact that its referent is not the world but a particular sub-organization of the world pulled together under the rubric of the imaginary. Think, for example, of the meaning of the phrase 'Your spouse is having an affair' in the following presentations – novel, newspaper, hearsay, or toilet grafitti. Though the statement is only a collection of signs, it does matter terribly in what form of distribution those signs are presented to the effect and truth-value of the statement.

As I hope to show, we can no longer smugly think of the novel as the culmination of the human spirit or the height of mimetic accomplishment. It is after all a cultural phenomenon with certain overt aims and a hidden agenda. While few would praise the current state of our culture to the hilt, it is all too common to find warm, unreflective praise for the novel as a form – even among leftists who are quite critical of other aspects of society. A colder view might see the novel as part of the process that got us to the world of the 'minimal self' in the first place.

II

In an attempt to re-establish the self, before entering the sociological, I would like to present at least one reader's seduction into the practice of novel reading by representing my own experience. If it seems odd to do so in a fairly academic book, let me cite the precedent of Rachel Brownstein's *Becoming a Heroine* as a precedent for the need for a dialectic between subject and object.

My earliest recollections of stories were the ones my father told as he returned from work every day. He would stand in front of the door to our apartment and recount in incredible detail what he did at work as a sewing-machine operator in the garment district of New York City. We would get a close focus on the unwrapping of lunch-time sandwiches, troubles at work, and so on – all in American Sign Language since my parents were both profoundly deaf. What my father said was usually repetitive and uneventful, but he clearly was delighted to make it into a story. And we would stand and watch him, prisoners in our domestic routines of childhood, knowing that he had voyaged out into the world each day and returned, Odysseus-like, to tell us of the Scylla and Charybdis of the New York City subways and of the Circe of the coffee wagon. Like all pre-literates, I received my stories in oral form – or as oral as sign-language can be.

There were books in my house, painfully few when I think about it now. I was read to from what was scraped out of this Mother Hubbard-like bareness. I can only recall three books. One was about a little black lamb who was rejected because of his color until he fell into a bucket of white paint, and then I think when it rained the other lambs realized he was black but still liked him (or so I like to think). It was rather unlike my family to have had so consciously an anti-racist book in the house, so I assume it got in without pedagogical intent – probably because of the fuzzy lamb's wool that you could rub in the hopes that your book was in some sense actually a lamb. I remember that no member of my immediate or extended family could enter the house without being forced by me to read this book at least five or six times. In keeping with pre-literate cultures, I liked repetition of stories.

The second book was one about five Chinese brothers who were to be executed and each one avoided his fate by using a single power they had – one to swallow huge amounts, the other by stretching very high, and so on. Recently I found this book at a sidewalk sale and reread it. It is extremely bloodthirsty and inherently racist. I think it was my favorite book as a child, but ironically I do not read it to my children.

The third book was *Curious George Sails a Boat* in which the instructions for making a paper boat out of newsprint were given at the end.

So in my own way I came to feel that stories came from books, that one could even feel a lamb in a book, learn to make things from books, and – if lucky and Chinese enough – even escape death.

My earliest recollections of actually reading a long work myself take place in third grade. I read *The Mysterious Island* by Jules Verne. I remember quite well the illustrations, and the fantasy of being on an island, but I cannot recall the characters at all – except for Captain Nemo, whose name was more familiar to me from my Viewmaster stereo slides of *Twenty Thousand Leagues Under the Sea*. It is so appropriate that I and many others entered novel reading through the genre of adventure. There was a lot more happening on the Mysterious Island, I thought, than on the back lots of the Bronx. Actually, now that I have written some fiction about the Bronx, I realize the opposite might have been true.

In school we were encouraged to read novels and had to record our progress in a kind of double-entry book-keeping notebook every day. We logged in the number of pages we read, and what we thought that day. ('Very exciting today.') The message was clear – reading was a form of accruing valuable capital that would help in later life. Strangely, I remember more about what Valerie Groditski was reading – Greek mythology and the story of Bellerophone and Pegasus – than I remember about my book. But the point I want to make is that what I remembered was *that* I was reading a novel. I was impressed with myself for being able to do so. I do not think that I was ever able to comprehend *The Mysterious Island* fully since, like Tristram Shandy, my progress was so slow that I would forget previous chapters as I crawled through the succeeding ones. But I got the message – novels were not only worth reading but anyone who was anyone (and who hoped to get out of the Bronx) would surely be someone who read novels.

Reading novels was part of our education. I tended to think the better part, not being particularly good at mathematics, and fairly bored with the history of kings and wars. I took out a few books from the local library – things from the 'Cowboy Sam' series. Some girls read *The Bobsy Twins* and some of the fellows liked *The Hardy Boys*. But whatever I read between third and ninth grade I really do not recall except that I believe I devoured the 'Lad: A Dog' series by Albert Payson Terhune and read one strange book called *Hello The Boat*, about a family that lived on a houseboat. My parents were not big readers, being both deaf and under-educated, and so the only books we had were the ones my brother, ten years older, brought home. Those books tended to be acceptable works of literature that contained at least one or two sexy passages.

I discovered the dirty books – in this case *Lady Chatterley's Lover* and Edmund Wilson's *Memoirs of Hecate County* – and read them as carefully as I ever read any text. It was through these books that the distance between reality and fiction became dangerously narrow. I suppose that I followed along in the adventures of Cowboy Sam and Lassie, but with these books I experienced pleasure directly. My neurons were pulsing with actual synaptic messages inaugurated by simple words on a page. In discussing this subject with other male literary folk, I have found some kind of pressing connection between this erotic discovery of novels and the general pleasure of reading, but that is not the subject of this study.

In ninth grade my English teacher had us read *Brave New World* and *1984*. We had to get written permission from our parents. I recall my mother signing the release form with some strange sense of her own powerlessness since she had to rely on me to tell her what the book was about and since she could not understand that school might be exposing us to something bad – that would have been a contradiction in terms. I think I told her that the books only had one little bit of sex in the middle. I think I was right. Those books entered directly into my bloodstream. I recently reread *1984* and was surprised by the fact that nothing in the book could surprise since I remembered all so vividly.

Beginning tenth grade I entered De Witt Clinton High School – a massive building in the Bronx whose architect had clearly designed all the major penitentiaries in New York State. Seven thousand boys, mostly of the dangerous persuasion, were marshaled in those walls and shepherded from one dull class to another. I was, however, safely ensconced in what was called 'The Scholarship Program' – a reference I always thought hopefully of, like Pip, in financial terms. The summer before entering this august institution, I was given a list of 'classics' – mostly novels – to read which, according to the regnant wisdom of the school fathers, might act as a kind of disinfectant to the odor of our slum-soaked minds.

I was required to read *David Copperfield* and about ten other such works. I brought the books to summer camp and became lost in their world. I myself was David – no question about it. I didn't learn to swim that summer, but I learned to float. I floated on Dickens' fantasy and, when David met his child-wife, I held hands with Zina Klapper. Literature and life were different, particularly when I was living in the yellow tenements of the Bronx, but when I was in the almost pristine nature of the Berkshires – thanks to the helping hand of the Jewish Federation of Philanthropies – the difference was not so great. And I prided myself that my parents were born in England – so much closer to real life.

I learned about adventure through *The Mysterious Island*, not through the knifings and sadistic gang wars of the dreaded Fordham Baldies. I learned about sex from D. H. Lawrence and not from Jill, the slightly fat girl who lived upstairs and played at being nurse with those of us boys unlucky enough to have been blown up during our daily re-enactments of World War II. I learned about the difficulties of life from David Copperfield and not so much from my immigrant parents who worked each day in garment-district sweatshops. I learned to speak 'properly' and recognize what was really important conversation from Dickens and not from the quick, precise movements of my parents' hands as they turned their day's experience into finger-signs that dashed through the air and leapt into the eyes. But more than that I learned that as a normal, educated human being I should sit down on the slip-covered chair in our living room, shut out the sound of my father sucking slivers of pot roast out of his teeth, shut out the endless Dodger games on the Magnovox television console, disregard my brother's grunts as he worked out with Charles Atlas barbells, and the sound of the dishes being washed so that I could stare for several hours at pages that told me about what was really going on in my actual home – the heaths of England, the moors of Scotland, the wilderness of Cooper's Catskills Mountains paved under the parking lot of the Borscht Belt hotel in which my uncle worked. That activity was judged as not only normal but exemplary. In that sense, I loved the novel.

At Columbia College, I joined not only the novel readers but the novel analyzers. The novel was not just a good read, not simply a raiser of moral and intellectual worth, it was a fantastically revered and sacred text. Grown men and women, with distinguished accents, fine clothes, and names like Lionel and Quentin were exhorting us to find meaning, search content, find formal alignments, read the author's letters, and make sense of the endlessly rich tapestry. I worked hard and made sense – although I always carried with me some consciousness of the paradox of my career. I can remember being at a party as a graduate student and asking Lionel Trilling if he did not feel silly being a grown man studying literature, wasting his time with books. Rather than getting the outraged reaction for which I was probably hoping, I was slightly deflated when he agreed with me. I later found out we went to the same high school.

And I fell in love, endlessly, with heroines – with Emma Bovary and Tess, with Sue Bridehead and Estella. I could taste them – they were so real to me, and I suffered painfully that they were not in the world. I chose for girlfriends women who reminded me of these characters, and these girlfriends in turn resembled these characters because they modelled themselves on the same books. We were all Pips and Estellas, bumping into each other in Chock Full O' Nuts, hoping to open the pages of our own passions and friendships over cream cheese and nut sandwiches on raisin bread and steaming coffee.

III

My personal history with the novel is only one story. There are millions of lives in this naked city of the mind. And with the individual story comes the cultural story. The human race was not born with a novel to its nose. The novel is a literary form with a beginning, a place, and a duration. Many societies have never developed the novel. Many never will. As people who grew up reading, as a society that came of age with the novel, we are eminently bad judges of this phenomenon. We are the worst people to write or talk about the novel because we are too much with it. The best critics of the novel would be illiterates, peasants in Alsace, tribal folk in Ghana, bedouin women and children. We cannot listen to what the novel is saying to us because the novel, as a cultural phenomenon, is one part of a gigantic defense mechanism. That is, it serves a defensive function in helping us carry on and live in the world.

I should add here that I will be using the word defense quite a bit and I do not want to imply that defenses are in and of themselves bad things. As ego-psychologists have pointed out, defenses are simply adaptive. They help us to live and to function in a world that does not always meet our needs or stroke our egos. If these adaptations are useful, then the personality is fine; if the adaptations or defenses are actually maladaptive, then they are hindrances to our well-being. For me a defense is a particular psychic construct that helps humans and by extension human society to cope. Defenses are frequently the nodal points by which humans make contact with reality and buffer that reality. As with biological defenses, psychological defenses are like the active sites on which our own needs impinge on the potentially relieving and potentially dangerous world. Our defenses empower us; and at the same time they can weaken us. Nevertheless, we all have defenses, and the particular combination of defenses makes us each individually who we are. Our defensive structure is like a fingerprint of our personality. To some this description may sound a bit callous and psychologized. Would falling in love be described as a defense? By this definition, the answer would be yes. Would falling in love then be bad or maladaptive? That would depend on your reasons for falling in love and what happened when you did. The point is not to deride defenses, but to see how they operate.

To return to the novel, I have found that the arguments I make in this book are simply echoes of those made by the staunchest pre-novelists – those folk so thoroughly outside the mainstream and even the flotsam of the novel that they are branded now as stupid, regressive know-nothings. They were the bad guys of literary history – and I am speaking of the Puritans. Odd as it may be for a left literary critic to ally himself with seventeenth-century Puritans, it probably makes more sense than alliances with trendy Tories like Swift, Pope, and Fielding. The Puritans did not like fiction and they did not like it for the main reason that it was not the truth. It was a pack of invented lies. Their point of view – so alien to a culture now addicted to fiction on the page and on the screen – is not to be dismissed lightly. Just because they were against Shakespeare, dancing, and fun does not mean they were all wrong. In their unique position outside of the mainstream, they correctly saw that novels had an effect on people who read them and that somehow people who read novels were involved in the false notion that what they read was linked to life. My argument throughout this book will be that novels are not life, their situation of telling their stories is alienated from lived experience, their subject matter is heavily oriented towards the ideological, and their function is to help humans adapt to the fragmentation and isolation of the modern world. However, unlike the Puritans, I like novels. I read them and will continue. I am not advocating burning books, I am advocating resisting them.

The word 'resistance' will be used in two distinct but finally related senses. Resistance is both a political and a psychoanalytic term. In the first sense, I mean 'resistance' as the way politically oppressed groups fight back against the powers that oppress them. Resistance can be armed or passive – both indicate the rejection of the power of the political over-structure and a sense of group solidarity against that structure. The second sense of the word 'resistance' is the psychoanalytic one. Freud says that resistance

> means opposition. All those forces within the patient which oppose the procedures and processes of analysis, i.e. which hinders the patient's free association, which interferes with the patient's attempt to remember and to gain and assimilate insight, which operates against the patient's reasonable ego and his wish to change. (*The Interpretation of Dreams* 517)

There is an inverse relationship between the political sense of resistance and the psychoanalytic one. In the case of the political, resistance aims at change – change of fortune, change of government, change of social aims. In the case of the psychoanalytical, the resistance is defensive reluctance or the blockage of change. Psychoanalysis aims to change or modify behavior and defenses, and the patient resists because change is terrifying. 'Resistance defends the neurosis, the old, the familiar, and the infantile from exposure and change' (Greenson 77). So we can say in shorthand that while political resistance is 'progressive' psychic resistance is 'regressive' or 'conservative'.

We might even say that political resistance and psychic resistance work in a dialectical relation in the world. Politically progressive forces will have to work to negate the psychic resistance of groups who in some sense are wedded to their oppression. Ways of seeing the world, ideological world views, are intimately related to the psychic apparatus, and in turn such ideological views serve as defenses against harsh social and political realities. Parenthetically, one of the problems with recent discussions of ideology (those of Althusser, Eagleton, Jameson, Macherey, for example) is that they lack a psychological model to describe the way ideology works on the level of cognition. Some of our best discussions of ideology still talk about the interpenetration of the subject and object in general terms or in terms relative to nineteenth-century philosophy. But even a brief consideration of the subject of ideology would indicate that ideology does not exist 'out there' but is intricately part of the affective and cognitive life of individuals. In order to understand how ideology works, it is necessary now for us to use the relatively large body of writing on the way the mind works – that is psychoanalytic methodology.

Many Marxists may well object that psychoanalysis is fundamentally ahistorical. That objection only furthers the notion that Marxists can and should extend psychoanalytic theories to make them more directly related to social conditions and historical periods. However Steven Marcus in *Freud and the Culture of Psychoanalysis* has demonstrated that even the unconscious – often seen as universal and unchanging – has a history and is part of material change. Using Kardiner, Erikson, and Kohut, he makes the point that 'the disposition of forces within the super-ego may within a single culture change across historical time . . . hence it is also possible to demonstrate within the course of development of one complex society and culture alterations within the unconscious' (184). Studies like Marcus' need to be done to understand the way that psychology participates in the historical continuum. But to turn away from what amounts to our only really systematic study of the mind may be to fall into the realm of solipsistic speculation and mechanistic views of the operation of the flow of ideas in society. It is true that psychoanalytic methods have been used in fairly ahistorical ways. Even with the best intentions, critics like Peter Brooks in his recent *Reading for the Plot* do tend to fall into universal and ahistorical readings in the name of psychoanalysis. Nevertheless, such practice should not make us move in the completely opposite direction of avoiding what is valuable in psychoanalysis just as we would not avoid using standard grammar because we object to the ahistoricity behind the logic of its proponents.

I should add that I am not advocating psychoanalytic readings of texts *per se*. My feeling is that such readings usually tend to be reductive and, in the case of psychoanalyzing authors, risky at best. The psychoanalytic session is based on a dialectical, face-to-face interaction between patient and analyst – a dialectic that is completely absent in the literary critical method. As such, any psychoanalytic reading of a text is simply risk-taking at best and at worst a violation of psychoanalytic principles. Nevertheless, psychoanalysis can help us in understanding not the content of literary works or even the psychological history of individual authors but the process of cognition and the ways in which literary structures operate on the conscious and unconscious mind. I add quickly here that such work must always be done in the context of the historical moment. In other words, literary conventions and techniques are not universal but of a particular historical moment and were originally developed to operate on humans of that time and place (although they may have varying effects on future readers). As such, they contribute to *relative* rather than *permanent* defenses. One might further argue that ideological structures are themselves of this category of relative collective defenses and as such they are subject to psychological scrutiny while yet being bound in a particular historical moment.

Another note about defenses. In using this concept I want to avoid the narrowness of psychoanalytic methods. For example, Norman Holland in *The Dynamics of Literary Response* and subsequent works does use and pay tribute to defenses as part of the reading process. But, as Susan Suleiman notes, Holland's earlier work privileges the text and the later work privileges the concept of individual identity (Suleiman and Crosman 30). The danger of using a concept like defenses is that it makes the reader become artificial, reified, or objectified. That is, the text or history is seen as variable, but readers are seen as absolute. Of course, this is not the case. As the work of Iser, Jauss, Fish and others has explained, the reader is not a simple and privileged being, but is in fact a kind of invented construct that is somewhere between reader and text. Nevertheless, even implied readers have 'defenses' that bind them emotionally to the text. Those defenses do not have to be seen as the same in all readers, but can be seen as components arranged differently for different groups at different times but nevertheless compiling an inventory that can be drawn on to discuss the dynamics of how people interact with ideology and with texts.

I will be using 'ideology' in this book in the confusion and richness of its current meanings some of which I trace in chapter 2. For the time being, I should say that the general uses of ideology fall into three categories that have been laid out by Raymond Williams in *Marxism and Literature*:

1   the belief system of a particular group or class;
2   a system of illusory beliefs – false ideas or false consciousness – as contrasted with true or scientific knowledge;
3   a semiological system or system of signs which produces meanings and ideas in society.

However, I want to add to these concepts of ideology my own qualification. Therefore, my best definition of ideology would have to be 'public ideas wedded to collective and personal defenses.' Political resistance, then, is involved with defeating psychic resistance through analysis and of course through action. The project here is part of what Adorno and Horkheimer call 'the self-destruction of Enlightenment' (xiii). Thought has to make itself the object of its own study. Political analysis is the attempt to show through teaching, public education, and other forms of praxis that various collective defenses and ideological constructions are effective in the short run but in the long run are damaging and neurotic. For example, the belief in industrialized countries that any person, if really set on it, can pull himself or herself up by the bootstraps and become relatively wealthy, is a collective defense that is useful in the short run in helping us to keep up morale and cope with difficult conditions, but in the long run defeats the attempt to change conditions towards a goal of greater financial equality. Obviously, such a defense operates personally as well as with the collective. Feelings of victimization and low self-esteem can be defended against by invoking a rosy future.

Having laid out provisionally what I see as a definition of ideology, and having then put forth a comparison between political and psychic resistance, and the role of analysis in both cases, I now want to focus the discussion of resistance more closely on literature and particularly on the novel. As one well-known text in psychoanalytic method advises, 'We have to distinguish between the fact that the patient is resisting, *how* he does it, *what* he is warding off, and *why* he does so' (Greenson 78). This advise is to the point in an analysis in which a patient is resisting therapy, but I have to complicate things by specifying *two* patients, not one. One patient is the reader, let us say, and the other is the novel itself. That is, the novel stands in relation to society as the reader stands in relation to the novel. The diagram I have in mind looks like this:

$$\text{reader} \longleftrightarrow \text{novel} \longleftrightarrow \text{society}$$

The novel provides a resistance to dominant trends in early modern culture in the sense that it provides controlled ideological locations, a sense of community and belonging through identification with characters, a special significance to conversation that elevates those who engage in it – to name a few aspects that I will develop in greater detail in the rest of this book. In this sense, the novel resists society and is a kind of mass cultural defense, as are ideological structures in general. As my title indicates, there is an ambivalence in this picture since 'resisting' in 'resisting novels' can be either a gerund or an adjective.

The reader, in the first part of the diagram, alternately succumbs to and resists the structures of the novel as well as resisting society through the reading of novels. Readers can adopt wholesale the useful ideological defenses against the realities of social life and at the same time they may resist such seductions as 'escapist' or 'fantasy.' That is, readers are both resisting society through the defensive structures of novels and at the same time resisting the dynamics of novel reading itself.

The level of resistance to the novel has varied during different historical periods. It is now very low in our own society, and far from resisting, readers acknowledge openly their right to 'escape' into literature. In the realm of film, which is now the dominant form of narrative, it would be unimaginable to argue against the strange habit of entering dark rooms for several hours to lose oneself in the images on the wall. However, a mere 200 years ago, one could have found all kinds of examples of resistance to novel reading. At the beginning of the nineteenth century debates still raged in religious circles about the suitability of reading novels and whether such readings furthered moral aims or inhibited them. And of course, at the beginning of the eighteenth century, the Puritan argument dove-

16

tailed with the feelings of many middle-class people in their strong disapproval of the very idea of fiction. The Puritans argued that since novels were 'lies,' reading them would only encourage immorality. At the inception of the novel, resistance to the novel was probably at its highest point.

When Puritans resisted the novel their action was logical because by being an insular group they managed to avoid becoming habit-uated to many of the conventions of the novel – so in some ways they were ideal naïve readers of the novel. The Puritans, also, because they sought to transform society by actively creating their own world, probably found the indirect and passive resistance to society offered by the novel a false or misleading form of resistance.

In this book I will be advocating a position of active resistance by readers against novels. That is, in the diagram, readers should interpret that first arrow as a relationship of resistance to the text. In advocating resistance, I advocate conscious effort on the part of readers to fight back the regularizing and normalizing features of the novel. These features, as I will show, operate on subliminal levels and in such innocuous notions as the fact that there *is* a character in a novel, that the character has conversations, that action takes place in locations, and that characters' lives fit into plots. However, readers in general do not want to resist novels, because novel reading helps people defend themselves against certain negative features of modern society.

Now, it is entirely possible for someone to object: 'But I do not read novels as if they were life. I am a critical reader, an informed reader, capable of discerning fact and fiction.' This position is fine and most of us are actually *that* kind of reader. But I am arguing that even with an ability to be aware at this level of consciousness, there is still a good deal of the process of reading that is unconscious. None of us invented novel reading. The process was inherited from pre-vious generations. We were socialized, trained, and in that sense are unconscious of many of the bargains we have already struck and forgotten in the process. One can be an aware reader and still subject to those circumstances of which one is aware.

One of the points I will be making is that novel reading as a social behavior helps prevent change. In saying this, I am of course aware that all of our great political leaders and theorists were also readers of novels and fiction. I am therefore not saying that if you read novels you will never do anything to change the world. Like any complex social formation, novels are highly ambivalent in their messages, as I will show in chapter 6 on 'plot' and in the conclusion which speculates on the special category of the political novel. Novels can offer in their heroes and stories various kinds of opposition to stasis and power, but at the same time it would seem that the formal elements of the novel add up to a social formation that resists change. Readers, of course, can react to the interplay between elements of plot and elements of structure in a variety of ways. Yet I would maintain that for the large mass of people, reading novels is an activity that prevents or inhibits social action as do so many leisure activities in a consumer society.

In psychoanalysis, patients resist change by repeating. Freud, in his essay 'Remembering, repeating, and working-through,' says that 'We have learned that the patient repeats instead of remembering, and repeats under the conditions of resistance' (151). The experience of novel reading is one of repetition. Having once become indoctrinated to the habit, the compulsion is repetitive in nature. Unlike a child who listens to a favorite story or a listener who attends to a story-teller in a folktale – both occasions in which repetition is a natural part of the act and a reinforcement of some kind of living human community – the reader of novels repeats the process without human contact and without necessarily repeating the particular story. Very few novels are reread, except in the rare cases of those of us who study literature. Usually the end of one novel demands the beginning of a different one. Committed readers live their lives in a continual chain of narratives broken and forged by the ends of previous novels and the beginnings of new ones. The search for the 'new' or 'novel,' a feature of a consumer economy (McKendrick, *et al.* 316ff.) encouraged the rage for a new novel or a newer one (Davis, (*Factual Fictions* 42ff.). The development of the idea of an author (Foucault, *Reader* 101ff.) as a locus of narrative encouraged reading as the sequential following of the author's next or newest work.

Further, the plots of novels tend to be repetitious in their limited variety. That is, eighteenth-century readers would find that most of their novels were essentially about potential and thwarted marriages. Each novel constituted a repetition and a variation on the theme. Even about 200 years ago, Susanna Rowson could remark that 'there are at the present day, about two thousand novels in existence, which begin and end exactly the same way' (Gilmore 10). In effect, the act of repetition in reading novels can be seen itself as part of resistance on the part of readers to change – on the part either of themselves or of the world. And the fact that within novels most protagonists undergo a dramatic change by the end of the novel – usually moving from innocence to experience or imprudence to prudence – provides a false or surrogate example of change that might satisfy any external need or desire for change.

In advocating political resistance to the novel, then, I expect to encounter psychological resistance on the part of novel readers who will balk at seeing their own defenses uncovered. Indeed, in many of the seminars, conferences, and lectures I have given based on the materials of this book, as well as in my classes, I have routinely encountered along with interest some angry resistance. I might interpret this resistance in two ways – the first is that what I am saying is simply wrong, and the second is that I am cutting my argument too close to the bone. Obviously, I prefer the latter viewpoint. Literary people do not want to have their defenses revealed any more than neurotics do – and literary folk have a vested interest in seeing things like novel reading as uplifting and universally beneficial. On some level, I am arguing that novels are wrong and even that they are bad, and such an argument cannot curry favor among novel readers. As I have pointed out, I read novels and enjoy them. But does that mean I cannot recognize that the very process I love and depend on is in effect part of the social mechanism that keeps me in my place? When Freud began in the early part of this century to uncover the workings of the unconscious, there was great resistance. Freud noted that the findings of psychoanalysis constituted a 'narcissistic injury' ('A difficulty') to humankind. And later in an essay entitled 'The resistance to psychoanalysis' he noted that psychoanalysis was 'an assault on the dignity of the human race' (169). And he added 'the situation [of resistance] obeyed a simple formula: men in the mass behaved to psychoanalysis in precisely the same way as individual neurotics under treatment for their disorders' (172). While I cannot claim to be launching anything as noble or high-minded as psychoanalysis, I think that an attempt to reveal the defensive side of literary endeavors will necessarily produce intense resistance. As Heinz Kohut writes, 'Analytic treatment as a whole offends the pride of the analysand, contradicts his fantasy of independence, and that is why he now resists treatment' (547).

Likewise, with literary analysands, analysis of this sort will necessarily offend the enterprise of reading fiction. But, in order to take such a first step, we might want to explore specifically the ways that novel reading is actually an activity with features of other defenses.

The first defense that is inherently part of reading is what psychologists call 'isolation.' In order to read, we have to ascribe a certain validity to what we read. If we were truly skeptical, we would be saying, along with our Puritan forbears, 'This is false, this is a lie,' and we would ultimately be unable to read a novel. To be able to read, then, we must cut off, as it were, or *isolate* certain features of our ideational life and separate them from the demands of reality. Reading fiction demands isolation of ideas and affects; that is, it demands the ability to say of these pictures, feelings, and thoughts in our mind's eye, 'These are not part of my emotional or cognitive being. They are simply part of what is *in* this book.' Obviously, when we are reading a book we are experiencing the elements of plot and character as part of our own lives, but we separate and isolate them and say '*That* was Emma Bovary suffering, and *I* feel sorry for her plight.' Isolation, as Freud noted, is one of the major forms of defense, since it keeps unwanted emotions or thoughts from entering consciousness in a disturbing way. Probably our modern distinction, at least for the purposes of cataloging genres, between fact and fiction is most strongly linked to this defense. Earlier times clearly did not make such a strong distinction in narrative (Davis, *Factual Fictions*).

Another defense mechanism is 'projection.' In projecting, people 'attribute to others wishes and impulses of their own which are unacceptable to them and which they unconsciously try to get rid of' (Brenner 102). Now, clearly, novel reading is premised on the notion of projection. In reading we project our own feelings and thoughts into characters, we attribute to them a range of passion and actions that we might never allow ourselves. That is why characters in fiction are always larger-than-life emotionally, why they are driven by passions much greater than our own, and why they can transgress so dramatically. If I get drunk, not too much happens; but if Tom Jones gets drunk, he winds up renounced by Squire Alworthy and thrown into the adventures of the road. Some people get bored with their marriages, but Emma Bovary turns the emotion into a flood of unbearable passion and destruction. In projecting unacceptable emotions into characters, we are doing the very thing we cannot do without damage in real life – we are blurring the distinction between fact and fiction. The space of novel reading obviously provides a safe place to allow reality testing to go haywire. However, part of my

20

critique of the novel has to do with this point that we can impair, to a certain extent, our ability to test reality. As Christopher Lasch has pointed out, our own era is characterized by just such a lack of distinction between self and other. Novels like *Don Quixote* and *Madame Bovary* inherently realize in parodic form this blurring of fact and fiction. As Brenner notes, 'if projection is used as a defense mechanism to a very great extent in adult life, the user's perception of external reality will be seriously distorted, or to put it in other words, his ego's capacity for reality testing will be considerably impaired' (Brenner 102). To a certain extent, novels intrude on our lives in this way.

'Identification,' another major defense, in which we convince ourselves that we are like certain 'ideal' figures, is so clearly a feature of novel reading that further discussion is not necessary at this point (although I will discuss the subject at length in chapter 4). Suffice it to say that a novel can barely succeed unless we place ourselves in some special relation to the hero or heroine, or in the case of anti-heroes of the twentieth century with the author or some ideal reader.

The defense of 'denial' is one in which a person denies 'an unpleasant or unwanted piece of external reality either by means of a wish-fulfilling fantasy or by behavior' (Brenner 100). Thus, we might say that simply reading novels is an escape or denial activity, as are other leisure-time endeavors. But more directly related to my argument, novels provided a collective wish-fulfilling fantasy that distracted readers from the realities of the early modern world and that continues to work that way in the modern period. The obsessive nature of the novel's involvement with sexuality, financial power, and giving logical order to human events pointed to wish-fulfillment at work in a world that was becoming increasingly dependent on erotic solutions to individual dilemmas, purely economic replacements for traditional structures, and an abandonment of religious order and explanation in an increasingly secular and alienated environment.

In running through these defenses, I do not of course want to imply that people who read novels are therefore neurotics or hysterics, but much more that society as a whole can develop collective defenses that match or parallel individual defense mechanisms. Further, I do not want to give the impression that I am discussing this issue in a purely universal way. My point throughout this book is that even in the case of such supposedly universal defense mechanisms as I have listed, there is a particular origin and poignancy to the combination

21

of defenses that developed in co-ordination with the rise of the novel. In other words, Atilla the Hun and Shakespeare might well have denied, projected, isolated, and resisted as individuals, but the particular combination of defensive needs in their society at a given moment can be ascribed at least in part to historical causes. If ideology is the interpenetration of individual defenses and social ideas, then the needs of people in the eighteenth century would have had to be met by cultural forms like the novel in order for the novel to succeed. In other words, large masses of people read novels because novels entertained them, of course, but also because novels *helped* them individually and collectively. What I want to look at in this book is the way that novels helped people.

But, of course, being helped by a defense is only being helped in a very attenuated way. Ego psychology speaks of defenses as strategies of adaptation which may or may not be effective. A man with an obsession is being 'helped' by not having to pay attention to what is really bothering him. So in some ways he is being helped but actually he is being hindered. Readers, with their collective obsession for following the lives of fictional folk, are being helped to avoid the various dehumanizing aspects of modern life, but paradoxically, as I will show in greater detail, are helped by being lowered further into that dehumanizing pit from which they are trying to escape. Yes, novels are part of the humanities and as such they inspire us, they humanize us, and they make us sympathize with the human condition. But they often do so by depressing us, dehumanizing us, and making us simply passive observers of 'the human condition.' If they lower us into that pit with a candle burning brightly, they only serve to show us the futility of the candle and the enormity of the darkness.

In advocating political resistance, then, I am advocating an awareness not unlike the awareness of the analysand. Overcoming the psychic features of resistance can lead, after the narcissistic wound and shock to one's pride, to an awareness that, while not eliminating behavior, can neverthless create a dialectic between the defenses and the ego. In reading, what would that mean? It would open the possibility for understanding the historical origins of novel-reading defenses, the present function of such defenses, and the ability to save ourselves as a culture from the passive and crippling effects of fiction as an obsession. This scenario does not envision a Luddite-like burning down of major publishing houses or planting bombs at local movie theaters, but a critical self-understanding of the role of fiction in our lives. There is a risk involved in disturbing the thin tissue on which the imagination rests. Some who read this book may curse it for rending the sacred veil that makes reading possible. But it is my hope that rather than interfere with what is obviously a pretty widespread pleasure, I can encourage a self-conscious enjoyment of all that comes within the pages of novels. Ignorance may be bliss, but ignorance of the laws of culture is no excuse.

2

The ideology of ideology

Fiction is history, human history, or it is nothing.

Joseph Conrad

Novels do not depict life, they depict life as it is represented by ideology. By this I mean that life is a pretty vast and unco-ordinated series of events and perceptions. But novels are pre-organized systems of experience in which characters, actions, and objects have to mean something in relation to the system of each novel itself, in relation to the culture in which the novel is written, and in relation to the readers who are in that culture. When we 'see' a house in a novel, there is really nothing 'there,' and, worse, there is really no 'there' for a 'there' to be. The house we 'see' in our mind is largely a cultural artifact. It must be described as a cultural phenomenon with recognizable signs to tell us what kind of a house, what class, whose taste, and so on. All of this description will depend on ideology – that is the vast signifying system that, in its interpenetration with the individual psyche, makes things 'mean' something to a culture and individuals in that culture. Ideology constitutes the sum of that which a culture needs to believe about itself and its aspirations as opposed to what really is. Ideology is in effect the culture's form of writing a novel about itself for itself. And the novel is a form that incorporates that cultural fiction into a particular story. Likewise, fiction becomes, in turn, one of the ways in which the culture teaches itself about itself, and thus novels become agents inculcating ideology.

When I say that novels are ideological, I do not mean that in the obvious way that a particular author might want to use fiction to make a political point. Susan R. Suleiman has written extensively in an able book on the subject called *Authoritarian Fictions: The Ideological Novel As a Literary Genre*. In this work she defines the ideological novel or *roman à thèse* as 'a novel written in the realistic mode . . . which signals itself to the reader as primarily didactic in intent, seeking to demonstrate the validity of a political, philosophical, or religious doctrine' (7). Specifically ideological novels in that sense do exist of course but, first, they are a rather small subdivision of the genre. As such, they present their ideological message or position in an 'authoritarian' way. Second, they operate ideologically primarily on the level of content. However I am arguing that novels in general are ideological but in more covert ways in terms of content and form.

Ideology's major function, according to Louis Althusser, is the 'reproduction of the conditions of production' (*Lenin* 127). The reproductive process here allows things to keep on going, and ideological structures need to replicate themselves in cultural forms and in the cognitive and affective processes of people. The novel in this sense is uniquely reproductive. Novelists create things that must look like novels, and they reproduce in others the desire to write novels. Readers will read and reread novels – learn the form and expect the next novel to fit the form. Readers will repeat the process, defining themselves as novel readers, and guarantee their title by reading more novels. The 'eternal truths' embodied in novels will become, in effect through the process of reproduction, eternal truths in fact. Novels make sense because of ideology; they embody ideologies; and they promulgate ideology. They exist by virtue of ideology and, as I argue, they owe their origin to the beginning of the modern concept of ideology (Davis, *Factual Fictions* 212ff.).

The novel is a form which depends on mimesis – the imitation of reality through realist techniques – and because of that fact, novels depend on their ability to make readers feel as if they are witnessing not art but life. In this sense novels parallel ideology, which attempts to destroy the veil of its own artifice and to appear as natural common sense. And in the same way that ideology presents itself as a

25

seamless whole – a complete and evident explanation of the state of affairs of a society – so do novels. Novels attempt to contain through representation the totality of a society at a given moment. Even if a novel is set only in a drawing room, that room will contain in its small and limited scope the social relations and thought-systems of the larger world. In Henry James' book, a golden bowl on a mantle becomes the embodiment of the complex and variegated fabric of social and psychological forms. With Jane Austen, the drawing room marks and contains the boundaries of the known world. With writers like Hugo and Dickens, the novel itself inflates to become the known world and even begins to suggest the world beyond.

The most interesting and layered definition of ideology that I have found has recently been synthesized by T. J. Clark in *The Painting of Modern Life*. Clark says that ideology indicates 'the existence in society of distinct and singular bodies of knowledge: *orders* of knowing.' We can tell that ideology is present in discourse because it shows up as

> a kind of inertness . . . a fixed pattern of imagery and belief, a syntax that seems obligatory, a set of permitted modes of seeing and saying; each with its own structure of closure and disclosure, its own horizons, its way of providing certain perceptions and rendering other unthinkable, aberrant, or extreme. And these things are done . . . as it were *surreptitiously* . . . most often tied to the attitudes and experiences of a particular class, and therefore at odds, at least to some extent, with the attitudes and experience of those who do not belong to it. (8)

Thus 'ideologies naturalize representation . . . they present constructed and disputable meanings as if they were hardly meanings at all, but rather forms inherent in the world-out-there which the observer is privileged to intuit directly' (8). Clark's definition strikes me as a good example of the way that ideology is being used now – a sort of state-of-the-art usage of the word. But the features of this definition have evolved over about 200 years, and in order for us to use the word adequately, it might be helpful here to trace the usage of the word and the ideology that accompanies the changing definitions of 'ideology.'

I want to take the time to trace the history of the concept of ideology, and I am taking a rather large chunk of this work to do so for a few reasons. First, the word ideology has in effect become the word of criticism in the 1980s just as deconstruction belonged to the 1970s and structuralism to the 1960s. And like those two previous concepts, ideology means many things to many people. While a number of writers, most notably Raymond Williams and Terry Eagleton, have explained the use of the word, I am still hard pressed to find a really thorough-going tracing of the development of the concept to the present moment. My choice in writing this book, as would be anyone's choice who now uses the word 'ideology,' could be to use the word and have readers figure out what I mean, or to define my own particular use (as I in effect have done in the previous chapter). But language is such that my particular definition will certainly have trouble reigning in general usage which has a life of its own. So in avoiding either of the previous choices, I opt to lay out the historical development of the word and then amend that with my own qualifications. For those readers thoroughly steeped in ideological studies, I would suggest skipping to the next chapter.

One point I would like to make in this chapter is that the history of ideology confuses two perspectives. Ideology is seen 'objectively' as a set of beliefs imposed by a particular group or class on the way most people think. But the study of ideology is not a neutral one because by unmasking and demystifying it places itself in adversarial role *to* ideology. It is therefore by definition a *critique* of ideology. As a critique, it seeks to change the status quo and therefore change the way we think. I want initially to place myself and my argument in this book in the more hopeful camp of those who aim to change ideology by consciousness. Resisting novels, as ideological constructs, is an activity that relies on a growing awareness that, to paraphrase Vico, since humans make ideology they can change it.

To begin, then, one must turn to the earliest use of the word 'ideology.' It has been traced to Destutt de Tracy who used the word to inaugurate a science of ideas. This 'science' fits into a trend in the European Enlightenment that in the simplest terms wanted to apply the rational to the human, subjecting human life to the same kinds of methods of analysis that had been applied to the more overtly organic and chemical side of nature. Destutt de Tracy's science considered human thought a sub-section of zoology, and it was this part of his science that he called 'ideology.' To speak rather broadly, one might say he was just retooling Locke and Hume in an attempt to find a scientific way of talking about the workings of the mind. This approach, one might note, was materialist as opposed to idealist. De Tracy thought of the experience of material reality as the foundation for ideas. Thinking was therefore manifested in 'signs' which Condilliac had seen as specifically more material than the intangible modulations of spirit Kant had suggested.

Even in these approximate beginnings, there was a serious bias and imprecision about the use of the word that would contaminate later thinking about ideology. Inherent was the positivist prejudice that once the way the mind works was understood through reason, then errors of the mind could be corrected through reason. In other words, at this point 'ideology' referred both to thought processes themselves and to the science that would correct the way the mind worked. As George Lichtheim has pointed out, the current imprecision over the use of the word 'ideology' finds its origins even at its moment of inception since the word is used to indicate both a system of 'normative' ideas and at the same time a critique of that system (7). The normative use suggests a description of universal processes of the mind while the critical approach suggests the possibility for change and opposition.

In 1795 the Institut de France was founded to provide the country with a nationwide system of higher education committed to the philosophy of the Enlightenment. Napoleon Bonaparte was an honorary member, and it was he who eventually fell out with the ideologues dominating the Institut and blamed them for the catastrophe into which his own policies had plunged the country. In 1812 he addressed the Conseil d'Etat:

> It is to ideology, to this shadowy metaphysics that, in searching deviously the first causes, would on these bases found the legislation of the people, instead of adapting the laws to the knowledge of the human heart and the lessons of history – to which one must attribute all the unhappinesses of our beautiful France. (Lichtheim 5)

Napoleon here pits the work of academic theoreticians against that of practical politicians. In essence, this is an argument about the value of tradition over new-fangled theories. But what is important for our purposes is Napoleon's recognition that this 'academic' study of the mind posed a political threat. More pertinently, one notices Napoleon's actual resort to a language of power and power itself as a response to the incursion of intellectuals into politics. Later Marx and Engels would continue to emphasize the political power behind ideology that would be seen as something to be combatted and something which those in power would be willing to defend by force. On the other hand, Napoleon inherently recognized what would be a major weakness in the critique of ideology – its excessive reliance on theory over practice. This view – what I might call the 'Napoleonic doctrine' – pinpoints the ultimate weakness of a critique that relies for its power on an analysis that must remain theoretical – even when attempting to be practical – since the project of studying how ideas work is caught in a permanent state of immateriality, despite the emphasis of Locke, Condilliac, and others on the materiality of the sign.

It was Marx and Engels who made the most significant use of the word 'ideology' after the ideologues. Whereas for Destutt de Tracy the word was a hopeful avatar of future academic study, to Marx 'ideology' pointed to the delusion that it was possible to comprehend the world through ideas *only*, without first understanding the relation between ideas and the material world. In this sense, Marx and Engels rejected the Enlightenment's faith in reason. In fact, the attack on Feuerbach and the Young Hegelians in *The German Ideology* centered around the major flaw in idealist philosophy – that the world could be understood solely with reference to mind:

> We do not set out from what men say, imagine, conceive, nor from men as narrated, thought of, imagined, conceived, in order to arrive at men in the flesh. We set out from real, active men, and on the basis of their real life-process we demonstrate the development of the ideological reflexes and echoes of this life process. The phantoms formed in the human brain are also, necessarily, sublimates of their material life process, which is empirically verifiable and bound to material premises. Morality, religion, metaphysics, all the rest of ideology and their corresponding forms of consciousness, thus no longer retain the semblance of independence. (14)

In this statement, Marx and Engels are being deliberately scientific and mechanistic, using words like 'reflexes' and 'sublimates' in an attempt to avoid humanistic notions of 'idea' and 'mind' and to stress that ideas must be bound to material developments.

29

Marx and Engels did not actually write a great deal about ideology. The subject occupies only a small fraction of their total work, and certainly nothing rivaling the sheer output on the subject in left literary circles over the last thirty years. When Marx and Engels use the term, they mean several different things. The first definition points to a chimerical world of ideas that is separated from material practice. A second definition includes 'truths' of those in power that are imposed on the majority to convince them about the correctness of the status quo. Specifically, Marx in his *Theories of Surplus Value* uses an interesting simile likening the concept of ideology to a Roman mythological thief, Cacus, who used to drag oxen into his cave backwards to make it seem that they were leaving rather than entering. Bertell Ollman points out that 'what stands out clearly from this example of Cacus and his oxen is that ideology does not so much falsify the details as misinterpret them so as to reverse what actually occurs' (227–8). Ideology becomes an explanatory device relevant to Marx because 'capitalism differs from all other oppressive systems in the amount and insidious character of its mystification, in the thoroughness with which it is integrated into all its life processes, and in the degree to which it requires mystification in order to survive (all other oppressive systems relying far more on direct force)' (229).

To this definition of ideology as false consciousness, Ollman adds that 'bourgeois ideology serves capitalist interests not only when it provides pro-capitalist solutions to pressing social problems but also when it confuses people, or makes them overly pessimistic and resigned, or makes it difficult for them to formulate criticism or imagine alternative systems' (231). This notion of ideology spins out a very significant thread that runs throughout the intellectual history of the critique of ideology. Capitalism is seen as infinitely wise and devious. Somehow it manages to confound even those members of the working class who should know better. Ideology in this sense is the spell cast by the omniscient, capitalist wizard. Ideology is seen as totalizing and infinitely confounding, and capitalists, as stupid as they may be in some ways, have managed to confound the lot of us. In this view, the only refutation of ideology is the 'science' of historical materialism – which can counteract the obfuscation of the Merlinesque captains of industry; and of course the inevitable dawning of consciousness and resolution of contradictions through revolution. Short of that violent action, the intelligence of workers and intellectuals remains something far more meagre than the thick power of the dominating intelligence. It is important to see how this theme of the total power of ideology will continue into the twentieth century – particularly once the study of ideology becomes focused on the study of literature and art. And in this context, the 'Napoleonic doctrine' that intellectuals are excessively reliant on theory over praxis is confirmed by the totality of ideology and the helplessness of intellectuals to do much about this domination.

A third use of ideology by Marx and Engels emphasizes that those structures of intellectual and cultural life – what is referred to as the 'superstructure' – are ideological because such systems embody the beliefs and myths of certain dominant classes. Certainly, these uses all dovetail and interconnect, but Marx and Engels were not terribly clear in their use of the term. Raymond Williams suggests that a weakness of their use of ideology is that it 'is simplistic . . . and belongs to the naïve dualism of "mechanical materialism," in which the idealist separation of priorities is reversed' (*Marxism* 59). The problem, as Williams puts it, is that ideology is thought of, in a strange reversal of the emphasis that Marx and Engels would have liked to place on this concept, as actually *separated* from material life. That is, 'there is *first* material life and *then*, at some temporal or spatial distance, consciousness and "its" products' as part of the superstructure (61). This unfortunate, mistaken detour in Marx's and Engels' thinking led to reductionist notions that art and literature are simply 'reflections' of the material base – in which sense ideology becomes like a tin can tied to the tail of material society.

Together with these founding ideas about ideology, and founding problems as well, is Marx's discussion in *Capital* of the fetishization of commodities. This concept is relevant to this discussion because it explains how objects, devoid of meaning in and of themselves, acquire a meaning through their role in the process of production. In its simplest form, the argument runs that a car has no inherent meaning, except as a vehicle for motion, but when the car is a Porsche and a woman in a leopard skin lies languorously on the hood, the object takes on meaning in the context of the culture. Since value is conceptual, objects gain or lose value through the system that produces them. So objects exist, in a cultural sense, absolutely by virtue of ideology – since it is a social system of signs that attributes meaning to things. This discussion in *Capital* has taken on new meaning with the advent of semiotics and structuralism. Also, since novels are themselves commodities, and within themselves fetishize other commodities, there is a significant relationship between this process of meaning and fiction in general, as I will discuss in later chapters.

Sigmund Freud is not normally thought of as someone who contributed to the concept of ideology, but I think it is impossible to avoid the permeation of many of his ideas into the subject. Some might object that Freud is hardly an historical materialist because he deals in universal phenomena that straddle the ages, classes, and so on. But, as Steven Marcus has most recently argued, Freud did have a strong conception of historical change. 'Like Darwin's theory of evolution, to which it owes a good deal in a very general way, psychoanalytic theory's explanatory powers are largely historical or retrospective' (*Freud* 166). This does not of course mean that Freud was a leftist theoretician or a political radical, but it does allow us to consider those concepts of Freud that permeated society and influenced later conceptualizers of ideology – particularly Mannheim, the Frankfurt School, and now Jameson and Eagleton.

The model presented by Marx and Engels of the superstructure as a reflex of the base is not so different from the idea that art is a sublimation of instinctual drives. What makes culture – art, literature, drama, philosophy, and religion – possible is the process of sublimation, that is, instinctual renunciation. For example, our notions of beauty are founded on a repression of anality, according to Freud. Art is a kind of reflex and stands in dynamic relation to the base of libido which is displaced upwards. Further, what is below the waist – sexuality or anality – is displaced upwards to the rational and creative faculties of the mind. The way the conscious mind works is in a superstructural relation to the dynamically repressed.

Culturally, Freud envisioned the same processes occurring. Art, religion, cultural habits, and so on were seen as reactions to repression of the libido. In Freud's work, the idea dominates with a kind of powerful centrality. First and foremost it predominates over the physicality of the body which becomes the site – in hysteria – for the subsuming of the body to the psychic construct. The 'idea' is so central that 'in mental life nothing which has once been formed can perish – that everything is somehow preserved and that in suitable circumstances (when, for instance, regression goes back far enough) it can once more be brought to light' (*Civilization* 16). Even history itself can be brought back through the psychoanalytic process without a documentary record. Freud does not hesitate to reconstruct the origins of humanity's acquisition of fire by examining myth and fairy tale and retrieving that moment when men hesitated or held back from micturating on fire (37). He finds the origins of society itself to be based on the Oedipal desire to overthrow the father and band together in a kind of fraternity and on the sublimation of individual sexual pleasure to the interests of the collective (46ff.).

The development of the unconscious further opened up the notion that no idea is what it seems, that all ideas and social formations have an unconscious component. This formulation was, as Freud says, 'an insult to the entire world' (*Introductory Lectures* 21) because it implies that ideas – even lofty and philosophical ones – are subject to uncontrollable and even offensive origins. Nothing human is exempt from the unconscious. While Marx had seen that social institutions arose from a material process – that social beings made ideas – Freud believed that instinctual life made, or at least conditioned, ideas and cultural life.

Marx and Freud, among others, agree that humans are unhappy in civilization. For Marx the villain was capitalism, for Freud the malefactor was the 'harshness' of the super-ego which 'in the severity of its commands and prohibitions . . . troubles itself too little about the happiness of the ego' (*Civilization* 90). On the social level, Freud postulates a cultural super-ego too which by forcing humans to renounce libidinal drives too harshly creates trouble in paradise.

> It [the cultural super-ego] issues a command and does not ask whether it is possible for people to obey it. On the contrary, it assumes that a man's ego is psychologically capable of anything that is required of it, that his ego has unlimited mastery over his id. This is a mistake; and even in what are known as normal people the id cannot be controlled beyond certain limits. If more is demanded of a man, a revolt will be produced in him or a neurosis, or he will be made unhappy. (90)

This cultural super-ego which has shaped civilization is similar, in some way, to Marx's concept of ideology because it controls what can be thought and does so totally. In culture, we cannot isolate the super-ego that dominates civilization any more than we can point to the location of ideology – except that we may specify more clearly the origin of ideologies and the mechanism of their institution (newspapers and mass-signifying systems of various kinds). Nevertheless, both Freud and Marx create a specter that dominates culture without specifying exactly how it works, and both end with little remedy – short of, in the case of Marx, the general overthrow of capitalism.

However, for Freud humans are not going to change much because their instinctual and psychic life will remain constant. Freud did not hesitate to move from the individual psyche to the psyche of the culture, and in his later career he applied the observations and findings of psychoanalysis to cultural history. Freud's desire to move from the individual to society is a logical one. After all, the study of the psyche is self-contained only to a degree, and once the origin of the drives and instinct can be accounted for on an individual basis, then one must move to the origin of the cultural formations that influence and house individual psyches. That is, the social component of psychoanalysis is demanded at some point. When one reads through such works as *Totem and Taboo*, *The Future of an Illusion*, *Civilization and Its Discontents*, and *Why War?* one is afforded a view of the mind of Freud as it ranges over the sweep of human cultural history and even into the future. One can only admire his genius and inventiveness, but this is finally a narrative approach abstracted from history and fact. It is a kind of mythos devoid of the same kind of scientific rigor that Freud proposed for his study of psychic life. And Freud must have recognized this fact, because in *Civilization and Its Discontents* he wrote that

> In none of my previous writing have I had so strong a feeling as now that what I am describing is common knowledge and that I am using up paper and ink and, in due course, the compositor's and printer's work and material in order to expound things which are, in fact, self-evident. (64)

Freud's treatment of history as simply an analogue of individual development is only a metaphor not a methodology. His prejudice toward the individual mind made collective history rather difficult.

The effect of Freud's work on later leftist thought has been considerable and in a sense immeasurable in its pervasiveness. But in picking up Freudian premises, the left also picked up Freudian biases. The analogy between ego development and the progress of civilization frequently shows up in discussions about ideology, which becomes not a material effect but a kind of impersonal and indefinable force, like libido, that creates and conditions thought. Histories of culture or literature that are simply about ideas and ideology operate, seemingly, on much the same basis as Freud's historical work. Placing ideology in the role of a universal and inevitable force, literary critics bow to the destiny of a kind of collective biology, as does Fredric Jameson when he talks about a 'political unconscious' lying under the movement of history. Ideology is there; we see it; we feel it; we analyze it. But it resists alteration through analysis, stubbornly refusing to retreat as a symptom. What is to be done about ideology is a secondary question embodied more in hope than action. Freud's pessimism about the super-ego's ferocity and about the inability of humans to triumph over the collective repressed of the race gave a lasting emphasis to the power of the idea and in that sense ideology.

Freud confirms several trends in the critique of ideology. First, the expert is needed to tell the subject the true nature of his or her thought. Second, Freud confirms what I have been calling the 'Napoleonic doctrine,' that intellectuals cannot change or shape political reality, though it is possible for the analyst to help change individual behavior. Mass ideation, however, cannot be substantively altered. Third, certain kinds of immateriality make it impossible to locate historically or politically such things as ideology or the cultural super-ego. While one might not want to see Freud as a major force in the critique of ideology, his influence is significant, as is his influence in so many spheres of the social sciences.

Those who are associated with this history of the critique of ideology have been characterized by their linking of what goes on in the human mind with material causes. The ideologues saw thought as a zoological process; Marx asserted that the ideational process of humans was bound by their social moment; Freud maintained that conscious thought was the superstructure or epiphenomenon of a deeper hidden, repressed instinct; and Karl Mannheim tied all human thought to the social process and to a kind of collectively unconscious motivation.

Mannheim wrote in *Ideology and Utopia* that 'the principal thesis of the sociology of knowledge is that there are modes of thought which cannot be adequately understood as long as their social origins are obscured' (2). Ideas do not rely on the individual psyche but on that of the social group. More radically put, 'strictly speaking it is incorrect to say that the single individual thinks. Rather it is more correct to insist that he participates in thinking further what other men have thought before him' (3).

For Mannheim, the error of previous thinkers in the western tradition was their belief that 'through insight into the origins of cognitive representation one could arrive at some notion of the role and significance of the subject for the act of knowing and of the truth value of human knowledge in general' (15). Introspection about how we think, of course, leaves out the role of the social world in creating thought. Meaning exists as part of a vast social system and therefore affects how we see that system. Hegel and the philosophers of consciousness, Mannheim asserts, created the thesis that experience could be organized rationally through the perceiving subject. 'Henceforth the world as "world" exists only with reference to the knowing mind, and the mental activity of the subject determines the form in which the world appears' (66). But as Mannheim wrote, 'the derivation of our meanings, whether they be true or false, plays an indispensable role, namely, it socializes events for a group. . . . In every concept, in every concrete meaning, there is contained a crystallization of the experiences of a certain group' (21–2). So any analysis of language or meaning cannot trace the genesis of the idea to an individual's personal history because each private history is really part of a complex intertwining of others' histories. One must instead focus on the 'interdependence of the individual life-history and the more inclusive group situation' (27). Like Marx, then, Mannheim would say that ideology, the collective system of meanings of a culture, is socially rather than individually determined.

While some of this explanation seems to stem from Marx, Mannheim has added the findings of psychoanalysis. Noting that the emergence of the unconscious is the most important feature of our age, he synthesizes Freud's discovery by noting that our ideas are unconsciously motivated – but unconsciously in the sense that the individual thinker is unaware or unconscious of the power of particular historical groups in determining thought.

In *Ideology and Utopia*, Mannheim presents a working definition of ideology which makes a distinction between, first, the critique of ideology and, second, the study of ideology:

1 a skeptical view of the ideas of an opponent 'the true nature of which would not be in accord with his interests. These distortions

range all the way from conscious lies to half-conscious and unwitting disguises; from calculated attempts to dupe others to self-deception.'

2 the more or less total thought system or outlook of an historical period or a particular class. (55)

Mannheim distinguishes between the traditional lack of focus on ideology as false consciousness on the one hand and ideology as a set of governing beliefs on the other. What both of these definitions rely heavily on is the idea of unconscious motivation – or, as Mannheim puts it, 'The common element of these two conceptions seems to consist in the fact that neither relies solely on what is actually said by the opponent in order to reach an understanding of his real meaning and intention' (56). The subject is unconscious of what he is actually saying because the ideas expressed are 'functions of his existence.' But Mannheim is quick to point out that the individual can never properly be considered the locus of ideology, but only of a fragment of the total picture. Therefore individual psychological study cannot hope to deal with the problem of ideology which is a group phenomenon. Further, because ideology totalizes the world and our view of it, it is difficult if not impossible to escape it. In this sense, Mannheim picks up on Freud's sense of hopelessness – we are largely helpless against the force of a dominant ideology.

Mannheim changes the notion of false consciousness a bit from that of Marx and Engels. 'To consider a statement ideological,' says Mannheim, 'one must consider one's opponent wrong – but not lying.' The further development of this process is that 'previously one's adversary, as the representative of a certain political-social position, was accused of conscious falsification. Now, however, the critique is more thoroughgoing in that, having discredited the total structure of his consciousness, we consider him no longer capable of thinking correctly' (69). Whereas in Marx's system it is possible for one human to escape the obfuscation of ideology by recognizing certain facts about the way the economic system works, in Mannheim the escape from ideology is much more problematic. People are not simply misled, they are *incapable* of thinking correctly. We have moved from attacking our opponents for lying to attacking them for thinking.

Ideology is for him the obscuring of the collective unconscious, as it were, of a particular group in power by their own interests.

Mannheim compares ideological thinking with its opposite – utopian thinking which sees the present status quo as purely negative. Utopian thought issues from oppressed groups within society. These two processes are diametrically opposed. Mannheim, unlike Marx, believes that *only* the intellectual can make sense of all this and restore some kind of order to the chaos of thinking.

We might say that Mannheim is particularly responsible for articulating the notion, presented in a different form in philosophical, political and Freudian theories, that the intellectual provides the only way out of the ideological trap. The earlier concept of the scholar as particularly able to view the complexity of the natural or supernatural world and its laws is replaced by a view of intellectuals as the only group somehow able to rise above the miasma of the ideological smokescreen. This is so because the intelligentsia is a relatively classless stratum although 'a large body of our intellectuals come from *rentier* strata, whose income is derived directly or indirectly from rents and interest on investment' (155). It does not take much perspicacity to point out that Mannheim's analysis may no longer be true. The independence of intellectuals from relying on their writing, teaching and professional activities as a source of income in Mannheim's period has now reversed rather dramatically. Professors now are so dependent on their primary social role as intellectuals that they can hardly be described as classless. Therefore, if we follow Mannheim's theory, they are now the *least* likely candidates to rise above the prejudices of ideology, but would logically tend to represent their own interests. In this sense, Mannheim opposes the 'Napoleonic doctrine' – pointing out that *only* intellectuals can change political life and perceptions.

Mannheim is not as naïve as I am making him out to be. He does not say that all intellectuals can understand the contradictions in society. But he does say that in the moral meritocracy 'the more outstanding intellectuals' could develop 'the social sensibility that was essential for becoming attuned to the dynamically conflicting forces' in a given nation (157). Reservations aside, the question is a vexing one. Georg Lukács argued at the time against this view, insisting in *History and Class Consciousness* that the proletariat was the only real source of true consciousness, or using Hegelian terms the 'identical subject-object of the socio-historical process.'

Mannheim fits into the critique of ideology in several ways. First, he continues the notion of looking outside of thought for 'true' thought. Second, he sees the possibility of an end to ideology and therefore fits into the line of thinkers who blur the distinction between studying belief systems and those who wish to change them. Third, he goes beyond Freud's universalizing tendencies by attempting to anchor the immateriality of the cultural super-ego in actual social practice. And fourth, he furthers the notion that only the expert can tell people what they are thinking.

Next in line in this brief sketch of ideology might be Antonio Gramsci, who redefined the discussion of ideology by introducing the concept of 'hegemony' – the notion that a ruling class does not 'impose' its ideology on the subordinate class but that the ideology must be willingly accepted. Hegemony implies that the dominance of certain formations are secured not by ideological compulsion, but by cultural leadership. This fine-tuning of Marx's theory of ideology is important because it makes ideology more concrete and tangible. We are moving away here from Freud's and Mannheim's general way of referring to the forces that shape thought (super-ego in the former case, ideology in the latter) as immaterial and totalizing. What Gramsci says is that dominance is not simply derived from the oppressed's passive and helpless acceptance of ideology received blankly and unquestioningly from the dominant though unnamed makers of ideology, but that dominance is created through a complex cultural interplay that involves consent and willingness to move within the culture. Gramsci shifts the problem from a focus on domination to a more complex situation in which the mentality of the oppressed permits them to accept the domination that shapes their perceptions. Gramsci, too, is trying to deal with *how* ideology is actually imposed. In this sense he is demystifying its processes by paying uncharacteristic attention to the way that ideology descends to everyday life and by naming them directly.

The intellectual and the artist become central figures. 'One of the most important characteristics of every class which develops towards power,' writes Gramsci, 'is its struggle to assimilate and conquer "ideologically" the traditional intellectuals' (*Modern Prince* 122). Intellectuals become kinds of gatekeepers of ideology and not only, as Mannheim would have it, decoders of ideology. The role of the intellectual in a revolutionary struggle is to replace old hegemonic forms with new ones more appropriate to liberation and equality. This view is more optimistic than that of Mannheim. Ideology is not seen as totalizing and all-powerful – rather, it can be changed, shaped, and used for new purposes. Unlike Mannheim, Gramsci did not separate the intellectual into a specially privileged group that could penetrate the obscuring quality of ideology. For Gramsci, intellectual life was not different from the life of most people – intellectual life was just more socially specialized.

One powerful distinction that Gramsci makes over and against someone like Mannheim is that the intellectual cannot be passive. 'The mode of existence of the new intellectual can no longer consist of eloquence, the external and momentary arousing of sentiments and passions, but must consist of being actively involved in practical life, as a builder, an organizer, "permanently persuasive"' (*Modern Prince* 122). Gramsci's intellectual is defined in the context of action. Obviously, this requirement is difficult to follow, and it points to the weakness of the critique of ideology as only a critique and not a practice. Gramsci is reiterating the 'Napoleonic doctrine' – but in this case standing it on its head. Previous thinkers and writers have largely relied on the power of analysis and of the word – which we have also seen is often simply a way of escaping one's political marginality through language. The immateriality of ideology – the fact that though much has been written about this subject it has been hard to say where or specifically what ideology was – has allowed a kind of 'immaterial' response to ideology. One may talk of superstructures, reflexes and distillates, but Gramsci signals for the left intellectual that a return to a material explanation in writing about ideology requires concrete political realities. It is perhaps not considered cricket to judge a critic by the extent of his or her own political involvement, but by the standards of Marx and Gramsci such judgment is not only pertinent but requisite. Gramsci links this emphasis on practice with the role of the intellectual in the hegemonic process – a process that involves both ideas and power in intimate contact. In a sense, Gramsci empowers ideology by detailing the material forms by which it operates in society through concrete institutions – schools, newspapers, libraries, and so on.

As we have seen, up to this point the concept of ideology has been an intriguing one for intellectual circles, but, with the exception of certain spats between Mannheim and Lukács, it has not been a subject that has merited lengthy disagreement. Perhaps, at best, there has been a confusion in definitions. But it is really with the French communist Louis Althusser that the most recent phase of the critique of ideology begins. What Althusser did was to combine Marxism with structuralism. These two subjects had been seen in the late 1950s and early 1960s, before the work of Althusser and Lucien Goldmann, as two mutually exclusive and antagonistic discourses among theoreticians of literature. In *For Marx* Althusser accomplished this melding of discourses by redefining ideology as the signifying system of a culture – 'a system of representations ... distinguished from science in that in it the practico-social function is more important than the theoretical function (function as knowledge)' (231). For Althusser, ideology 'is not an aberration or a contingent excrescence of History: it is a structure essential to the historical life of societies' (232). With this very important step, Althusser almost single-handedly transformed ideology's traditionally negative sense into a positive one. (Even Mannheim, champion of the scientific study of ideology, advocated ultimately that ideology be replaced by some kind of true consciousness or knowledge.) Althusser significantly points out that 'in no sense' does he condemn 'ideology as a social reality: as Marx says, it is in ideology that men "become conscious" of their class conflict and "fight it out;" in its religious, ethical, legal and political forms, etc., ideology is an objective social reality; the ideological struggle is an organic part of the class struggle' (12). In *For Marx*, there is no footnote to the above citations, and indeed this is a curious reading of Marx's view that ideology was a negative structure to be overcome only by changing the material base. But for Althusser, ideology is itself the battleground on which the class struggle can be fought. This view radically departs from Marx by placing an entirely new centrality on ideology and intellectuality. In the history of the critique of ideology, though, this move seems a logical culmination of a trend through which the intellectual had come to love that which he could not destroy – ideology becomes the positive force and analysis the tool.

According to Stuart Hall, Althusser introduced the idea that ideology, by being a site of class struggle in itself, was to a certain extent distinct from Marx's characterization of ideology as a reflection of the dominant powers (dominant power/dominant ideas). The fact that one could not now read off the ideological position of a social group or individual from class position, but that one would have to take into account how the struggle over meaning was conducted, meant that ideology ceased to be a mere reflection of struggles taking place or determined elsewhere (for example, at the level of the economic struggle).

It gave to ideology a relative independence or 'relative autonomy.' Ideologies ceased to be simply the dependent variable in social struggle: instead, ideological struggle acquired a specificity and pertinence of its own – needing to be analyzed in its own terms, and with real effects on the outcomes of particular struggles. (*Culture, Media, Language* 82)

With the structuralist connection, the sign is essentially severed from the material process, becoming itself the arena of contention. And what we are faced with is an analysis which in some ways is not terribly different from an approach based only on a history of ideas which sees battles as fought in a purely intellectual realm. The critique of ideology now focuses on the immateriality of the sign, relying on language theory rather than political or social science. Saussure's main point that language was unmotivated and arbitrary, that is that words did not inherently 'mean' things outside of a system of binary oppositions, has been seen as necessarily outside materiality (Jameson, *The Prisonhouse of Language*, 14ff.).

In relative opposition to the purely structuralist approach stands Michel Foucault's work, very heavily based on research as well as a devotion to system. Interestingly, Foucault flies in the face of the trend being described since he rarely uses the word 'ideology.' Naturally, since his work focuses so heavily on the relationship between knowedge and power, one might assume that the project is inherently about ideology. Foucault's central notion of 'discourse' provides a way out of the lack of specificity that ideological discussions tend to generate. He carefully defines discourse as 'the interplay of the rules that define the transformations of these different objects [treatises, writings, etc.], their non-identity through time, the break produced in them, the internal discontinuity that suspends their permanence . . . in other words to formulate their law of division' (*Archeology* 33). In other words, discourse is the ensemble of rules governing a set of related texts, concepts, and strategies – whether the treatment of madness or the penal reform movement. Because Foucault studied documents, records, treatises, manuscripts, and also spatial arrangements (the architecture of prisons or of courtrooms), he was not necessarily required by his method to examine what forces created those documents. In Foucault's work, what is paramount is the ensemble of documents and the rules that govern their order. One could say that 'discourse' serves for Foucault the function of 'ideology.' But Foucault avoids that term partly because it would be necessary to talk about issues of class, dominance, and the way that particular discourses are actually created. He steers clear of the issue of class, by assuming that any discourse or state apparatus must inherently exist in relation to power. By examining institutions like the prison, Foucault must automatically deal with power and ideas. Though he may analyze *how* power infiltrates quotidien life he rarely speculates *why* 'power' conceives of things in a particular way. As he has said, 'in thinking of the mechanisms of power, I am thinking rather of its capillary form of existence, the point where power reaches into the very grain of individuals, touches their bodies and inserts itself into their actions and attitudes, their discourses, learning processes and everyday lives' (*Power/Knowledge* 27).

Does Foucault avoid the pitfalls of the critique of ideology by avoiding the term? His very careful mapping out of the concept of discourse allows him to skirt questions of the historical mechanism of ideology. On some occasions he uses the word in a more or less classically Marxist sense as when he discusses 'the moral ideology of the bourgeoisie' (*Power/Knowledge* 21). But he also uses ideology to describe the way the proletariat thinks when he notes that 'there is in particular a proletarian ideology into which certain bourgeois ideas about what is just and what is unjust about theft, property, crime and criminals have infiltrated' (23). Here and in other places, Foucault sees lower-class perceptions as controlled or infiltrated by bourgeois thought. In fact, he says that what the lower class thinks is 'not necessarily a revolutionary ideology' (26).

But Foucault specifically denies the importance of ideology when he says that western Marxism has 'had a terrible tendency . . . in favour of consciousness and ideology' (59). For Foucault, the Marxist notion of ideology is too tied up with consciousness alone. The critique of ideology is really an idealist project, despite its association with materialism. What is troubling 'with these analyses which prioritize ideology is that there is always presupposed a human subject on the lines of the model provided by classical philosophy, endowed with a consciousness which power is then thought to seize on' (58).

Foucault would also correct thinkers like Herbert Marcuse who say that repression of knowledge is the central role of those who control power. Marcuse, according to Foucault, 'thinks of power as essentially negative working through censorship, exclusion, blockage and repression, in the manner of a great Superego.' But Foucault notes that if, 'on the contrary, power is strong this is because, as we are beginning to realize, it produces effects at the level of desire – and also at the level of knowledge. Far from preventing knowledge, power produces it' (59). Foucault's emphasis on desire places his analysis closer to Gramsci's concept of hegemony.

The emphasis on desire is a hallmark of Foucault's work – although 'desire' seems to be as vague a word as 'power.' Desire centralizes the body and sexuality and adds to the concept of ideology the notion of volition. In this sense, it is not so different from Gramsci's concept of 'hegemony' – by which the oppressed are drawn to their oppression through a volition that ratifies power. But Foucault, like others, does not talk about desire as a psychological construct. In focusing on the defensive nature of ideology, one could readapt the concept of desire with greater specificity. Foucault strategically chooses those professions that more or less directly affect the body through treatment, incarceration, sexual conditioning, and medical study. He can therefore gloss over some less direct kinds of control. The subject Foucault frequently avoids is literature – a subject whose authority is somewhat more ambiguous and whose effect is more generalized than those he chooses. In so doing, he avoids getting entangled in the stickier web of literature whose relation to power is more ambiguous than subjects like incarceration. Certainly a literary work is not governed by the law, regulated by the American Medical Association, or housed in a panopticon of incarceration. *Whose* power is asserted is a far more complex question.

In talking about power globally, does Foucault simply exchange the vagueness of the concept of ideology for the vagueness of the concept of power? For Foucault, power is an absolute. In this sense, Foucault wants to avoid the crudities of vulgar Marxists who point the finger at the ruling class and use their intentions as an ultimate justification. Foucault emphasizes that analysis should not concern itself with power at the level of conscious intention or decision; that it should not attempt to consider power from its internal point of view and that it should refrain from posing the labyrinthine and unanswerable question:

"Who then has power and what has he in mind?" . . . Let us not, therefore, ask why certain people want to dominate, what they seek, what is their overall strategy. Let us ask, instead, how things work at the level of those continuous and uninterrupted processes which subject our bodies, govern our gestures, dictate our behaviour, etc. (97)

The continuing theme in the critique of ideology recurs here in the centrality of the role of analysis. Foucault, so interested in the micro-procedures of social discourses, avoids completely the full line of descent of that discourse. He keeps himself at the level of effect. The obvious problem with such an approach is that it tends toward the minute, the particular, the contextualized. Motivation is ignored, and action is delayed. Like the critique of ideology, the study of discourse is an intensely intellectual endeavor requiring the isolation of the scholar. And as a defense against the powerlessness of the scholar, the enemies remain abstract and global. Take for example the general nature of the following quote:

but the impression that power weakens and vacillates here is in fact mistaken; power can retreat here, re-organise its forces, invest itself elsewhere . . . and so the battle continues. (56)

Power here seems to be a kind of abstract bogey. If one can speak of power so globally, then the major difference Foucault introduces into the critique of ideology is simply a shift from the abstraction on the level of ideological consciousness to the abstraction of power as a function of the institution.

Another major contributor to the contemporary critique of ideology has been Raymond Williams. Over the past thirty years his works have taken a more explanatory mode in the direction of Marxist conceptualizations of ideology and literature. For the most part, his recent books have focused on explaining the origins of words and concepts. The tone is that of the helpful philologist who believes that we can understand our world better by better understanding our words. Williams' earlier works are characterized by an interest in more or less thematic interpretations of literary works to reveal their concern with social problems. Incidentally, Williams, as we have noted, has stated that the concept of ideology is simply not useful since its meaning is too ambiguous. As he wrote in *Marxism and Literature*:

> it is an open question whether 'ideology' and 'ideological', with their senses of 'abstraction' and 'illusion', or their senses of 'ideas' and 'theories', or even their senses of a 'system' of beliefs or of meanings and values, are sufficiently precise and practicable terms for so far-reaching and radical a redefinition. (71)

However in a later book, *The Sociology of Culture*, Williams turns around and uses the concept of ideology quite willingly – seeing it as revitalized by recent structuralist recuperations. Williams sees his new attitude as emerging from a practical convergence between the anthropological and sociological senses of culture as a distinct way of life and the more specialized sense of culture as artistic and intellectual activity. It is specifically in the area of ideological studies that Williams locates this new convergence, and particularly in the notion – which one must attribute to Althusser – that ideology denotes the vast signifying system which is the way culture represents ideas to itself and which involves all social practice. Williams, then, sees in the method of sociology an answer to the problems of how one actually talks about the specific ways in which ideology works. His main contribution to sociology is to show that it can explain things in the realm of the arts – where it is has presumably been remiss.

Williams' systematic work turns out to be not so different from his earlier nonsystematic work. In the first place, he wants to explain the signals, devices, and functions of literature as a result of history and class. Second, he wants to trace the history of certain words and concepts to show how their significance can be ascribed to history and class. For Williams the problematic of the critique of ideology is rendered less difficult by a recourse to the scholarly. Of course, all the thinkers we have been considering are scholarly, but Williams is the most likely to trust implicitly and without pre-stated defense traditional scholarship. So tracing the history of a key word through its 200 years of use is a retooling of traditional philology and Williams uses this kind of information rather uncritically. In this sense his work is also the most closely associated with traditional literary history and scholarship – except that he has always focused on the subject of class, worker conditions, rural and urban life, and so on.

His careful considerations of the growth of social formations integrate the work of Mannheim with that of literary critics. Williams' work is also focused on the past, on large blocks of time, and on general practices (like drama), so that explanations tend to be broad and general with scholarly and theoretical applications rather than immediate or practical ones. Yet, of all the critics of ideology of the present moment, Williams is the least likely to generalize ideology as the abstract bogey that is insurmountable and unimpeachable. His work therefore neither places the critic in some kind of fantastic warrior relation to the dragon of ideology nor is the intellectual seen as the defeated victim of ideology. There is a kind of quiet English faith in the project of the scholar and the heuristic value of study and historical revelation emitting from the university.

Fredric Jameson's further contribution in *The Political Unconscious* continues an expansion of the concept of ideology so that it becomes virtually synonymous with all forms of collective thought. He tries to resolve the vexing question of how ideology – particularly as it is manifest in novels and the mass media – can both impose constraint and domination on a mass of people and at the same time arouse in them the desire to overthrow such domination. As Jameson puts it:

> if the ideological function of mass culture is to be understood as a process whereby otherwise dangerous and protopolitical impulses are 'managed' and defused, rechanneled and offered spurious objects, then some preliminary step must also be theorized in which these same impulses – the raw material upon which the process works – are initially awakened within the very text that seeks to still them. (287)

To resolve this contradiction, Jameson makes the most expansive move in the history of the critique of ideology. He says that the reason so-called conservative ideological material can also awaken revolutionary impulses is because '*all* class consciousness – or in other words, all ideology in the strongest sense, including the most exclusive forms of ruling-class consciousness just as much as that of oppositional or oppressed classes – is in its very nature Utopian' (289). Providing the widest expansion of ideology, Jameson's vision includes not simply false consciousness to be combatted, but links revolutionary and conservative thought into the same category.

Blurring Mannheim's distinction between utopian and ideological thought, Jameson links the two, and thereby makes ideological anything short of actual thought within a real utopia. Jameson's argument is relevant because it is particularly about the novel. For him the novel, and modernism in general, can at once be a product of ideology and at the same time 'a revolt against that reification and a symbolic act which involves a whole Utopian compensation for increasing dehumanization on the level of daily life' (42). That is, Jameson's resolution of the problem of ideology is to have it both ways – to say that culture apes ideology but is capable of revolting against it as well.

Jameson's other contribution to the critique of ideology has to do with his concept of the 'political unconscious.' This formulation sees history as the unfolding of a hidden narrative – the slow progression towards a socialist state. As Jameson puts it:

> It is in detecting the traces of that uninterrupted narrative, in restoring to the surface of the text the repressed and buried reality of this fundamental history, that the doctrine of a political unconscious finds its function and its necessity. (20)

History is virtually an allegory of this narrative subtext. The critic then can read history as a text, an ideology obscuring the real political unconscious of the era. The power of this observation, however true or untrue, is that it assigns to the intellectual a kind of prophetic and interpretive role. However powerless the intellectual may be, he or she is standing on the right road to the future of power. Paradoxically, the influence of Freud and his concomitant sense of hopelessness is somewhat present in the idea of a political unconscious. Like the psychic unconscious, the repressed can only be made clear with the help of the analyst. Analysis through the specialized negative hermeneutic Jameson suggests is the only solution short of a new kind of 'collective' analysis. Ideology becomes not simply what is immaterial but analyzable – like the super-ego – but so vast, broad, and universal that it may indeed be impossible to escape it.

Whether Jameson is correct or incorrect in his theories, his contribution to the critique of ideology can be summarized as an expansion of ideology so that it becomes in the broadest sense neutral, analyzable, and homogeneous. The critic, empowered with armaments, enhanced by the most recent theoretical insights, can envision himself or herself in some kind of predestined war. The critical act becomes an action of unmasking, of opposition, and of a sort of terrorism. The irony here is that the field of operation is quite limited and the effect of such an attack is not actually felt much beyond the campus walk.

Terry Eagleton believes not only in the power of ideology but in the recuperative powers of criticism. In *Literary Theory*, Eagleton has written a kind of primer to aid readers in understanding the variety of critical schools. His point is that all criticism is political, whether it claims to be or not. Eagleton argues that literary criticism really is an illusion, the product of a culture that ascribes a special role to literature, and that we would be better off thinking of cultural analysis or the analysis of discourse instead of literary criticism.

Eagleton, perhaps the most influential discussant of the critique of ideology in our own period, best represents those writers who see ideology as totalizing and infinitely intelligent. In this view capitalist society has taken over the complete signifying system so that no social action and no piece of art or literature can successfully escape. In the midst of this totalized view stands the intellectual who can only hoist the occasional grenade into the intellectual edifice of deception. Analysis provides, as it has throughout the critique of ideology, the strongest and virtually only weapon. Criticism becomes a kind of laboratory for figuring out how signifying systems work. But hidden is the implication that no matter how smart the intellectual is, the system will always be smarter, more recuperative, more resourceful, and ultimately more powerful. The intellectual's powers are no match for Goliath, and hurl stones though he or she may there will be no dent in the tough, seamless exterior of the signifying system. The real message of such studies, hidden as they are, is that intelligence is not intelligence without power. That as smart, as competent, as computer-assisted as the intellectual may be, his or her intelligence is a poor match for the stupid intelligence and deviousness of the ideology-makers.

Eagleton's work continues certain dominant trends. Although emphasizing egalitarianism, Eagleton still untimately comes to rely on the expert and on the strength of analysis. Again, one sees the ambivalence between studying ideology as false consciousness (with the aim of changing it) and studying it as a set of belief systems (with the aim of analysis). By widening the definition of literature to include popular culture, Eagleton tries to make the category of literature as large as Jameson and Althusser have made the category of ideology. Such a continuing expansion of the categories have created a new 'end of ideology' thirty years after Daniel Bell proclaimed the exhaustion of political ideas in the 1950s. What Bell was announcing (or more accurately calling for) was the end of one-sided passion: 'if the end of ideology has any meaning, it is to ask for the end of rhetoric, and rhetoricians of "revolution"' (406). But over the next thirty years there has been a good deal of intellectual current under the bridge from which Bell was hoping ideology would jump. But ideology has come to an end in a different sense by expanding the definition to include everything from history or thought to literature and consciousness. It has become transformed into a huge and seamless text requiring not vaporizing or destruction but scholarship, interpretation, and devoted reading. In this sense, we are now in the period of the end of ideology.

Lest we announce prematurely the death of ideology, we have to acknowledge that ideological studies have clearly become a challenging area for a wide variety of disciplines from sociology to political science to literature. But the direction in which these studies need to go is clearly determined by the direction from which they have come. In this overview, a telling split occurs in the early twentieth century. Mannheim moved from Freudian interest in the individual to emphasis on the collective – but no one has moved back to the individual. What I mean is that there has been a distinct lack of interest in the ways that individuals interpenetrate with collective systems. Thus the individual has gotten lost in the social fabric and at the same time the concept of ideology has grown so global and general as to become itself an object of reification and mystification. The task ahead, at least in this study, is to try and combine our vast knowledge of the human psyche with our vast knowledge of the social conditions that shape its development. In each case, we need to particularize. How does the individual accept and rely on the group? It is here that my emphasis on the defensive structure of ideological formations becomes essential. Without individual and collective defenses, the very mechanism of ideological reproduction will remain mechanical, as it has been in so many of these explanations. At the same time, a defensive theory will help to combine both the critique of ideology and the study of a system of ideas

The ideology of ideology

– just as psychoanalysis provides both a critique of the analysand and the systematic study of his or her mind. Finally, an emphasis on the way that literary works in particular use specific techniques for ideological purposes can ground generalizations about the transmission and formation of ideology on specific social practices.

In presenting the history of the concept of ideology, I am attempting to show how difficult it is to rein in the meaning of one's own use of the word. When I use the word I am not using it in, for example, the Jamesonian sense or the Foucauldian sense. One cannot narrow such usage because the word itself has become part of ideology. I cannot restrict the sense of words like 'liberty' or 'human rights' or even 'structuralism' precisely because such words are themselves the objects of a struggle for meaning. Nevertheless, if absolutely pinned down, I would have to say that I use the word in three general and overlapping ways: that is, as a system of beliefs of a particular group or class; as false ideas or false consciousness; and as the general cultural system for the creation of signs and meanings. These three definitions will move in and out of focus as the concept is used in different contexts, and to these I add the mechanism of their dispersal by interpenetrating defensive structures.

My aim in laying out this little history of ideology is to show the force of the conflict between the 'Napoleonic doctrine' and the materialist view. The former consistently sees the work of intellectuals as separated into the world of theory. The latter sees ideology as a product of material culture, and thus sees intellectuals as actively able to intervene. Resisting novels means siding with the view that knowing is part of the process of changing. In saying this I cite Adorno and Horkheimer who wrote 'We are wholly convinced – and therein lies our *petito principii* – that social freedom is inseparable from enlightened thought' (xiii). But a genuine enlightenment means that we must not be fooled by our own words. In the case of the novel, this means not wishing for what is not there. If novels are ideological structures, then they will be ideological throughout. Though writers like Jameson may wish to see revolt in modernism and in the novels of this period, the predominant message of ideological structures is not towards revolt. It will be the burden of the rest of this book to show in what formal and structural ways novels are molded in the image of the ideological.

51

3

'Known unknown' locations: the ideology of place

Contemplating these essential landscapes, Kublai reflected on the invisible order that sustains cities, on the rules that decreed how they rise, take shape and prosper, adapting themselves to the seasons, and then how they sadden and fall in ruins. At times he thought he was on the verge of discovering a coherent, harmonious system underlying the infinite deformities and discords, but no model could stand up to the comparison with the game of chess.

Italo Calvino, *Invisible Cities*

Having just traced the range of the developing concept of ideology, it is now necessary to prove that such a concept has any validity for the novel. In the following four chapters I will be exploring the way in which ideology infuses various conventions of novel writing. It has been fairly commonplace to state that the novel is permeated with ideological themes, but the point I wish to make is that not only on the level of content, but even at the level of sheer form, ideological factors are operating. So I have focused on the most obvious requirements in the prestructure of the novel – location, character, dialogue, and plot. No novel can exist without these basic building blocks, and yet these building blocks have the appearance of universality, timelessness, and common sense. They do not appear necessary to the novel – but can apply to any form of narrative from a folktale to a play. That is precisely why I have been drawn to these seamless and shockingly plain categories. If I can show, as I hope to, that these seemingly neutral requirements of the novel themselves carry with them a good deal of ideological significance, then I hope to demonstrate the complicity of the novel in a much more inextricable way than simply pointing to 'what novels say.'

Before creating a character and a plot, one of the major tasks for a novelist is to establish a place or series of places in which characters will perform actions. While it may be more or less obvious that novelists must create locations, I want to stress that spaces in novels – and the whole enterprise of creating space in a dimensionless medium – is qualitatively different from the use of space in other literary and non-literary forms. Space in novels, particularly realistic novels, must be more than simply a backdrop. That is, paradoxically, novelistic spaces must have dimensions and depth; they must have byways and back alleys; there must be open rooms and hidden places; dining rooms and locked drawers; there must be a thickness and interiority to the mental constructions that constitute the novel's space. It is almost impossible to imagine the novel as a form divorced from a complex rendering of space. And while modern novels have variously eschewed character and plot, very few have dispensed with location, even if they have avoided realistic description. (Most of this chapter, though, will be more relevant to realistic, rather than surreal, narratives.) As Seymour Chatman writes: 'In verbal narrative, story-space is doubly removed from the reader. . . . Existents and their space, if "seen" at all, are seen in the imagination, transformed from words into mental projections' (101).

This simple idea that novels need to create locations is actually a fairly complex one. First, I want to stress that the creation of deep or thick space is not a universal given in all narratives. In fact, most narratives in most cultures before the advent of the novel in Europe in the eighteenth century, use a fairly flat, simple backdrop that lacks the thickness of novelistic space. Therefore the next part of my argument is an historical one that grounds the development of novelistic space in a particular set of social and historical processes.

Novelistic space as I will show is involved in a series of more or less hidden, ideological presuppositions about the nature of property and lands, foreign and domestic, the relationship of various races and classes to those lands, and the ways Europeans at various times found it necessary to represent, describe, and control terrains and property – their own as well as others. In other words, the very idea of a 'setting' could only happen as a result of a complex series of historical and cultural developments that occurred during the time of the novel's development in Europe. Likewise, as with other novelistic conventions, the seemingly neutral idea that novels must take place in locations was actually part of a collective structure of defenses that gave eighteenth-century society a way to justify the ownership of certain kinds of property. In the simplest terms, locations are intertwined with ideological explanations for the possession of property.

Before beginning this argument, I need to make a point which I will have occasion to stress throughout this work. In constantly emphasizing the distinction between reality and fictional representation, I may be seeming to say the obvious – that place, character, or dialogue are different within novels than without. Someone might well object 'What is the point? We all acknowledge that representation is not the same thing as reality. So what?' The 'what' in question is really a 'how.' I am not so much arguing that places in novels are different from real places – I want to see how. This book is nothing more than the analysis of modes of representation. When someone objects that a representation will necessarily be different from reality, I am only adding that we cannot simply take comfort in the fact of representation, but must analyze the mode – what is left out, what is included, what cannot be represented. In art, the argument might go: 'Of course there are bodies in many paintings but we need to look at the way the body is represented in different cultures and styles to understand the function of the various types of representation.' In the end, no one will disagree that a painted hand does not really look like a human hand. But the 'how' of the representation is what is central.

My major argument places the novelistic use of space in the at first unlikely political development of colonialism. When Columbus set foot in the West Indies and when Cortes conquered Mexico, these explorers were, I believe, discovering land in a way not so different from the way in which novelists like Defoe discovered the ability to control property through literary representation. Tzvetan Todorov has shown the relationship between the political and linguistic or semiological incorporation of foreign lands in his *The Conquest of America*, and this chapter is a kind of meditation on that subject as it applies to the novelistic depiction of terrain. Perhaps the mentality I am describing is best summed up by Daniel Denton who in 1670 returned from America and wrote a book describing the area from New England to Maryland and 200 miles inland. This area he called 'a known unknown part of America' (4). This chapter will try to detail the process of description, and show how the attempt to transform terrain into a literary representation can create a 'known unknown' space – an ideological representation of property that at once attempts to make it known and at the same time objectifies and falsifies it.

To begin with, one might want to locate three kinds of spaces in novels. The first is an actual geographical area such as the London of Dickens or the Paris of Balzac represented within the novel. The second kind of a location would be a fictitious place totally created by the novelist – a Wuthering Heights or a Middlemarch. A third instance would be a renamed, actual location purporting to be purely fictional such as Fitzgerald's East Egg and West Egg or Mrs Gaskell's Milton, which is understood to be Manchester. All of these depictions – even the ones of Paris and London – are ideological in the sense that they contain embedded social meaning. No author can actually recreate a place, but in using Paris or London – as well as Middlemarch or Wuthering Heights – the location becomes in effect reshaped through the intersection of the literary imagination and the social mythology. So in speaking of these locations, I intend to consider them ideological in the sense I have just described.

Certainly there were descriptions in earlier narrative, but they rarely achieved the depth and thickness of accounts in novels. In fact, I would assert that the very idea of an extended description of *any* place seems not to have been of general interest in medieval or renaissance Europe before the historical period roughly coinciding with the beginning of the novel.[1]

Of course, there had been travel literature since Herodotus' *Histories* and Xenophon's *Anabasis*, but while such works might relate the anomalous details of foreign life and occasionally describe monuments, there are few if any extended and detailed descriptions of particular locations. Percy Adams in his *Travel Literature and the Evolution of the Novel* demonstrates how, because the two forms are

55

uniquely interrelated, they both share an ideological view of terrain. Many English or European travellers were serving political, economic, or propagandistic purposes when they wrote about foreign lands. As Adams notes, 'a chief motive for Hakluyt ['s books on English sea travel] . . . was the desire to establish not just a British empire but good trade relations, to discover new commodities of trade, to arouse the interest of English statesmen or businessmen' (77). And the novelist, too, as I will show, had a stake in creating locations that could be claimed by language and used to justify and control property.

One important genre, aside from travel literature, that by definition must fall into description and creation of space, is military history. Xenophon's *Anabasis* is perhaps the earliest example of a military history that is also a travel journal. And since military history is primarily concerned with the claiming of space by force, it is in some sense a precursor of the ideological control of space inherent in the novelistic description. Rare, in these accounts of battles, is description for its own sake. In Julius Caesar's writings one is likely to find general accounts such as 'Caesar disembarked his army and chose a suitable spot for a camp,' or 'Next day the enemy took up a position on the hills at a distance from the camp' (Hart 37). But there is an absence of great detail. However, occasionally writers like Tacitus in his *Annals* give a more detailed description, as in the following:

> They marched to a level area called Idistaviso, which curves irregularly between the Weser and the hills; at one point an outward bend of the river gives it breadth, at another it is narrowed by projecting high ground. Behind rose the forest, with lofty branches but clear ground between the tree trunks. (Hart 42)

In all these cases, the detail is there in the service of recreating the battleground. But since the battleground is not imaginary but can be visited – as we might visit the scene of the Battle of Agincourt – the description of it is quite different from the creation of a 'known unknown' location which is firmly rooted in its fictionality. Because the battleground is so intimately known, in a sense, and so well celebrated or reviled, it is not up to the author to recreate the place. Also, in military history, the historian is ultimately more interested in the mass movement of soldiers, as is obvious, according to one military historian who points out that the paintings of battles focus more often on armies than on terrains (Keegan 64).

Nevertheless, the attempt of the novel to capture space and the aim of military history come together in the parodic *Tristram Shandy* when Uncle Toby sees the entire world in terms of the Battle of Namur, and sets about recreating the battleground in his backyard to explain where he got his wound. Although Uncle Toby is foolish, his nose is onto the correct scent since he is responding to an essentially narrative question ('Where did you get your wound?') with a space-fabricating answer.

One could of course argue that in allegorical works like *The Romance of the Rose* there were extended architectural details. But the importance of the space in such works is directly linked to the symbolic function of the location. Detail is there to be interpreted not to create a space that can be controlled. Detail for aesthetic rather than moral or schematic purpose is virtually absent. Symptomatic of this phenomenon in painting are the landscape backgrounds of Tuscan renaissance works and the allegorical use of terrain in medieval art. In his *Landscape Into Art* Kenneth Clark divides the history of landscape painting similarly, describing how the medieval 'landscape of symbol' gave way to a later 'landscape of fact.' The development of landscape painting as a genre came rather late to Europe and coincides with the literary trend I am describing here. Clearly there is a convergent movement to try and control, enumerate, and represent property. In *Ways of Seeing* John Berger makes the argument that landscape painting gave to patrons 'the pleasure of seeing themselves depicted as landowners and this pleasure was enhanced by the ability of oil paint to render their land in all its substantiality' (108). Part of the field I am trying to discuss in this chapter has to do with the urge of early modern Europeans to create, describe, and record space. Barbara Stafford has written an entire book, *Voyage into Substance*, on the way in which late-eighteenth-century painting for the first time systematically and scientifically attempted to describe and encompass the visible world. There is most certainly a changed attitude toward space during the early modern period, as I will show further, and the question is how did this change come about?

Were there any previous models for novelistic use of space? Novels might be closest to the Greek epic in their sense of space. Epics clearly take place somewhere, and though Troy might not be as clearly defined as Middlemarch, one can nevertheless envision the walls, the towers, the lone tree on the plain, the river, the armies, and so on. One can remember Odysseus' home with the feasting halls, the bedroom with the memorable bed, the swineherd's shack, Calypso's island, Circe's bed. Homer does not spend much time telling us *precisely* what these places look like, but within the imaginative structure of epics, space expands and is important.

Even in Greek art, according to Kenneth Clark, the landscape serves mainly 'decorative ends.' Where there is landscape, as in the Odysseus series in the Vatican, 'these are backgrounds, digressions, like the landscapes in the Odyssey itself' (1).

But the interior of, for example, Robinson Crusoe's cave strikes one as much different, so much more specific. Of course there is specificity in Achilles' sheild, but the detail is there for its significance and commentary on the rest of the story. For the most part the detail of the island is much more irrelevant and yet more important than the epic's.

One can make the argument, along with Georg Lukács in his *The Theory of the Novel* and Erich Auerbach in *Mimesis* that because the epic is authorless – in the sense that the concept of the author had not yet developed and the bard's subjectivity was subsumed in his function – the relationship to objects will be different in the epic and in the novel. Since the epic is without subjectivity and author, according to Lukács and Auerbach, it is also without perspective or depth. Its objects are bound together on an hierarchical single plane that assigns meaning in relation to social function. In the epic, social position and deed are identical and in this sense social position and object are interchangeable (Bernstein 59). Naturally described objects will participate in that system hierarchically. Tripods, goblets, cattle, and women are marked with value equivalents. In a novel like *Robinson Crusoe*, however, objects and terrain have only a use value, but they have no clearly assigned hierarchical and symbolic value. Hence, Crusoe can observe the irrelevance of gold and money – whose exchange value is meaningless in his primitive island economy. The point at which the novel diverges from earlier forms, theoretically speaking, is the point at which objects are included and described outside of an exterior, fixed system of meaning such as that provided by allegory. The new system of meaning by which objects are inscribed is the more ambiguous one of ideological meaning.

Further, one must recall that the epic is primarily not about *place* but about *memory* and voice. The listeners recall the fame and the exploits of past heroes, and the place where all this happens is primarily a backdrop to the exploits. The dominant presentation is made through the voice of the bard whose presence ratifies the tale telling. In a novel, there is no presence. The physical book itself is just the husk, the casing, of something not there.

Drama, of course, has a different relation to space. Playwrights need not manufacture an interior space since the action takes place within the defined location of the stage; the problem is how to make us believe that the location is not merely a stage but is in some way Elsinore or Venice and that the space offstage is not the reality of props and burly stagehands but is continuous with the onstage decor.

Because space is so obvious in drama, its importance diminishes. Shakespeare rarely gives much indication of what a particular location is to look like. Place is not described to be delimited as it is in the novel. Elsinore or Venice is simply as you like it. This casual attitude toward space stands in sharp contrast to novelists' deep concern to shape and claim location. One immediately thinks of the contrast between the islands occupied by Prospero and Crusoe. In *The Tempest*, Shakespeare does not go beyond indicating the existence of an island after the initial scene of foundering at sea. Act I, scene ii begins merely with the instructions: 'Enter Prospero and Miranda.' Shakespeare's point is that the action takes place on an island – any island – and the lack of specificity is not important. For Crusoe, the terrain, the location, the habitation is *everything*, taking the place of plot and even character. By contrast, *The Tempest* does not even describe Miranda's and Prospero's house.

One notable exception to what I have been pointing out is Petrarch's attempt to describe Mont Ventoux in his well-known letter. He gives a very limited vision of nature but several factors are operative here. First, this work is more in the nature of a private than a public work. Second, it can be interpreted allegorically. And third, it is an anomaly – and did not catch on in any dominant way for centuries.

Of course, one must recall the obvious from time to time – that there are actually no objects or landscapes in novels, that the novel can only imitate *accounts* of or *descriptions* of landscapes since the novel is exclusively a linguistic phenomenon, as Mikhail Bakhtin and Barbara Herrnstein Smith, among others, have pointed out. So we are discussing in essence the various conceptions of the language's ability to encapsulate and contain objects – the presuppositions behind various kinds and degrees of belief that a particular culture can use language to contain or describe objects. In talking in such general terms, the pitfall is of course that not all groups of readers may accept the values of this convention. Unfortunately I do not have the space or occasion to examine the range of readers who might or might not accept the convention, but my sense is that a majority of readers – past and present – have been able to create a belief in the existence of interior space. In making my argument, I do not want to imply that this historical explanation will condition all future readings of these texts. Obviously, not all readers at all times will find in *Robinson Crusoe* the ideological constraints on place I am describing. But in a culture that continues to rely on linguistic (and now electronic and chemical) representations of extended terrain, these issues will play a prominent part in perception.

To move from these general observations to more particular examples, I will now look at four major works from different centuries – Daniel Defoe's *Robinson Crusoe*, Balzac's *Le Père Goriot*, Hugo's *Les Misérables*, and F. Scott Fitzgerald's *The Great Gatsby*. Of course, such a random selection will prove nothing in and of itself. I simply want to trace a development and continuity in the novel's use of space. Any reader will perhaps find counter-examples to the ones I have selected. That is inherently the problem of any book that treats the novel, which is in itself a massive and untreatable corpus. But in the spirit of this book, which keeps to a rather slim and respectable 'reading list,' I hope to illustrate my points.

My argument in following paragraphs will be that Defoe began *Robinson Crusoe* using the earlier, non-novelistic sense of space as simply a backdrop and then moved to a more complex rendering of space. Defoe made this move partly as a solution to the limiting 'problem' of how to develop a story of a man on an island for several hundred pages and partly with an intuitive sensitivity to a growing interest in controlled property.

To understand this claim more clearly, consider the opening section of *Robinson Crusoe*. The first actual scene, after a few details of Crusoe's upbringing, is the one in which his father counsels him to do what middle-class kids have always done. That advice is placed in a 'setting' with the simple phrase: 'He called me one morning into his chamber' (5). This scene uses the older, non-novelistic sense of space – the traditional space of the ballad ('As I was a walking' or 'In the town where I was born') – when Crusoe describes in a few sentences the facts of his identity and his family. Let me distinguish here between 'setting' and 'terrain.' A 'terrain' is an actual place in the world; a 'setting' on the other hand is a terrain incorporated into a story which serves as a very generalized backdrop to the action which will occur. 'Settings,' however, are not detailed or specific.

In the hands of a novelist like Dickens, as we will see, that scene might have been treated quite differently. We would visualize fully the father, his features expressing his sentiments, and the room which would act as an index to the state of life of the family, and these details would accumulate to a full statement. If one compares Defoe's description of space, only the words 'his chamber' actually defining the setting, with Balzac's nine-page opening description of Madame Vauquer's boarding house in *Le Père Goriot*, the remarkably large distance description has traveled over the 100 years separating these works gives us some indication of the importance the illusion of space has to the nineteenth-century novel.

But here, all we have is the simplicity of the words 'his chamber.' The space is claimed by the adjective but not by the novelist. Settings such as this one are generalized and not detailed or specific. But as this novel of claiming and possessing progresses, Defoe also – by the necessity of his limited plot – has to claim the interior space of the novel in a rather newer and different way than any preceding European writer. This use of novelistic space I will call 'location.' Just as Hollywood looks at a terrain and then turns it into a location, so novelists go beyond *setting* and *terrain* to transform their space into an intentional *location*. In the course of writing *Robinson Crusoe*, I want to argue, Defoe moves from tale or ballad-like setting to the novelistic equivalent of 'shooting on location.' And as I want to show, locations are ideological precisely because they delimit action and enclose meaning while appearing only to describe neutrally. Paradoxically, as in the cinema, locations do not really exist anywhere since they are created for the moment of filming. Even if a location is a street in New York City, that street must be remade, lit, cleared, or arranged for the camera. Locations are in this sense 'known unknown' spaces since by making themselves known to the viewer they, at the same time, become unknowable – outside the parameters of normal perception. In effect, the façade of the frontier town on the Paramount lot and the desert island of Crusoe are comparable. The more Defoe describes the island, the more it becomes unknowable by furthering its existence as a purely linguistic phenomenon. The more a filmgoer gets to know the layout of Dodge City the more duplicitous the experience becomes since there is no continuous Dodge City, but only a series of shootable locations connected by the film editor's skill.

One way to explain this interest in location of the early European novel is to connect it with property relations during this historical period. English power over the colonies in *Robinson Crusoe* is particularly relevant. That is, *Robinson Crusoe* is largely about the claiming of an island that does not 'belong' to Crusoe except in the sense that he is a European and builds something there. But Crusoe's claiming is not simply the manifestation of a military might, although he does demonstrate that too, but of establishing an ideological right to the island. Defoe causes the claiming of the island to be interpenetrated with morality, thought, and desire. Crusoe's and Defoe's ways of thinking about the island are inseparable from the island; thus the island becomes an occasion for examining that way of thinking. In this sense, the creation of a place becomes part of the process of ideological control. As Geoffrey Sill has pointed out, *Robinson Crusoe* was written 'to answer's a specific reforming end, and to arrive at this end by systematizing the ideas of nature, kingship, providence, opportunity, and self-restraint into a coherent, new personality [and is therefore] . . . a work of ideology as well as a work of fiction' (158). In effect, Crusoe's advice throughout the work connects a series of injunctions about work, the world, religion, sexuality, sovereignty, knowledge, and so on, but these can manifest themselves purely on the level of location.

Another clue to a growing interest in property can be found in English property laws. The history of such laws shows a greater and greater interest in turning real property, that is land, into a commodity like any other. Under the feudal structure of tenure, the tenant did not own his land nor did the lord, who received the land from the king. Actually, all land was the king's land but under the system of feudal obligations the king could not be said to own the land either because he 'owed a duty to recognize and protect the possessions of the tenant' (Baker 199). Land in effect was not owned and therefore could not be transferred or sold. The history of 'uses' and 'settlements' is too vastly complex to explain here, but the point is that by the eighteenth century land could be sold and transferred under the 'strict settlement' which had certain provisions, particularly that restrictions could only be placed on land for one generation. Giving owners the power to sell represented a realization of 'the economic fact that . . . a settlement of land was a settlement of wealth, which need not be tied to specific pieces of land' (Baker 247). In other words, the value of land could be commodified, bought, and sold, and did not inherently reside in the land. The movement in law is toward the creation of controlled, commodified property.

In novels, space – such as Crusoe's island – is given a specific or relatively specific purpose. In life the meaning of spaces is much more diffuse and varies from person to person and culture to culture, according to Yu-Fu Tuan in *Topophilia*. Likewise in the colonization of space, specific purpose was attributed by an exterior culture whose task was then to see that meaning as inherent in and indigenous to the colonized space. Or, as Edward Said has written in *Orientalism* about the study of the Middle East:

> that Orientalism makes sense at all depends more on the West than on the Orient, and this sense is directly indebted to various Western techniques of representation that make the Orient visible, clear, 'there' in discourse about it. And these representations rely upon institutions, traditions, conventions, agreed-upon codes of understanding for their effects, not upon a distant and amorphous Orient. (22)

At roughly the period that Europe was creating the representation of its colonies, its novelists – at least Defoe – were colonizing another kind of space, a space perhaps more complete and total because it was inside the mind of that particular captive of the novel who was the middle-class reader.

What was being claimed in a tentative way was not merely the castles of the imagination, but the very way the world was seen and European society was conceptualized. Of course, colonizing is not merely a literary exercise, but the project of colonizing cannot exist without the help of ideological and linguistic structures. A country must do more than simply steal another country: a series of explanations, representations, and rationalizations must intervene to justify political action. Even the inhabitants of the targeted colony must, for a successful colonization, accept the domination of the language and symbols of this takeover. To win hearts and minds, one must occupy hearts and minds – in the dominant as well as the occupied countries.

The very project of writing a novel relies on the specificity of locations and the detail of creating a description or a texture to a location we come to believe is 'there.' In essence that space must be controlled, and therefore becomes 'property' which is after all controlled space or location. Thus, we may say that property is a precondition for the novel since novels must be set in controlled or claimed places. Middle-class readers, reliant for their existence on the relatively new emphasis on movable and controlled property, might have found this emphasis congenial. (Of course, in saying this, one must exercise caution. Novelists were rarely if ever conscious of their ideological roles except insofar as novels were overtly for or against something. It would be foolish to say that Defoe or Richardson were trying, formally, to arrive at ideological structures. They were probably trying to devise structures that worked in those times and places, with only the most intuitive sense of what 'worked' meant. I want to stress that these novelists were not latent Marxists or bourgeois propagandists working away with a particular project in mind.)[2]

We have a tendency to think that the way we conceptualize space is the way space has always been thought of. But writers like Yu-Fu Tuan and Clarence Glacken show us that different epochs have regarded nature and space differently. Particularly, it is Tuan's point that with the rise of the modern state came a change in the way Europe regarded space. The modern state is too large to be perceived as a natural unit, the way for example the Greeks held allegiance to their home region, to their city, but not much farther than that. But 'the modern nation as a large bounded space is difficult to experience in any direct way; its reality for the individual depends on the ingestion of certain kinds of knowledge' (100). In effect, the modern state required the recreation of its space through ideological means. Modern patriotism is therefore a product of language and information dispersal in rather a different way than earlier types of patriotism linked to a land bounded by directly perceivable horizons. The novel's embuing of space with ideological significance seems to be part of a larger project of the modern state which attributes meanings to locations at home and abroad.

Power and physical space were fairly consciously manipulated by those who created the system of the modern state. For example, cities in medieval Europe were built haphazardly with streets small, narrow, and criss-crossed. When a ruler like Louis XV wanted to display the royal prestige of the centralized state of 1746, he had to impose on the medieval pattern of Paris nineteen *place royales* with radiating streets forming stars, and at the center of each star a statue of the Divine Monarch (Tuan 159). To create the central pull of the modern state, urban landscape had to change and in effect become ideological. The radiating and converging avenues of Paris stood for political power as well as aesthetic ease, as did the British Empire's creation of a colonial center in New Delhi with its massive avenues and radiating vistas counteracting the crazy quilt pattern of Old Delhi. T. J. Clark has written brilliantly of the 'Haussmanization' of Paris in the nineteenth century in which the old quarters were demolished to make even more avenues and vistas. The purpose of this decoding and recoding of the city was to turn ideology into physical, public signs. As Clark notes, contemporaries wanted 'the city to have a shape – a logic and a uniformity – and therefore construct one from the signs they have, however sparse and unsystematic' (33). Like the novel, architecture and urban design served to make public the private. As the Goncourts' journal noted in 1860: 'The interior is passing away – Life turns back to become public' (34). England's industry in building over the pre-existent Delhi is not unlike Crusoe's remarkable reshaping of his environment.

To return to the text of *Robinson Crusoe*, Defoe begins his work, as I have pointed out, with a non-novelistic use of space as had most writers before him. Early in the novel, settings are simply nautical notations plotting the co-ordinates of the tropical and the equatorial (10). These nautical references give the impression of a cartographic mastery over unknown worlds, but no thick space is created for the reader, who at this early point in the narrative is provided only with the tale, the teller, a few anecdotes, an inventory slip, and a map. What space there is signifies that of the unknown, the exotic, and the dangerous. Most of the countries Crusoe visits before arriving at *his* island are undescribed places that tend to echo with 'dreadful noises of the barking, roaring, and howling of wild creatures.' At one, Crusoe writes that it was 'impossible to describe the horrible noises, and hideous cries and howlings, that were raised as well upon the edge of the shore' (22). And another setting yields one animal who emits 'the most hideous roar that ever I heard' (24). For Defoe, inarticulateness is the recurrent feature of unclaimed territory that cannot be understood through recognizable European signs.

These lands are hostile, peopled and animaled with horrors, hence not worth colonizing (at the moment) and therefore not describable. I would fine-tune the definition of 'terrain' here to say that it becomes location (that is, the novelistic use of place) only when a nation, character, or author seeks to control that property: the attempt to describe it in a novel would then be the literary equivalent of the act of political, legal, or military control. The desire to describe and the desire to possess politically are not simply related metaphorically, as I have indicated, because political occupation needs ideological justification. The idea of description is profoundly dependent on cultural notions of what one can claim, envision, or comprehend in words. In his book on early American discoverers, Wayne Franklin singles out a description by the conquistador Cortes of a market in Mexico. This account ends on a note of indescribability and befuddlement:

> Finally, besides those things which I have already mentioned, they sell in the market everything else to be found in this land, but they are so many and so varied that because of their great number and because I cannot remember many of them nor do I know what they are called I shall not mention them. (3)

While Cortes cannot describe the confusion of things, he nevertheless uses his language to claim and refashion the object. Cortes' confusion is the rule rather than the exception among travel writers who 'universally had trouble representing what they saw' (Stafford 28). But, as Franklin stresses, Cortes' concern does not accidentally relate to description and reporting. 'More than any other emblem of identity, language seemed capable of domesticating the strangeness of America' (5). Such descriptions filled out the void of the colonies so that they could be made understandable to Europeans – remade in Europeans' own descriptive terms. In short, according to Franklin, in the New World 'the reportable was the feasible and the conceivable as well' (4).

Particularly in the affective and aesthetic realms, the colonies presented untold problems to European cognition. Dutch settlers found 'the great valley views [of the Hudson] too measureless, heavens too vast for charting' (Van Zandt vii). The very idea of 'wilderness' was too imposing and strange for settlers – even well into the nineteenth century – since Europe had virtually eliminated any pretension towards wilderness. The first Puritans dealt with the impenetrability of the wilderness by laying on Biblical iconography (Carroll 6). Even the lowly Catskills range remained an object of awe and wonder until well into the nineteenth century – before general familiarity with and exploration of the wilder Adirondacks and the Rockies and Sierras. As Roland Van Zandt notes, speaking of the Catskills, 'it was the unique quality of the American wilderness, that became a major obstacle in the intellectual assimiliation of European canons of aesthetic judgment' (153). Late eighteenth-century European aesthetic focused on the Lockean doctrine of 'association,' in which the observer appreciated the landscape by the series of mental associations it called forth particularly concerning 'ruins and relics, myths and legends, of all past human history' (153). But the problem with America was that there were no ruins and relics, its myths were hidden behind the obscure cloak of native American signs and symbols, and the wilderness resisted such associations. As Barbara Stafford points out concerning ruins and relics, 'the enfeebling of material objects was intrinsically inimical to voyagers who believed that distant or strange lands and their marvels existed without the need for human intervention' (4). In other words, the spaces of the colonies were without preordained meaning or ideology, so that meaning had to be supplied from without. The paintings of the Hudson River School – particularly those of Thomas Cole, John Frederick Kensett, Jasper Francis Cropsey, and Frederick Church – along with the writings of authors like James Fenimore Cooper, gave a meaning to the wilderness, inscribed the natural forms with intelligible iconography and so turned them into ideological space. Reading the descriptions in a work like Cooper's *The Pioneers* one feels the fully realized attempt to transform the Catskill wilderness into a space made intelligible to the Euro/American mentality:

The mountain on which they were journeying was covered with pines, that rose without a branch some seventy or eighty feet, and which frequently doubled that height, by the addition of the tops. Through the innumerable vistas that opened beneath the lofty trees the eye could penetrate, until it was met by a distant inequality in the ground, or was stopped by a view of the summit of the mountain which lay on the opposite side of the valley to which they were hastening. The dark trunks of the trees, rose from the pure white of the snow, in regularly formed shafts, until, at a great height, their branches shot forth horizontal limbs, that were covered with the meager foliage of an evergreen, affording a melancholy contrast to the torpor of nature below. (19)

The fullness of description bearing with it the notion of the wilderness made intelligible and transformed into a sublime poem of nature is a kind of benchmark of the novel's abilities when compared with earlier notions of description and space. Clearly, too, Cooper's forest was appearing in his mind as a painting by Cole (who did illustrate scenes from *The Leatherstocking Tales*).

The inherent contradiction in describing but being unable to completely subsume the New World under descriptive control focuses attention on the colonizing European's attitude toward the native's linguistic abilities. It was necessary to think of the native as essentially bereft of language. Since natives could not describe their own space they could not be said to own it in the same way as the European – and here the ability to describe land has its legal consequences as well since deeds and land claims require a specialized kind of linguistic notation. So, if land required description, it was European description it required. Typically, one settler in South Carolina noted that Indian language lacked

> terms to express abstract and general ideas, which is an evident proof of the little improvement of the understanding among them: time, duration, space, substance, matter, body, and many such words have nothing equivalent in their languages, not only those of a metaphysical, but likewise those of a moral nature, cannot be rendered into their tongue, but imperfectly, and by a circumlocution; they have no words that correspond exactly to those of virtue, justice, liberty, gratitude, ingratitude, etc. (Milligan 517)

It goes without saying that lacking those concepts, such people could not be seen as responsibly owning or describing their universe – moral or otherwise. Tuan points out that the dichotomy between visitor and native renders the native voiceless, particularly when the native is a so-called primitive:

> Only the visitor has the viewpoint. . . . The native, by contrast has a complex attitude derived from his immersion in the totality of his environment. The visitor's viewpoint, being simple, is easily stated. . . . The complex attitude of the native, on the other hand,

can be expressed only with difficulty and indirectly through behavior, local tradition, lore and myth. (63)

It is the complexity of the native's view of the environment that stands against the visitor's incomprehension and consequent simplification. Simplification permits colonists to flatten the object of their desire so that it may be taken without guilt or shame. This same process allows novelists and painters to transform the complexity of the topological to the aesthetic and the ideological.

In *Robinson Crusoe* this theme of linguistic incompetence continues, since although Friday has a modicum of intelligence he never sufficiently masters English to allow him legitimate linguistic status (in the way that the Portuguese captain is 'permitted' by the convention of the novel to be represented in Standard English without knowing a word of it). Friday's claim to the island is perhaps stronger than Crusoe's, since Friday lives in the region, but it is Crusoe who 'discovers' it and becomes the 'governor' of the domain, and Friday never is thought of as staking a claim. It is Crusoe's language combined with his industry that makes his claim special. In the same ideological triangulation language, industry, and moral right are thought distinctively European and therefore the qualities that transform the shapeless nature of the New World into describable locations. Indians, on the other hand, were considered lazy, slothful, and morally bereft – hence incapable or unworthy of their land. As one contemporary writer put this notion:

a rude and unpolished *America* peopled with slothful and naked *Indians*, instead of well-built houses, living in pitiful huts and cabbins, made of poles set endways; then surely the brute Beasts condition, and manner of living, to which what we have mention'd doth nearly approach, is to be esteem'd better than Man's, and wit and reason in vain bestowed on him. (Glacken 483)

And to put a finer point on the argument, Buffon wrote of the native Americans that they 'lack the force and vigor to change the physical environment, as other peoples, especially in the Old World, had done' (Glacken 588). That is, novelist and settler come together in their industrious transformation of terrain into location. Journals, novels, travel accounts, and so on grant, through the skilled use of language, a kind of possession of that which is described. Obversely, the native American's linguistic inadequacy renders him less dangerous, according to one settler in South Carolina, since Indians act as a buffer between whites and black slaves. If the Indians were driven off, 'their ground would be soon taken up by runaway Negroes from our settlements, whose numbers would daily increase, and quickly become more formidable enemies than Indians can ever be, as they speak our language, and would never be at a loss for intelligence' (Milligan 480).

The slaves' ability to speak English is what makes them dangerous since linguistic competence allows the ability to control and master. The major contradiction for Europeans is that while the natives do not have adequate language, the European with a competent language faces a kind of crisis of representation in which his language is both able and unable to subjugate the unknown by description. Inherent in this contradiction is the idea I raised earlier of the 'known unknown' – by which description itself transforms the object. In this case, the object is transformed from an impenetrable set of signs to a colony ready for domination. In the case of the novel, space is objectified by description to become a representation, that is, a controllable but unreal space – hence an ideological location.

The frequency with which Crusoe uses phrases like 'nothing can describe' or 'which I cannot describe' (37, 39) may also be thought of as part of a novelistic frustration about creating a space out of nothing, especially a nothing which is so terribly 'other' as to be outside the discourse of a reasonable Englishman.

Although terrains may have been converted to places with purposes or functions in some earlier works (for example, Hell in *The Divine Comedy*), the schematic meaning of those places was always foremost. However, the intentionality of Crusoe's island is much less obvious, embodied subtly in objects and acreage, much the same way that ideological structures work without overt compulsion or even visibility. On the other hand, while we are meant to believe in the fullness of Dante's space, we always remember the allegorical meaning, the schematic justification.[3] The third ring of Hell means something, but what does the 'other side of the island' mean? Defoe himself, as a novelist, was in suspect terrain when he created the space of Crusoe's island – and it is the anxiety of creating space that is recorded by Defoe.

Through an overdetermined combination of colonially influenced thought patterns, middle-class interest in controlled property, and the arbitrary limitation of *Robinson Crusoe*'s plot, Defoe comes to create an extended, non-allegorical space almost by necessity as Crusoe first explores the island, builds his house, and settles the location. Crusoe's first attempt to describe the island amounts merely to a negative list of objects:

> I began to look round me to see what kind of place I was in, and what was next to be done, and I soon found my comforts abate, and that in a word I had a dreadful deliverance: for I was wet, had no clothes to shift me, nor any thing either to eat or drink to comfort me, neither did I see any prospect before me but that of perishing with hunger, or being devoured by wild beasts. (39)

Without the available concept of extended description, inventory is about the only permissible form of representation. Inventory revolves around the presence or absence of useful objects. According to Svetlana Alpers in *The Art of Describing*, this tendency toward the representation of objects would classify Defoe as more of a describer than a narrator, if one kept her distinction between the descriptive Flemish painters and the action-oriented Italians. Alpers equates this tendency toward the 'descriptive' with the 'realistic' (xxi). As the Flemish painters were drawn to the painstaking representation of objects, Crusoe's first descriptions seemed to have been made around useful things as part of Defoe's realistic effect. Also, Kenneth Clark notes that the earliest non-symbolic landscapes were made up of inventories of objects, as are for example the medieval tapestries filled with detailed illustrations of flowers and plants. 'The art of painting, in its early stages, is concerned with things which one can touch, hold in the hand, or isolate in the mind from the rest of their surroundings' (11).

Most of the objects[4] Crusoe lists are of European origin – either brought to the island or manufactured there. They amount to a relative inventory of wealth and power. It is curious that only when the island is littered with the flotsam of civilization – and thus made sensible and recognizable to Crusoe – can it be claimed enough to be described. In his well known commentary in *Capital* on Defoe's work Marx wrote that 'all the relations between Robinson and the objects that form this wealth of his own creation, are here so simple and clear as to be intelligible without exertion. . . . And yet those relations contain all that is essential to the determination of value' (77).

In other words, the objects embody ideologically the whole system of European economic relations.

Crusoe's private act of settling the island can be seen as a kind of parody, intended or not, of what England was doing throughout the world, and the only thing that makes Crusoe's task less distasteful is that the island appears uninhabited and empty. But, as Johannes Fabian points out in his history of anthropology, 'political spaces' are not the same thing as 'natural resources.' The former are

> ideologically construed instruments of power. . . . It has long been recognized that imperialist claims to the right of occupying 'empty', under-used, undeveloped space for the common good of mankind should be taken for what they really are: a monstrous lie perpetuated for the benefit of one part of humanity. (144)

If the cannibals of the second half of the novel had appeared earlier, Crusoe no doubt would have had to shoot them – making much more obvious the power relations implicit in his activity, thrift, industriousness, and so on.

When Crusoe views his island as a collection of objects to be used, he is still within the pre-novelistic discourse. In effect Defoe is following the line of discoverers' journals which also view the New World colonies as inventories of goods. The records of the East India Company during the sixteenth and seventeenth centuries reveal a dearth of any extended descriptions of India before the eighteenth century. Typical of the type of letters sent back to England from India is one from an employee of the company who wrote in 1614: 'But to speak in general of the country itself, it is a place of good trade and divers good commodities to be had, especially indigo' (Foster 144). 'Speaking in general' of India meant speaking of its natural resources. There is little sense that one might want descriptions of the country aside from the value of its raw materials.

Another example might be Sir Walter Ralegh's trip to Guyana in 1595. His account *The Discovery of the Large, Rich, and Beautiful Empire of Guiana* is more centrally about 'large' and 'rich' than it is about 'beautiful,' since the book was written to secure the invasion of this choice island. Very rarely is any terrain described at length except in terms of its objects of utility, and then only gold is central. As Ralegh himself says, 'Where there is a store of gold, it is in effect needless to remember other commodities for trade' (113), so he often just skips them. Descriptions deviating from this singleness of purpose are unnecessary: 'To speak of what past homeward were tedious, either to describe or name any of the rivers, islands, or villages of the Tiuitiuat which dwell on trees, we will leave all those to the general map' (106). And what description there is falls into the catalogue of useful objects for settlers: 'It hath so many plains, clear rivers, abundance of pheasants, partridges, quails, rayles, cranes, herons, and all other fowl: Deer of all sorts, porks, hares, lions, tigers, leopards, and divers other sorts of beasts, either for chase, or food' (111). The country is described as a warehouse simply waiting for consumption. Or, to shift the metaphor, Guyana is a country Ralegh aptly notes 'that hath yet her maidenhead, never sacked, turned, nor wrought' (120).

In an era in which these early explorers talk overtly of brute force, we know that the more covert and subtle control of ideology is not fully necessary. The refashioning of the terrain through language and extended description is a development in political control and the rise of the modern state, with its concommitant reliance on covert rather than overt compulsion. It was during the eighteenth and nineteenth centuries, when colonizing was seen not strictly as a business venture but more as a humanizing of the world, that the primacy of ideology and language in changing and refashioning terrains into locations became more central. As I have noted, the records of the East India Company during the seventeenth century are simply business transactions, trading accounts, and so on. What is striking is the absence of any sense of moral justification or description in these records. Only as the project of colonizing begins to include the idea of saving the world and civilizing it does one begin to see justification.

Interestingly, the history of landscape painting follows a similar pattern from the inventorial to the ideological. Seventeenth-century Dutch landscapes tended to be fairly topographical, simply showing the viewer what was there and amounting to the kind of catalogue we have been discussing. The English did not seem to have developed indigenous pastoral painting, according to John Barrell, and preferred to have mainly portraits of themselves and their estates (9). Thus the development of landscape grows out of an intimate connection with property. As Kenneth Clark notes, 'The landscape of fact, like all portraiture, is a bourgeois form of art . . . [reflecting] the desire to see portrayed *recognizable* experiences' (29).

But when the English did arrive at landscape painting in the eighteenth century, they began to shift from descriptive landscapes to more interpretive or ideological ones. This movement corresponds to what Kenneth Clark describes as a progression from the 'landscape of symbol' to one of 'fact' to, finally, the 'landscape of imagination.' Ronald Paulson points out in *Literary Landscape* that 'the history of landscape painting is a movement from description to self-expression, from either topography or emblematization toward "landscapes of the mind."' (9). In effect, landscape began to be perceived as capable of embodying ideas and to contain significance. Linked to the notion of ideology is the notion of order since, as Paulson points out, painting landscapes comes out of the desire to master nature and control it. 'To control something that seems uncontrollable, whether one is an artist or a farmer or a gardener, one must package, label, verbalize, and humanize it' (18). Following Jay Appleton's theory, we can add that the entire idea of landscape is to provide the viewer with prospect and refuge. As Appleton puts it:

> Habitat theory postulates that aesthetic pleasure in landscape derives from the observer experiencing an environment favourable to the satisfaction of his biological needs. Prospect-refuge theory postulates that because the ability to see without being seen is an intermediate step in the satisfaction of many of those needs, the capacity of an environment to ensure the achievement of *this* becomes a more immediate source of aesthetic satisfaction. (73)

So landscape as a control of space serves to protect the viewer from the dangers of the terrain and at the same time transform the hostile environment into a refuge. Such a notion not only serves Crusoe's interests but the interests of readers as well. In this sence, Ian Watt misses the point when he says 'wherever Crusoe looks his acres cry out so for improvement that he has no leisure to observe that they also compose a landscape' (70). Actually, by creating a refuge, Crusoe is in effect transforming his island *into* landscape – that is, he is shaping wilderness into inhabitable, controlled space which will provide the maximum in possibilities for prospect and refuge.

One has the impression that between 1750 and 1850 the entire world was painted and sketched in detail, mapped accurately, and described, so that the visible world now had its correlate in the pages of books and the surfaces of canvasses. The conquering of the world and the establishment of Empire was reproduced, transcribed, contained and organized – largely through explorers' and novelists' use of description and painters' use of landscape – to become what Roland Barthes called in another context an 'empire of signs.' Even the aesthetic program of landscape had its connection with property relations. In her book on landscape painting and its relation to exploration, Barbara Stafford notes that 'the purpose of the long-standing practice of having naval draftsmen take coastal profiles was to provide . . . [a] . . . clear . . . indication of the shape of unmapped land. . . . Panoramic views drawn from high points of land were connected with triangulation surveys' (124).

One exception to my argument about the ideologicalization of space in the eighteenth century is raised by Clarence Glacken who points out that the massive deforestation of Europe which occurred during the Middle Ages had an ideological component in religion.

> It would be remarkable, therefore, if no bridge was built from theology to farming, grazing, and the forest – that is, if no divine purpose was seen in man's ability to sustain himself by suing the earth and changing it to meet his desire. (294)

And as Glacken notes, the Renaissance too saw further the 'power of man to transform not only the elements but the landscape' (464). But it was really during the late seventeenth and into the eighteenth century that the formally religious view and the generally humanistic view merged into a thoroughgoing politico-social transformation of the visible world. According to Glacken, a plan like the following one by John Evelyn to transform the king's forests would have been impossible before 1664:

> [If oak were planted] at handsome intervals, by which grazing might be imporved for the feeding of deer and cattle under them . . . benignly visited with the gleams of the sun, and adorned with the distant landscapes appearing through the glades and frequent valleys, nothing could be more ravishing. We might also sprinkle fruit-trees amongst them for cyder, and many singular uses, and should find such goodly plantations to boast of our rangers, and forests infinitely preferable to any thing we have yet beheld, rude and neglected as they are. (488)

Here we see the qualities I have been pointing out: moral and even political significance attributed to space and combined with an aesthetic view.

Description even more profoundly implied the taking over of space if one considers that it was the obligation of every British subject landing in a new or unclaimed territory to place a monument there claiming the dominion of English rule. Gulliver realizes this obligation in his *Travels* when he notes that 'it was whispered to me, that I was bound in Duty as a Subject of *England*, to have given in a Memorial to a Secretary of State, at my first coming over; because whatever Lands are discovered by a Subject, belong to the Crown' (257).

An actual traveler's journal, that of Francis Rogers written in 1702, still reflects this kind of inventorized relation to description. Even the title to his handwritten journal evokes a pre-novelistic, printed news ballad: 'Brief Observations of the Most Remarkable Occurrence that hapn'd in a Voyage to the East Indies.' Arriving at Tenerife, he simply catalogues objects:

> This Island is very pleasant, being always green, the orange and lemon trees having all the year round blossoms, and the fruit green and ripe on the same tree, which is very pleasant to behold, and the trees affording a fragrant smell (Ingram 146)

Another entry in the journal is for the island of Mohila:

> This Island is high land and very woody and pleasant, and affords good cattle, but small; plenty of goats and fowl, very cheap; but no sheep or hogs, I think, they being a sort of Mahometans. (157–8)

Both of these descriptions are pre-novelistic in their limited scope. Terrain is skipped over in a single leaping bound in favor of useful objects or remarkable facts. It is worth noting attempts at more extended descriptions during this transitional period when the indescribable was beginning to be described. Take Rogers' description of a mountain which offers one of the first extended descriptions that combine inventory with detailed settings. However, we need to bear in mind that Rogers is describing the famous mountain at Tenerife which had become a kind of eighth wonder of the world because of its unusual geography – rising straight out of the ocean as it does:

This island is very high land, but especially the Peak, which is accounted the highest land in the World. When we were there the Peak was covered with snow at the top, as they say it is the year round, although t'was hotter than our Summer with us, the clouds flying a great way beneath the summit of the Peak which was in a clear transparent blue sky, like a clear frosty weather night with us.

A different island – more to the point – was detailed in William Dampier's 1697 account of Juan Fernandez Island. This of course was the island on which Alexander Selkirk was stranded and it was from Dampier's account along with that of Woodes Rogers' that Defoe is thought to have taken a good deal of his deep background for *Robinson Crusoe*. Dampier still cannot get beyond the inventory. He begins with navigational plotting and then notes that Juan Fernandez is

> full of high Hills, and small pleasant Valleys, which if manured, would probably produce any thing proper for the Climate. The sides of the Mountains are part Savannahs, part Wood-land. . . . The Woods afford divers sorts of Trees; some large and good Timber for Building, but none fit for Masts. The Cabbage Trees of this Isle are but small and low; yet afford a good head, and the cabbage very sweet. . . . The Savannahs are stocked with Goats in great Herds. . . . The West end of the Island is all high Champion Ground without any Valley, and but one place to land; there is neither Wood nor any fresh Water, and the Grass short and dry. (114–15)

In line with what we have seen, this description emphasizes objects of utility. The land is described so that its usefulness can be gauged and presumably so that future travelers may be provided with a kind of survival map of the land.

In contrast to this traditional form of description, in George Anson's journey around the world from 1740 to 1744 one sees more of a novelistic, extended description. In fact, the introduction to the printed version of Anson's journey, published in 1748, is nothing less than a plea for accurate description. As the editor writes: 'For every authentic account of foreign coasts and countries will contribute to one or more of these great ends [navigation, commerce, and national interest], in proportion to the wealth, wants, or commodities of those countries, and our ignorance of those coasts' (9). The editor praises Anson's *Voyage* for its accuracy saying that 'I can venture to affirm, without fear of being contradicted on a comparison, that no voyage I have yet seen, furnishes' similar details (10). This puff is then followed by a plea that travelers to distant lands should aim at accurate description: 'I cannot . . . but lament, how very imperfect many of our accounts of distant countries are rendered by the relators being unskilled in drawing, and in the general principles of surveying' (15).

Sketching is particularly singled out since people who know how to draw objects 'observe them with more distinctness, than others who are not habituated to this practice' (16). In accordance, Richard Walter, the chaplain on the *Centurion*, wrote that sailors should be encouraged to draw since 'those who are habituated to delineating objects, perceive them more distinctly than those who are not similarly accustomed' (Stafford 46). The logical extension of this attempt to record comes with the use on voyages of the camera obscura in the 1790s so that 'with this compact, portable "de-lineator" a person of but moderate skill could do more work of "the utmost truth," than the ablest draftsman' (Stafford 427). The emphasis here forges a powerful link between the visual arts, the description of terrain, and economic advantage. Property controlled is property extolled through representation. In Holland, landscape painting was used as a kind of mapmaking. Even the Dutch word *landschap* could refer to both what the surveyor was to measure and what the artist was to render. The word itself had a purely administrative meaning designating 'a collection of farms or fenced fields, sometimes a small domain or administrative unit' until it was used in English at the end of the sixteenth century in its more aesthetic sense (Tuan 133). The connection between describing, painting, and mapmaking was often related powerfully to recording and establishing landownership, whether in Holland or abroad. Obviously, too, any legal deed of land or charter would owe its existence to accurate description and delimitation of the land to be possessed. In addition to the graphic arts, writing also allows the confrontation of ideas on paper with the object represented, and can be included here. The sailing directions issued by Henry Hudson include a significant caution: 'Send those on land that will show themselves diligent writers' (Franklin frontispiece). Hudson realized that description of any kind records the colonial space and is part of the conquest, settlement, and use of that space.

The cataloging of knowledge was among other things a primary goal of such describing. Johannes Fabian points out that the ethos of early 'scientific' explorers included a parallel desire, in the words of the ill-fated explorer La Perouse, to 'complete the history of man.' Fabian adds, using Foucault's idea of the *épistème*, that 'complete' is used in the sense of

> *filling out* (as in 'to complete a questionnaire'). In the *épistème* of natural history the exercise of knowledge was projected as the filling of spaces or slots in a table, or the marking of points in a system of coordinates in which all possible knowledge could be placed. (8)

This goal is post-novelistic and ideological. The point is to fill out the entire idea-system of a culture and subsume it under the European vision without necessarily appearing to do so. The eighteenth century's passion for taxonomies and cataloguing in the natural sciences, economics, and philology is also transferred to this branch of knowledge. For example, a description of South Carolina written in 1761 stresses this inclusiveness, saying that

> every material fact or circumstance in this description is indexed under its proper head . . . so that if there be ten, twenty, or more particulars mentioned concerning any one species of product, and there are about forty about rice, the index will show in what pages each of them is to be found. (Anon. 194)

In addition to controlling through indexing, this work includes pages of tables of weather, wind conditions, import and export figures, numbers of black and white inhabitants – all rendering intelligible and ordering the disorder of the colonial experience. Such inclusiveness was consonant with the art of describing. As Barbara Stafford writes, 'An insistent empiricism underlay the explorers' method of perception and saved them from complete bewilderment and inarticulateness in the face of an unedited nature' (40).

Parenthetically, this empiricism in turn worked back from the ethos of exploration to that of landscape art. Early painters of landscape did not explore the terrain that they painted. According to

Kenneth Clark the mountains of the Gothic painters appear unreal to us because 'medieval man did not explore them. He was not interested' (11). Likewise, the old masters did not paint from nature (62), and it was Claude Lorraine in the seventeenth century who first painted from the observation of nature. Clearly, an interest in exploring extended to painters who then engaged nature directly. An even stranger example of the interrelation between observation and landscape occurred during the eighteenth century when people would buy 'Claude glasses' so that they could see the landscape as it would have appeared in a painting by Claude Lorraine – that is, as it *should* be seen.

In this light, the description in Anson's *Voyage* is remarkably different from the pre-novelistic ones of Ralegh, Dampier, and Roger. Anson's accounts are too long to print in their entirety here, and that fact in itself is worth noting – a simple inventory is no longer sufficient given the complex goals of England's attempt to colonize less 'civilized' lands. A colony, under such a large humanizing project, can no longer be thought of simply as a warehouse of products to be inventoried but must be represented as a system of values, ideas, and ways of thinking. Of particular interest in this regard is Anson's own description of Juan Fernandez Island. The quality of the description – still filled with objects of utility – expands not only to mark, but to define and fill out the space, to claim it in quite a different way from Ralegh, Roger, or Dampier. Take for example the following excerpt:

> the irregularities of the hills and precipices in the northern part of the Island, necessarily traced out by their various combinations a great number of romantic vallies; most of which had a stream of the clearest water running through them, that tumbled in cascades from rock to rock, as the bottom of the valley, by the course of the neighbouring hills, was at any time broken into a sudden sharp descent: Some particular spots occurred in these vallies, where the shade and fragrance of the contiguous woods, the loftiness of the overhanging rocks, and the transparency and frequent falls of the neighbouring streams, presented scenes of such elegance and dignity, as would perhaps with difficulty be rivalled in any other part of the globe. It is in this place, perhaps, that the simple productions of unassisted nature may be said to excel all the fictitious descriptions of the most animated imagination. (119)

Anson's mode is novelistic and nature is seen herself as a novelist who can write a pretty 'romance' with her streams that exceed all 'fictitious' description. We have moved here from a landscape of fact to a landscape of imagination – or ideology as it were. Or, as another early voyager to New York put it, 'You may be behold Nature contending with Art, and striving to equal, if not excel many gardens in England' (Denton 4). In this sense, nature is seen as inscribing space with a European aesthetic, as if nature intuitively knew that art was a European phenomenon. A new form of Claude glasses is being applied which, instead of infusing the terrain with the tint of old master varnish, colors the perception of nature so that it conforms to European values. Since nature creates its space with the European in mind, it follows that natives of the New World do not possess Art – hence do not appreciate the inherently 'civilizing' nature of their own country's aesthetic message. A visitor to the New Netherlands in 1656 depicts the Indians as bereft of art as well:

> The paintings of the Indians are of little importance, being confined to the colouring of their faces, bodies, and skins which they wear. . . . Their paintings are not spirited or ingenious . . . they paint representations of canoes and animals, which are not well done. (Van der Donck 39)

Nature, under the rubric of European art, is only capable of representation in European terms.

With writers like Anson, notions of space change too. Rather than being a virgin with treasures to be taken, as Ralegh had seen Guyana, now the New World incorporates the civilizing power of art and culture. So nature writes a novel with her hand, or more often may be thought of as presenting a theatrical experience to the viewer. Later Anson describes setting up camp in a place that nature had created as a kind of theater for viewing her productions (120). The island is laid out *for* the viewer – not simply as a catalogue of objects of utility, but to suggest that the New World inherently embodies a certain theatricality and narrativity. The stage is set and America awaits the castaway or the colonial. As Wayne Franklin points out, discoverers' accounts frequently imply that the discovered territory is laid out especially for a viewing by the Europeans. Such scenes, according to Franklin, show 'us a man struggling to find his proper perspective, that single organizing viewpoint from which the great size of

81

America can be reduced to proper dimensions' (27). According to Jay Appleton's prospect-refuge theory, these Europeans would be seeking the safe and mastered position from which to apply the colonial fulcrum that will shift the landscape to their side.

Defoe almost seems to stumble on this kind of description that creates ideological space. Before Crusoe expands his description of his first dwelling, two things occur. He shoots his gun for the first time, and he establishes a storehouse of commodities. The firing of the gun is presented by Defoe as a symbolic act with the repercussions of the shot heard around the world. 'I believe,' says Crusoe, 'it was the first gun that had been fired there since the creation of the world.' This boast is promptly cut down to size by the reaction of a small cat who sees the gun 'but as she did not understand it, she was perfectly unconcerned at it, nor did she offer to stir away' (44–5). The incomprehension of this furry native is amusing, muting Crusoe's triumph, but signaling the incomprehension of the cannibals – who are justly afraid of firearms. Their ignorance of this high technology is a sign of their general inability to understand or describe the European world and sets the stage for Crusoe's assertion of the superiority of English – both as a language and as a culture. Likewise, his storehouse, 'the biggest magazine of all kinds now that ever were laid up, I believe, for one man,' does not satisfy him, but does mark a kind of tremendous industry and the power of primitive accumulation. These two primal acts of colonizing – power and industry – seem to give Crusoe the right to claim the land, and Crusoe's extended description now can begin:

> In search of a place proper for this [building a dwelling], I found a little plain on the side of a rising hill, whose front towards this little plain, was steep as a house-side, so that nothing could come down upon me from the top; on the side of this rock there was a hollow place worn a little way in like the entrance or door of a cave, but there was not really any cave or way into the rock at all.
>
> On the flat of the green, just before this hollow place, I resolved to pitch my tent: this plain was not above an hundred yard broad, and about twice as long, and lay like a green before my door, and at the end of it descended irregularly every way down into the low-grounds by the sea side. It was on the N.N.W. side of the hill, so that I was sheltered from the heat every day, till it came to a W.

and by S. sun, or thereabouts, which in those countries is near the
setting. (48)

The description is hardly luminous – no setting sun and swaying
palm trees – but it serves a function, marks a point, and creates a
map. The account may be thought of as the first, or one of the first,
extended descriptions in the history of fictional narrative. It opens a
space that continues to increase as the house is prepared.

> Before I set up my tent, I drew a half circle before the hollow
> place, which took in about ten yards in its semi-diameter from
> the rock, and twenty yards in its diameter, from its beginning
> and ending.
> In this half circle I pitch'd two rows of strong stakes, driving
> them into the ground till they stood very firm like piles . . . this
> fence was so strong that neither man or beast could get into it or
> over it. (48)

The very circumscription of the land which precedes Crusoe's
building is a dramatic illustration of the way that describing –
literally drawing or enclosing the plot of land – claims the area,
protects it from intrusion, and in effect creates the internal space of
the novel. Colonizing the island requires the creation of ideological
space, and so Defoe in addition to describing in extensive detail must
make the island a location that unobtrusively embodies meaning.
The island is not conceived of allegorically, but each effort and each
location illustrates – even formally – some aspect of Defoe's belief
system. The bone-littered side of the island must contain Crusoe's
judgment of it; the corn sprouting must embody a divine significance; the fortifications must be the occasion for a discussion of
prudence. Place must become location – that is, terrain with a
purpose.

After this long descriptive section, Defoe seems to drop the
possibility of extended description. Crusoe's further explorations of
the island revert to the limited ballad-type description and almost
every exploration that follows focuses on things. We do get descriptions of the bank of a brook with 'many pleasant savannah's, or
meadows; plain, smooth, and covered with grass' but it is the
tobacco next to the grass that interests Crusoe, and so on. The
description is a catalogue of wealth, an inventory of nature's

possessions that are simultaneously his. Defoe, after beginning the possibility of extended description, rarely if ever returns to it.

It is interesting that shortly after Defoe was compelled more or less to include this description, he performed a kind of truncation of the novel by including Crusoe's 'own' journal. It may not be far-fetched to see this action as a way of shutting the Pandora's box of description of space that Defoe had inadvertently opened. Perhaps the difficulty of such a continuous, sustained, and consistent type of description turned Defoe back to the rather telegraphic style of the journal. I would speculate that Defoe was daunted by the necessity of this descriptive set-up and felt that one way of avoiding the tedium of creating space in such detail was to escape to a journal where the issue of place could be avoided. Defoe would come back to a few extended descriptions in *The Further Adventures of Robinson Crusoe* but in other works – even colonial ones like *The History of Colonel Jack* – the descriptions tend to be pre-novelistic (in the sense that they are either perfunctory or merely inventories of objects).

Defoe did not totally eschew description in his later career. In a 'non-fiction' work (and one must use that term between quotation marks with Defoe because it is so difficult to tell when he is fabricating and when he is not) such as *A Tour Thro' the Whole Island of Great Britain*, Defoe states his aim as 'a description of the most flourishing and opulant country in the world. . . . Here is the present state of the country described, the improvement, as well in culture, as in commerce, the increase of people, and employment for them' (1). But Defoe's aim of description stops far short of creating a physical space. When he does describe, he mainly describes architecture – and that he often does in great detail – including a proposed plan for the Royal Palace at Whitehall, but characteristically this extended description remains in the realm of the imaginary since the building does not yet exist. Ending that description Defoe says, 'But I return to the description of things which really exist and are not [like the Palace at Whitehall] imaginary' (365).

One of the few other detailed descriptions in his guidebook is that of Stonehenge which is a kind of 'known unknown' location. In Defoe's attempt to describe the place, he notes that according to local superstitions no human can accurately count the total number of stones. Rationally, Defoe tries to account for this by noting that since the stones are partially buried 'it cannot be known easily, which belong to one stone, and which to another, or which are separate stones, and which are joined underground to one another' (197). Aside from uncountability, which he dismisses a 'mere country fiction,' he cannot explain what the shape is actually since 'the form of this monument is not only described but delineated in most authors, and indeed 'tis hard to know the first but by the last' (197). He cannot explain how the stones got there or how they could be moved by man. And he concludes that since 'the true history of it is not known ... I think the making of so many conjectures at the reality, when they know they can but guess at it, and above all the insisting so long, and warmly on their private opinions, is but amusing themselves and us with a doubt, which perhaps lies the deeper for their search into it' (198).

I have taken a bit of time with this account because I want to show that since Stonehenge resists description, it therefore in Defoe's mind defies control. It is then a kind of 'known unknown' and as such cannot become the physical space that the island was. Paradoxically, Stonehenge can never be replete with *presence* the way the fictional can because until a space acquires ideological dimensions it cannot become part of social memory and collective culture. Stonehenge simply 'is,' therefore it resists meaning and even technical description.

In *Robinson Crusoe*, Defoe began a trend to make description of place seem as if it were a neutral requisite to plot, but as I hope I have suggested, location is a transformation of terrain. The seemingly neutral idea of describing a place and setting action in it carries with it the freight of a middle-class interest in controlled property of which the colonial experience is a compelling metaphor. Novels claim space and turn it into a system of meaning – just as countries claim other countries and turn them into systems of meaning. The Paris of Balzac is not Paris any more than the New York of Fitzgerald is New York. As readers, we are forced into the belief that location is really terrain. But locations have purposes and functions. The way that these locations embody meaning is ideological – they are indirect, naturalizing their signs, imitating the terrain, becoming the secret sharer of the original – and finally replacing the original, in the way that Dickens' London becomes the template in advertising and the popular mind for jolly old England. The ideological function of this act of appropriating space may serve to convince us that places can be summarized, controlled, and intended for specific purposes – a conviction that is the cornerstone of the early modern and modern periods.

As the early visitor to New Netherlands knew, description encapsulates an area that is known and yet unknown. And Cortes' confusion reflects at the same time both his ability and his inability to possess the New World. The novelist, too, can describe and encapsulate through language, but must also realize that any description is a simplification, a simulacrum, of any space. By making it known, the novelist makes the space unknown. That is, description is a familiarization of space and at the same time a defamiliarization. To describe the space and to control it is at the same time to objectify it – to change sensual reality into words and to make it part of a system that imbues objects with exchange value. As Karl Marx noted in *Capital*, in an industrialized society 'exchange value is *the only form* in which the value of a commodity can manifest itself or be expressed' (I: 128). Novels, by using landscapes and the objects in them not for their usefulness but as part of a system of meaning, regard these things for their symbolic exchange value as part of a symbol-system alone. For example, according to Fredric Jameson in *The Political Unconscious*, description in the work of Balzac is associated not simply with the object but with the social system's interest in objects. The 'Balzacian dwelling invites the awakening of a longing for possession, of the mild and warming fantasy of landed property as the tangible figure of a Utopian wish-fulfillment' (157). Lukács' notion in *Soul and Form* of the novel's movement between mimesis and form-giving – that is, between novelists' goal of imitating reality and their other goal of shaping reality – makes us realize that giving form to exterior reality can make that reality, as it were, unreal, just as Marx described the process by which commodities become fetishized through the process of reification. It is no coincidence, I am maintaining, that novelists began to conceive of linguistically incorporating land and space in a way that created an alienated or reified space at precisely the historical moment (Marx and others have suggested) that Europeans began to experience a parallel defamiliarization of their own space and their relation to property and objects. This is not the place to describe or assert that process. I can only point to the creation in the novel of that ideological structure of novelistic space, with all its valences, and suggest that space's existence as a kind of 'known unknown.'

At this point, one might well ask why I have taken an excursion through these explorers' accounts to try to explain something as fairly obvious as the fact that plots in novels take place in *some* kind of setting. After all, is this not like going back to the story of Joseph's coat to try and explain the nature of papal costuming? What I am trying to say is that something as obvious as setting is also something not so obvious. The very fact that extended description of the kind I am discussing rarely occurred before the novel's advent ties this kind of description to newly emerging forms by which European culture explained itself to itself. Looking forward, one might well raise the argument that what I am describing is fine for the eighteenth century but has little or no relevance to the novels of the nineteenth and twentieth centuries. To a certain extent this objection is valid, although I would expect that the conditions for the origins of a narrative form would remain somehow valid and integral to that form as it developed and changed. Particularly, I would agree that later novels have become somewhat less interested in place and more interested in the self and the language of the self, psychologically and philosophically. In the following chapters I will follow this development, but for now I want to follow the trend set by Defoe. That is, one might legitimately wonder if this particularly eighteenth-century insight into space might have any relevance to nineteenth- or twentieth-century works.

For the nineteenth century, the extended description became the rule rather than the exception. Writers like Balzac, Scott, and Dickens are known, sometimes disparagingly, for their detailed descriptions. Places in classic novels live in our own memories – Fagin's den, Satis House, Bleak House, Wuthering Heights, Madame Vauquer's boarding house, Raskolnikov's cubicle-room. The extended description, begun fitfully on Crusoe's island, grew during the nineteenth century to its full ideological significance, as did landscape painting which reached its height in that period. And the novel becomes, oddly, the form that *makes* places exist. In the nineteenth century, the idea of location expands in a crucially significant way – place becomes not the floating island or the isolated room, but becomes linked with history. We may say that in *Robinson Crusoe* location was important as controlled property – *any* property; that the interest in property as such was linked to a general ideological interest in acquiring property and in the interchangeability of property linked to the interchangeability of money or surplus value.

Saleable or moveable property, like money, held its aura in the eighteenth century by virtue of its phantom-like existence dependent solely on its exchange value. Adam Smith celebrated that invisibility and mystifying insubstantiality of capital by pointing to the regulations of the 'invisible hand.' The South Sea Bubble scandal and other attempts of Whigs to take advantage of the free-floating capital of middle-class progress remind us that free-floating capital was still a bizarre object of awe and mystification. So Crusoe's almost magical relation to money and property mirrors that awe and mystery.

But capital in the nineteenth century is a different story. Property no longer exists in the cultural lexicon simply as sheer value. In the previous century a character simply had to come up with property in connection with noble birth to be a success, as did Tom Jones, Pamela, Humphrey Clinker, and Evalina to name a few. But by the nineteenth century, property had to be justified as well as justly gotten. While Jameson is correct in pointing to the way that description evokes a longing for property, by the nineteenth century such a longing needed to be disguised by ideological means. Just as the representation of sexual longing in novels had to be controlled by directing it toward worthy institutions like the family, so the desire for wealth had to be seen as something more than crass greediness. Elizabeth Bennet has to *not* care about money to get it. Pip suffers for wanting it. Heathcliff gets it and is thought less of for his methods, as are Bullstrode and Lydgate. Bleak House dissolves on the struggle over money. Property needs justification. That is, it needs the underpinning of ideological support. Thus, property can no longer be thought of as undifferentiated and universal. It needs to be particularized through history – placed in a specific location and accounted for by its ideological place in society.

If we take Balzac's opening to *Le Père Goriot* which includes, I would guess, the longest description ever written until that time of a place – Madame Vauquer's boarding house – we can see evidence of placing property in its historical setting. The book begins:

For the last forty years the elderly Madame Vauquer, *née* de Conflans, has kept a family boarding-house in the Rue Neuve-Saint-Geneviève between the Latin Quarter and the Faubourg Saint-Marcel. . . . Yet in 1819, the time when this drama begins, an almost penniless girl was living there. (27)

One notices the attempt to place the opening in a specific time that is integrally part of the location – not just *any* boarding house but *this* one at *this* time. Furthering the specificity, Balzac quickly adds that his story will not be understood except by the people who live in Paris at this particular time:

> Will it be understood outside Paris? One may doubt it. Only between the heights of Montmartre and Montrouge are there people who can appreciate how exactly, with what close observation, it is drawn from life.
>
> They live in a valley of crumbling stucco and gutters black with mud, a valley full of real suffering. (27)

The ensuing seven-page description places the location historically, and also imbues the place with a full range of ideological meaning. The neighborhood is 'the grimmest quarter of Paris' and next to the house is a chipped and scaling statue of the God of Love, which even Balzac notes 'provides an allegory for those who are fond of symbols' (29). The sitting room is 'depressing;' the rooms smell of 'decay;' the furniture is 'old, cracked, decaying, shaky, worm-eaten, decrepit, rickety, ramshackle and on its last legs.' These details are imbued with the moment and with ideological meaning. In fact, the description cannot make sense without ideology. What Maison Vauquer means can only become clearer in contrast with the other ideological location of the wealthy Faubourg Saint-Germain. As Vautrin nastily puts it, 'We eat Ma Vauquer's messes and have a taste for the fine dinners of the Faubourg Saint-Germain; we sleep on a pallet and long for a mansion!' (126).

By writing about his Paris in the books that make up *The Human Comedy*, Balzac creates Paris. Each book opens in a different locale, a different house, but each one is a window on a world that only exists by virtue of the novelist. For Balzac, Paris becomes the ultimate location of meaning. Each street and house ceases to have an independent existence and becomes a signpost along the way, a semaphor for cultural observation.

Likewise, Dickens made or remade London, particularly for his reforming purposes. He is rarely writing about a universal London, but writing about a London with contemporary problems and proposed solutions. His property is never there without ideological justification. Paradoxically, the advertising executives for companies that promote tourism to England insist on seeing what they call 'Dickens' London' as if it were universal and timeless – still extant today somewhere overshadowing race riots in Brixton and the glorified mundanity of the royal family. However, it is true that Dickens caused his specificity to become universal simply by getting tangled in the very process of novelistic description, since as we have seen such description tends to universalize, based as it is finally on the timeless qualities of controlled property.

To a certain extent, Dickens' contemporaries realized that description changes location better than Dickens did. In writing about London, some saw that London had become a 'known unknown' location by the process of Dickensization. One particular instance might be illustrative. In the preface to the first cheap edition of *Oliver Twist*, Dickens points our attention to 'a description of "the filthiest, the strangest, the most extraordinary of the many localities that are hidden in London." And the name of this place is Jacob's Island' (xi). This is the squalid locale of Fagin's den and is referred to in the pages of the book as Saffron Hill. An excerpt might help to refresh the memory:

> A dirtier or more wretched place he had never seen. The street was very narrow and muddy, and the air was impregnated with filthy odors. There were a good many small shops; but the only stock in trade appeared to be heaps of children, who, even at that time of night, were crawling in and out at the doors, or screaming from the inside. The sole places that seemed to prosper amid the general blight of the place were the public houses, and in them the lowest orders of Irish were wrangling with might and main. Covered ways and yards, which here and there diverged from the main street, disclosed little knots of houses, where drunken men and women were positively wallowing in filth; and from several of the doorways, great ill-looking fellows were cautiously emerging, bound, to all appearance, on no very well-disposed or harmless errands. (86)

Parenthetically, we might want to notice the complete ideologization of the description – in which each detail accumulates to reveal lower-class degradation and the discomforting racist view embedded within it. Also the picture is impressionistic – focusing on movement and people rather than on urban architecture and layout. The impression given has more of the suggestiveness of a Turner or a Constable canvas than the detail and clarity of a Hogarth or a Reynolds. However, one can feel the thick quality of the description, even though it lacks pointed specifics.

The relevant point for our purposes is that Dickens' description of Jacob's Island took on a relative life of its own. In his preface, Dickens first notes that since he described this slum very little had happened to reform living conditions; but that recently the Bishop of London in a meeting had suggested changes in Jacob's Island. As Dickens said, he was at that meeting and the bishop 'did me the honor to mention that I had described Jacob's Island. When I subsequently made a few observations myself, I confessed that soft impeachment' (xii). Dickens continues to note that an opponent of this reform, Sir Peter Laurie, addressed another meeting a few days later in which he asserted that Jacob's Island did not exist, saying that

the Bishop of London, poor soul, in his simplicity, thought there really was such a place, which he had been describing so minutely, *whereas it turned out that it ONLY existed in a work of fiction, written by Mr. Charles Dickens ten years ago* (roars of laughter). *The fact was admitted by Mr. Charles Dickens himself at the meeting.* (xii)

Dickens goes on to comment wryly on this logic that

when Fielding described Newgate, the prison immediately ceased to exist; that when Smollett took Roderick Random to Bath, that city instantly sank into the earth; that when Scott exercised his genius on Whitefriars, it incontinently glided into the Thames; that an ancient place called Windsor was entirely destroyed in the reign of queen Elizabeth by two Merry Wives of that town, acting under the direction of a person of the name of Shakespeare; and that Mr. Pope, after having at a great expense completed his grotto at Twickenham, incautiously reduced it to ashes by writing a poem upon it. (xiii)

Dickens' irony notwithstanding, it is clear that something strange has happened in the cultural imagination when an area such as Jacob's Island was better known to the middle-classes through its literary incarnation than its own virtual existence. For Dickens, the place only exists insofar as its ideological and historical place allows. After all, Dickens is not just describing for art's sake, but for reformist purposes as well. However, for Laurie, by virtue of the fictional description, the location has changed and become an ideological if not a fictitious construct. Dickens rightly attacks Laurie for a kind of myopia, but the myopia operates on a larger scale than Dickens might wish to admit.

A similar situation arises with Thomas Hardy who created in his novels the imaginary countryside which he called Wessex. But his imaginary land gradually came to take on a life of its own, as did Jacob's Island. As Hardy writes in his preface to *Far From the Madding Crowd,*

> I did not anticipate that this application of the word [Wessex] would extend outside the chapters of these particular chronicles. But it was soon taken up elsewhere, the first to adopt it being the now defunct *Examiner,* which, in the impression bearing the date July 15, 1876, entitled one of its articles 'The Wessex Labourer', the article turning out to be no dissertation on farming during the Heptarchy, but on the modern peasant of the south-west counties. (5)

Hardy's refashioning of the pre-Norman location into an ideological and fictional recreation was obviously in line with current thinking, as if England could colonize not only the world but its own past as well. The public acceded willingly as Hardy noted, saying that 'the appellation which I had thought to reserve to the horizons and landscapes of a partly real, partly dream-country, has become more and more popular as a practical provincial definition; and the dream-country has, by degrees, solidified into a utilitarian region where people can go to, take a house in, and write to the papers from.' Thus, the colonization of the imaginary leads to concrete and perceptible gains in reality.

Let us take another example from the nineteenth century. In *Les Misérables* by Victor Hugo, the novel form reaches a kind of fullness and perfection in terms of plot, character, and location. Paris is evoked with an encyclopedic fullness. Taking the idea of description to its most inclusive conclusion, Hugo spends hundreds of pages describing Paris, evoking it, examining its argot, its gamins, its changed environs, and even the history of its sewers. He treats Paris as if he were an explorer recording the terrain and history of a foreign country. And Paris was in some ways a foreign country to him because he was forced to leave it during the Second Empire and remain in exile on the Channel Islands for many years. It was during this period that he wrote *Les Misérables*. In this sense, his recreation of Paris had to become a monumental simulacrum – and Paris would become a 'known unknown,' in effect.

What justifies Hugo's descriptions is the constantly informing voice of history. Property is made part of the historical process. And in this sense Hugo becomes the greatest historical materialist among novelists particularly when he devotes scores of pages to a description of the battlefield and the battle of Waterloo. Waterloo for Hugo inaugurates the symbolic beginning of the nineteenth century and therefore the beginning of the history of his period. Even the name of the place 'Hougomont . . . built by Hugo the squire' (280) incorporates not only the history of Europe but the author's familial history, if only by phonemic similarity.

In this section of *Les Misérables*, Hugo pays powerful attention to the particularization of landscape, since it was an unseen trough in the middle of the battlefield that led to the miscalculation on Napoleon's part that led, in turn, to his demise. History, in effect, is *contained* in the now quiescent terrain. Hugo begins by saying that he recently visited the battlefield and walked over the landscape. The visit evokes history, which is inscribed in the objects and natural features there:

> The farm buildings occupy the southern flank of the main yard. A portion of the original north gate, shattered by the French, still hangs from the wall – four planks nailed to two cross-pieces bearing the scars of battle. This north gateway, in which a makeshift door has been installed, was like any other farm entrance, wide double doors attached directly to a wall made of stone in its lower part and brickwork above. The struggle for it was particularly violent, and the imprints of bloodstained hands were for a long time to be seen on the surrounding masonry. It was here that Bauduin was killed. (I:281)

History speaks from the terrain. Even though the bloodstains are no longer there, the historical record, of which this novel is part, mutely testifies. As Hugo says more directly:

The fury of battle still lingers in that main yard; its horrors are still visible, its violence graven in stone, the life and death of yesterday. The breached and crumbling walls, their holes like gaping wounds, cry out in agony. (I:281)

History justifies even the most minute detail of description and creation of space. Take for example 'the spoon-shaped iron [door]handle sloping downwards' that Hugo pauses to notice. Its relevance does not serve, like Crusoe's artifacts, simply for the creation of a realistic effect or to act as a representation of movable property. Its existence and our notice of it is justified on historical grounds – 'As a Hanoverian lieutenant named Wilda grasped this handle to take shelter in the house, a French sapper cut off his hand with an axe' (I:283). Further, Hugo gives to the landscape a literary significance saying that a courtyard 'is divided into three parts, one may almost say, three acts' (I:284). The whole story of Waterloo is written, in effect, in the surrounding landscape so that all the village people know it, read it, and can charge a fee to visitors for the story. Hugo contrasts the enormity of the struggle with the simplicity of the financial transaction: 'All of this so that a yokel today may say to the traveller, "For three francs, Monsieur, I will tell you the story of Waterloo"' (I:285). But in the very next sentence Hugo becomes in effect the yokel, saying 'We must use the privilege of the chronicler to turn back to the year 1815, to the period shortly preceding the events related in the first part of this book' (I:285). Hugo is acting in a manner not so different from the yokel, making the terrain speak its mute message, changing the actual space into a literary location – and profiting from it financially as well. But as the chronicler, Hugo has history behind him whereas the yokel only has pecuniary interest and local legend.

History, it turns out, is better fulfilled in the novel than in history books because novels can truly allow space to speak. So Hugo can even now dig out from the landscape the word 'merde' originally hurled by the defeated but unbowed Cambronne to the English general who asked for surrender. For Hugo, this crude reply was the height of experience:

to demolish the European coalition with a word, fling in the face of kings the *cloaca* known to the Caesars, make the crudest of words into the greatest by investing it with the splendour of France, insolently conclude Waterloo with *mardi-gras*, complete Leonidas with Rabelais, compress this victory in a single word . . . this is sublime. (I:312)

And part of Hugo's ideological justification of the novel is that *only* the novel, not history books, can exhume from the archeological landscape this triumphant but profane word. As he notes:

From respect for the decencies of language this word, perhaps the greatest ever uttered by a Frenchman, is not repeated in the history books; the sublime is banned from the record. At our risk and peril we have defied the ban. (I:311)

This cloacal vision of greatness is perhaps not uncoincidentally evoked in Hugo's other mammoth description, that of the Parisian sewers. As Hugo says, 'This story of mankind is reflected in the history of cloaca' (II:368). However, unlike Cambronne's triumphal scatological salvo, the Parisian sewer is 'the resting-place of all failure and all effort.' Like Swift's view of the outhouse as 'the last result of all designs' (*Poetical Works* 621), Hugo's sewers are described in encyclopedic detail as the underside, literally, of human accomplishment.

To political economy it is detritus, and to social philosophy a residue. It is the conscience of the town where all things converge and clash. There is darkness here, but no secrets. Everything has its true or at least its definitive form. (II:369)

Like the battlefield at Waterloo, the location of the sewer contains history within itself. 'Crime, intelligence, social protest, liberty of conscience, thought and theft, everything that human laws pursue or have pursued has been hidden in it' (II:368). Only the novelist, who is not daunted by digging through the muck and seeing things as they are, can reveal the history hidden in the objects.

But again, what redeems the sewers is that they *have* a history, and a history that only the novel can write. No other printed form at the time could conceivably have included such a history – which would actually now be considered part anthropology and part sociology. And when Jean Valjean escapes through the sewers, whose history has been made clear to the reader, then Valjean adds his own history

to the history of escapes and concealments. Alongside the justification of history is of course the quasi-symbolic image of the convict
who is considered ordure by society, being flushed out through its
cloaca. But by so heavily tying his story to history, Hugo manages to
make this ploy seem less a part of allegory and more a part of
ideology.

It might not be far-fetched to remember that Freud linked the desire
to amass property with anal eroticism. If we take cognizance of that
fact, then we might venture to say that Hugo intuitively knew that
sheer property without a higher moral justification – that is, the
sewer, which Hugo saw as a 'mistake' (366) – is nothing more than
dross; but that the excremental in the cry of Cambronne by being
linked to moral right and the course of history rises and becomes art.
And the material ground of the battlefield becomes transmuted
through sublimation and language into the sublime. In the same
sense, the creation of space through language, the project of the
novelist, attains through rationalizing and sublimation significance
far greater in some sense than the mere material existence of
place.

One final example from the twentieth century might serve to close
this discussion on location. F. Scott Fitzgerald's *The Great Gatsby*
was published in 1925. Like Defoe's and Balzac's work, *The Great
Gatsby* 'invites the awakening of a longing for possession' (Jameson,
The Political Unconscious 157). Locations, real and invented, are always tied up with an ideological structure of desire and ownership. The
book itself is one extended meditation on the value of value and the
meaning of money. Gatsby is little more than a cipher projected into
the world by his own wealth whom various people including the
narrator and the reader try to decode. The general setting divides
between New York City and the Eggs (West and East) but there is
also always the inherent comparison between the East Coast and the
rest of the United States, since Nick is a visitor who must go back
home to write his narrative. Each of these areas 'mean' something
above and beyond their literal place, yet their meaning is not clearly
allegorical. The difference between nineteenth- and twentieth-
century depictions of space, and here we are painting the picture with
broad strokes, is that the historical and ideological justification for
space has dropped out. So while we have little trouble understanding
the sign-systems depicting the squalidness of Maison Vauquer or
Jacob's Island, or the historical significance of Waterloo, we have

many problems interpreting Fitzgerald's landscape, as we have for the landscape of Conrad, Joyce, Kafka, or Calvino.

For example, the contrast between West Egg and East Egg is an ideological one, dripping with what Jameson calls 'commodity lust' (*Political Unconscious* 157):

> I lived at West Egg, the – well, the less fashionable of the two, though this is a most superficial tag to express the bizarre and not a little sinister contrast between them. My house was at the very tip of the egg, only fifty yards from the Sound, and squeezed between the two huge places that rented for twelve or fifteen thousand a season. The one on my right was a colossal affair by any standard – it was a factual imitation of some Hotel de Ville in Normandy, with a tower on one side, spanking new under a thin beard of raw ivy, and a marble swimming pool, and more than forty acres of lawn and garden. It was Gatsby's mansion. Or, rather, as I didn't know Mr. Gatsby, it was a mansion, inhabited by a gentleman of that name. My own house was an eyesore, but it was a small eyesore, and it had been overlooked, so I had a view of the water, a partial view of my neighbor's lawn, and the consoling proximity of millionaires – all for eighty dollars a month.
>
> Across the courtesy bay the white palaces of fashionable East Egg glittered along the water. (3–4)

Fitzgerald, unlike Defoe, is comfortable with the extended description. He realizes that as an author he must write these kinds of accounts which have become by now the freight and baggage of the novelistic discourse. Each element of description is part of a larger ideological explanatory system that accounts for wealth and property and explains what it means. The white palaces of East Egg and the gaudy mansion of Gatsby speak of different kinds of wealth here. The narrator's anaclitic proximity to Gatsby's wealth is contrasted to the rental values of his and Gatsby's places. Even the modest, conversational pause in 'the – well, the less fashionable' bespeaks a momentary class embarrassment translated to the level of the linguistic sign for hesitation. The details – marble swimming pool, new ivy, and expansive lawns – participate in this system of meaning.

Fitzgerald expands his descriptive landscape to include the famous eyes of Dr Eckleburg which look out over the wasteland separating the Eggs from New York. These eyes are part of the cere landscape 'where ashes grow like wheat into ridges and hills and grotesque gardens; where ashes take the forms of houses and chimneys and rising smoke and, finally, with a transcendent effort, of men who move dimly and already crumbling through the powdery air' (15). This metaphoric account of the landscape, unlike the description of Gatsby's estate, signals directly to the reader the need for interpretation. Although the reader may pinpoint this location on the map as Astoria, Fitzgerald completely takes over the literal landscape with his meaning and system.

A good deal of literary criticism has gone into trying to interpret those huge eyes on the billboard and the landscape of ashes, but since the meaning is not allegorical, no single interpretation can fully decode the meaning. In reading, one feels that the landscape here must be filled with meaning. And one cannot read *The Great Gatsby* without trying at least once to ferret out the meaning from the landscape. What Fitzgerald is doing is essentially the same as Defoe – involving the descriptive space in a larger system of ideological meaning – but his variation, the variation of much of modernism, is to make the meaning more purely aesthetic. That is, the symbol of Dr Eckleburg's eyes does not enclose any single meaning but points to and frustrates the very process by which readers seek to arrive at meaning by reading novels. The *meaning* of the landscape of ashes is simply that the reader should be looking for a meaning. The ideological presupposition is that such aesthetic objects are endowed with meanings, and the interpretive process of arriving at those meanings will somehow release that secret as well as other secrets about life in general.

Like Nick, who feels that if he only could understand the meaning of Gatsby he would understand all other meanings, or like Marlow in *The Heart of Darkness* whose attempt to find meaning in Kurtz's 'the horror' is emblematic of all attempts to organize meaning, the reader looks to locations in the novel to embody meaning and meaning-systems. Thus New York, rather than being the absolutely puzzling and meaningless place it is, becomes a universal fantasy location for the realization of the artistic and alienated self: 'At the enchanted metropolitan twilight I felt a haunting loneliness sometimes, and felt it in others' (38). 'The city seen from the Queensboro Bridge is always the city seen for the first time, in its first wild promise of all the mystery and the beauty in the world.' Then seeing rich blacks in a chauffeured limousine, Nick laughs: '"Anything can happen now that we've slid over this bridge," I thought; "anything at all"' (45). New York becomes a timeless place that means life, and the people who really live in it – blacks, and Jews like Meyer Wolfsheim – are at the center of an existence that is unavailable to the WASPs and middle-Americans like Nick. Wolfsheim can sway an institution as cherished as the World Series and ultimately controls a figurehead like Gatsby.

What New York is cannot be answered by a quick trip over the Queensboro bridge. While Fitzgerald provides a way of inscribing the landscape with meaning, he also recognizes that what he has done is artificial and even, though he might not be willing to use the word, reifying. He has made the real city into a simulacrum, a known unknown – simplifying the contours of the skyline into a recognizable single line of thought. And it is probably not uncoincidental that Fitzgerald decides to end his novel at the moment that the first Dutch explorers landed in the New World:

> I became aware of the old island here that flowered once for Dutch sailors' eyes – a fresh, green breast of the new world. Its vanished trees, the trees that had made way for Gatsby's house, had once pandered in whispers to the last and greatest of all human dreams; for a transitory enchanted moment man must have held his breath in the presence of this continent, compelled into an aesthetic contemplation he neither understood nor desired, face to face for the last time in history with something commensurate to his capacity for wonder. (120)

The blankness of the new world is a blankness free of human meaning. Like Conrad's Marlow viewing Africa in *Heart of Darkness*, the viewer cannot ascribe a meaning to the landscape. Or, in the way that Anson described his island theater, the new world is a place whose meaning remains to be performed. And for Fitzgerald, typically, the view he attributed to the explorer is not pecuniary, ambitious, or chauvinistic, but 'aesthetic contemplation.' Fitzgerald's colonial metaphor is not purely accidental, because in a way his work acknowledges that his use of place, replete with meaning, makes his locations 'known unknown' places. Even the act of renaming Great Neck and Little Neck as East Egg and West Egg embeds in the story the little known fact that the Dutch explorers originally gave two inlets in Long Island the names 'Great and Little Egg Harbors' (Van

Der Donck 8). The possibility of a location that was completely free of ideological or systemic meanings is the fantasy of Nick who, in the moment just preceding his revelation about the Dutch explorers, has to erase an obscenity scrawled on Gatsby's mansion. It is as if Fitzgerald is wishing to erase the naming and defacing of places and to return to the primordial lack of organized meaning for which the New World originally stood. But obviously the novelist is bound to and cannot erase the very necessity for meaning in the novel's construction of places.

From Defoe through Balzac, Dickens, and Hugo, one can see a shift in the relationship to description of location. The artificiality of creating a location is worked through the template of colonial explorers' descriptions whose aim was to create a space out of a chaos through language and endow that space with meaning. By the nineteenth century the sheer joy in commodifying property shifts to moral justification largely through the defending shield of history, that most ideological of defenses. But by the twentieth century justification by history drops out in favor of a kind of aesthetic justification – a justification by works of art. Either property is merely possession, as it is in so many popular forms of narrative, or it is an aesthetic object needing literary hermeneutics as justification. Italo Calvino's book *Invisible Cities* becomes a kind of paradigm for the modernist cause. In it cities which never existed are described in detail by Marco Polo to Kubla Kahn. Like the city of Tamara, they are all aesthetic enigmas:

> Your gaze scans the streets as if they were written pages: the city says everything you must think, makes you repeat her discourse, and while you believe you are visiting Tamara you are only recording the names with which she defines herself and all her parts.
> However the city may really be, beneath this thick coating of signs, whatever it may contain or conceal, you leave Tamara without having discovered it. Outside, the land stretches, empty, to the horizon, the sky opens, with speeding clouds. (14)

These cities exist in timeless, ahistorical settings, and they seem to offer a meaning that we cannot grasp. Their meaning is in effect literary and artistic – since they do not evoke property lust or historical necessity.

100

And it might not be off the topic, since the subject of the visual arts had been touched on earlier, to note that the genre of landscape painting ended with the beginning of the modern period of painting. The landscape is virtually absent from the work of the cubists, abstract expressionists, minimalists, pop and post-structuralist artists. The disappearance of controlled property in painting has given way to the reality of painting itself as property. The artist's works are understood as objects of value rather than views of the world around. The property the artist creates is bought and sold rather than the patron's lands and mansion. Justification based on ownership, as Berger had noted, applied to the landscapes of the eighteenth century, or justification based on historical subjects – as was clearly the case with the many English and French painters of the nineteenth century – has given way to the primacy of form and the demand for an interpretation which is always inadequate or impossible in relation to the painting. So one might make a case for certain parallel developments in the visual and narrative arts in relation to space, although it is hardly the task of a chapter such as this.

In all these cases, the fact that there *is* a space in the novel, that there *are* locations, perhaps now no longer seems to be simply a neutral fact or an obvious convention. Whatever period we are discussing, the necessity for considering location as replete with ideology and serving the purposes of a social defense has to be considered. Property is always *there* of course, but in novels it is *there* with a vengeance. For the 250 years or so following Defoe, this newly made interior space of the novel continued to create islands in the mind, cities of the plain, and boudoirs without dimension in which plot and character are forever entwined. These places, that pretend to be open spaces of the real, are actually claustrophobic encampments of the ideological. As such they are not ancillary to but the absolute concomitant of the novel's discourse.

4

Characters, narrators, and readers: making friends with signs

We can say that what is proper to narrative is not action but the character as Proper Name.

Roland Barthes, *S/Z*

'You say right,' quoth Adams, 'knowledge of men is only to be learnt from books.'

Henry Fielding, *Joseph Andrews*

Novels are particularly compelling because they make us believe that in reading we are actually getting to know about people and life. Of course readers know that characters in novels are not really people, yet it is difficult if not impossible to follow any novel if one constantly bears in mind that a character is a totally fabricated construct. And novels that try and point out the made-up quality of their central character are, at best, intellectually interesting but somehow not really novelistic and, at worst, tedious and unreadable. While reading we do not want the centrality of the character's existence to be tampered with any more than we want to be reminded about harmful additives and chemicals while enjoying our favorite ice cream.

Even the most hardened deconstructionist who knows that all things in novels are only signs and tactics must – to get through a novel – allow some particular clusters of signs the kind of priority they need to become living, breathing characters. Experts in literary theory probably read novels somewhat differently from most readers – searching for formal connections and ruptures – but few would deny that the very idea of character is so entrenched a part of the novelistic discourse that it constitutes a kind of limit or regulation. What I want to do in this chapter is to understand not simply the commonplace that of course novels have characters, but how that very requirement pre-forms ideologically the reading or writing of a novel. What I will argue is that the simplification of personality required to produce a character in a novel is itself once again an ideological statement about the role of the individual in relation to society since the early modern period. In focusing on this simplification, I want to account for at least three requisites for the novel's central characters – beauty, passivity, and their ability to invite identification – and further to show how the relationship between narrator and reader is defined, in a sense, by these traits.

Simply to follow a novel, most readers have first and foremost to perform the rather startling (upon examination) action of believing that inside the novel is not only a three-dimensional space but a person with some kind of physical and psychological depth and contour as well. Typically of this kind of belief, Georg Lukács says of Willi Bredel's novels that there is missing 'what is needed to make them [the novels] come alive, i.e. living human beings, with living, changing and developing relationships between them' (*Essays* 24). As I have tried to show in the case of location, the very act of believing that there is space and claiming it is at root ideological, and here even as astute a critic of the novel as Lukács can fail to recognize the ideological dimension of formal elements. What I mean is that Lukács assumes novels can and should be filled with 'living human beings.' The feeling we have that 'living, changing' people are what novelists create is a mass cultural assumption – not a universal given – and requires a major perceptual and defensive change of the kind that the novel as a discourse encourages and requires. And, as with location, I would argue that before the novel an extended description of personality and psychology simply did not exist. The exact causality is here difficult to pinpoint. Indeed, it is likely that, here as elsewhere, an overdetermination of cultural and social forces were at

103

work creating ideology as well as literary forms. Numerous works have already pointed to the connection between the growing interest in autobiography, biography, and the novel,[1] and one might add that the novel seems to have taken over the technology of description of the self in its development.

It should be stressed at the outset that there has been in the post-modern period an attempt to create narratives that call attention to the artificiality of that construct we call 'character.' Baruch Hochman notes that although earlier literary forms were self-conscious (in works like *A Midsummer Night's Dream*, *Don Quixote*, *Tristram Shandy*) 'the difference between postmodernist and earlier literary practice in the generation of character is that even in the process of signifying and underscoring the artifice through which characters are projected, a Shakespeare invites us to envision them as *substantial hypothetical beings*,' whereas post-modernist fiction 'frustrates our construction of character altogether' (26). The post-modernist argument of writers like Duras, Robbe-Grillet, Borges, or Calvino are cases in point, syncopations against the beat, arguments against the grain. Their novels can be read, but in essence they are anomalous, contentious pieces of counter-practice. What most of us call novels are works substantially intertwined with character.

What then is the difference between characters in narratives in general and novels in particular? Historically speaking, there is a distinction between the epic form and the later novel form. Most of us might intuit a description of the difference between, say, an epic and a novelistic hero. Lukács himself, in *The Theory of the Novel*, points out that in the earlier epic form personality is less important than the events and their relation to a larger and integrated social system:

> In the epic, the central figure and its significant adventures are a mass organized in itself and for itself, so that the beginning and the end mean something quite different there, something essentially less important: they are moments of great intensity, homogeneous with other points which are the high points of the whole; they never signify anything more than the commencement or the resolution of great tensions. (82)

But 'the development of a man is still the thread upon which the whole world of the novel is strung and along which it unrolls' (82). Most people would agree that the epic personality is a limited one, not characterized by the extension of description of the novel. In fact Lukács' main point is that the epic is essentially without a subject or subjectivity, or as Erich Auerbach has noted in *Mimesis* Greek heroes 'have no development. . . . Homeric heroes . . . wake each morning as if it were the first day of their lives' (14). The novel, according to Lukács, is synonymous with the development of subjectivity. If we look to other forms of narration that preceded the novel the issue of personality is also muted. J. M. Bernstein, commenting on Lukács, notes that although 'allegorical narratives . . . may employ bio-graphical form as a vehicle for the representation of meaning . . . the meaning revealed will not necessarily belong to the individual whose life story occasioned its manifestation' (148). And in drama, for example, character can be complexly revealed, but the observer is uniquely outside the actors, except for the awkward convention of the soliloquy or dramatic monologue. But the experience we have of reading novels is more intimate, personal, and penetrating. Theater-goers may feel that they have come to *know* Hamlet, but novel readers understand that more than simply being acquainted with Jane Eyre, they have been required to *be* her. And, strangely enough, it is not unusual to feel that we know a particular character in a novel better than we know some of our own friends or acquaintances.

At the other extreme from the epic character are the characters in, say, Henry James' *The Golden Bowl*. Here the reader gets little else *besides* the thoughts of the characters and the narrator. We can argue over Achilles' motivation in his choice to fight or not to fight, but Achilles' character spins on *only* that choice. As Lukács has pointed out, one does not get much of Achilles' train of thought on unrelated topics: we see little ambivalence about his refusal to fight, and when his friend Patroklos is killed, he does not hesitate to return to the battle. If Achilles is thinking about all this, the listener to the epic is not permitted to enter that realm of discourse. Indeed, we have to assume that Greek culture did not really need the kind of representa-tion of the human psyche that would include such speculation in a subjective form. However, James, on the other hand, presents not only the Prince's decision to buy the golden bowl, but the thousand thoughts, feelings, intimations, and nuances of that choice. Here the choice is only the occasion for the train of thought that follows and precedes it. As Lukács notes, 'Where psychology begins, there are no

105

more deeds but only motives for deeds' (*Soul* 39). We may assume that if Henry James were living in ancient Greece his narratives would have been absolutely unreadable to the culture which would have been puzzled as to why anyone would represent the subjective aspect of human life.

This is not the place to analyze at length why it is that the Greeks did not develop psychologically their epic characters, although it can be argued that in the realm of philosophy the Greeks had contributed much to self-consciousness and 'examined life.' In *The Glory of Hera* Phillip Slater has suggested that Greek family life created a cultural narcissism that perpetuated a public, boastful, over-achieving personality with distant and diluted personal relationships. One could speculate that such a relationship would not encourage the kind of introspection and subjectivity characteristic of the novel. Slater leaves out economic and historical conditions that might have selected out this kind of child-rearing practice, but his observations give further evidence to Lukács' and Auerbach's emphasis on the lack of subject and subjectivity in epics. George Thomson's *Aeschylus and Athens* uses a more historical but more mechanistic method to describe the Greeks from an anthropological viewpoint as a primitive tribal society whose view of their own subjectivity was conditioned by kinship systems and gift exchanges in a way much different from the social organization of the modern world. It is thus pretty clear that the levels of subjectivity which fascinated Henry James would have been incomprehensible to an Homeric bard. Later Athenians, it could be argued, would have been more sensitive to subjective questions. But the fact that their objections to the epic as a form did not revolve around such issues is also a telling point.

There are two objections to meet here. The first is the common-sense notion that 'Of course all narratives have characters – so what is the fuss?' Such an objection constitutes a tremendous simplification since the very idea of character is itself not universal. Maggie Verver could have become a character to a Greek reader only with great difficulty – that is, the collection of signs that James arranged pointing towards an internalized character would for the most part not have been able to be organized into the concept of a being by a Greek reader or listener. I do not mean that Greeks were more primitive and James was more sophisticated. The problem would be one of cultural priorities and differences. What we know about

Achilles relates almost entirely to his social rank and role in society – his individuality is less significant and his thought processes are almost irrelevant. And if Homer had not been preserved in western Europe by the complex cultural bucket brigade that landed his works in early modern Europe, I would wager that Achilles would not make sense to an eighteenth-century, middle-class novel reader, whose central concerns lay with a new interest in subjectivity, love, marriage, and overcoming class restrictions – all of which were subjects utterly outside the issues that created Achilles. Undoubtedly all cultures have narratives in which named personages are represented in story form, but those names can mark out entirely different concepts of what character is, depending on the variety of historical period.

That is, the very idea of character in the novel is itself ideological. Wayne Booth implies this point – although using the phrase 'world of values' where I use ideology – when he says that 'the very effort of the narrator to wrestle explicitly with his character's world of values can make even the most insignificant character seem of world-shaking importance' (199). Or as Fredric Jameson has noted, 'the lived experience of individual consciousness ... has a quasi-institutional status, performs ideological functions, and is susceptible to historical causation' (*The Political Unconscious* 153). Character, at least literary character, or what Lukács and Jameson, among others, call the 'subject,' is closely linked to historical and cultural factors and indeed cannot be understood outside of history. This notion of the historical conditioning of the subject goes against one of the powerful ideological myths of the novel – the universality of character. It is one of the tenets of early modern humanism that art provides its consumers with eternal truths – that a Hindu, a Minnesotan, and a Bantu will all, given the opportunity, recognize the universal application of Oliver Twist or Tom Jones. Rather than seeing character as a universal given, I want to lay the foundation for understanding character in its historical and cultural particularity. In recent work on character as part of narrativity, the assumption is always made that characters are universally decodable or that there is what might be called a 'conservation of character' such that a residue of character will always be *there* in the mind of any group of readers. Seymour Chatman correctly objects to these assumptions that 'the differences between modern characters like Leopold Bloom or Marcel and Prince Charming or Ivan are so great as to be qualitative rather than quantitative' (112). There is, in effect, an historical dimension to character studies.

The second point worth noting is that Lukács' analysis, while useful to this argument, is fundamentally in error when it comes to his use of the term 'subject.' As with his comments on Willi Bredel, Lukács falls into the error of thinking of the novel as containing subjectivity or as describing a subject. It may seem obvious or deliberately dense of me but I want to make the point that there are no subjects in novels. The only subject is the reader. Characters do not exist, are only a collection of instructions, signs, or themes. The novel conveys the illusion of subjectivity, but – as we all know in our more rational moments – the novel *only* conveys the illusion. It could of course be argued that I am privileging the reader by saying that he or she is the only subject. Indeed are readers more 'real' than characters? Are we not all – reader, author, and characters – collections of signs constructed out of ideological raw materials? Wolfgang Iser uses the term 'implied reader' to describe the construct which is neither reader not text but the interrelation between the two. 'The concept of the implied reader is therefore a textual structure anticipating the presence of a recipient without necessarily defining him [or her]. . . . Thus the concept of the implied reader designates a network of response-inviting structures, which impel the reader to grasp the text' (34). Even in reader-response theories, there is necessarily posited a reader who is situationally *present* and who, though perhaps a collection of signs too, is first and foremost a) in the world and b) in relation to texts that only 'take on their reality by being read' (34).

The ideology of the novel involves as a prerequisite, however, the opposite view that there *are* real characters in novels who *do* have a kind of provisional reality. For example, Seymour Chatman and Baruch Hochman have argued that character has to amount to more than signs on a page or sets of instructions. Chatman asserts:

> Of course Hamlet and Macbeth are not 'living people;' but that does not mean that as constructed imitations they are in any way limited to the words on the printed page. . . . Why should we be any less inclined to search through and beyond the words of Shakespeare for insights into the construct 'Hamlet' than through and beyond the words of Boswell for insights into the construct 'Samuel Johnson'? (118)

Hochman refers to literary characters as 'substantial hypothetical beings' (26) and argues that 'the possibility of abstracting or "liberating" the characters and contemplating them as they are in themselves must be affirmed,' which amounts to 'acknowledging life as the source of the whole spectrum of characters in literature and granting that we perceive people on models analogous to them' (58). In both these arguments, the point is made that character is in a sense more than just words, that we construct characters of people who are living and people who are in fiction in not terribly different ways, and that Dr Johnson, Oliver Twist, and the corner grocer are known mainly by signs and paradigms. I certainly would not want to deny that fact. But both Chatman and Hochman are forgetting or downplaying the notion that fictional characters have a different level of existence and creation than people we meet. Fictional characters are created for a purpose – and that purpose is at least twofold. One is that they are designed to elicit maximum identification with the observer. The second is that their existence is part of a monolithic structure created by an author. They exist insofar as they move a text forward; actual humans may be equally mysterious to us, but they only become a text under scrutiny. Humans do not require a text to exist, although they may well become a text in the course of existing.

The case of Dr Johnson is apropos. His own life was not purposeful, but in the process of creating a persona he created a variety of fabricated selves – and he was aided in so doing by Boswell. Nevertheless, independent information can be attained about characters who are not fictional: corroboration, evidence and proof, justification, and concurrent testimony can all intervene to change the nature of the paradigm presented or constructed. In fiction, no counterveiling information is present aside from what the author gives us. Chatman refers to what he calls 'open' characters, who are complex enough to resist closure and therefore are like people who 'in the real world stay mysteries no matter how well we know them' (118). But their openness is unlike the openness of actual people since the cause of this void in our knowledge is absence not lack of access.

In large what I am talking about is the difference in situation and context between knowing a real person and knowing a fictional character. Here Wolfgang Iser in *The Act of Reading* can help because he spends a good deal of time trying to distinguish the differences between literary speech and ordinary speech – that is, between language in a literary work and language in our lives. As Iser notes, 'the sentences in the work of art seem just like those used to describe real objects, although the two types have completely different functions to perform.' Iser's solution is to see that

> the parting of the ways between literary and ordinary speech (speech act) is to be observed in the matter of situational context. The fictional utterance seems to be made without reference to any real situation, whereas the speech act presupposes a situation whose precise definition is essential to the success of that act. (62–3)

Thus although the same processes may indeed occur somewhat in knowing real and imaginary people, we must not be fooled into discounting the purpose such an interaction serves within its proper context. Knowing a fictional object is always characterized by the removal of that object from actual presence. Iser refers to Ernst Cassirer's statement

> that the concept, in accordance with its characteristic attitude must, unlike direct perception, move its object off into a kind of ideal distance, in order to bring it within its horizon. The concept must annul 'presence' in order to arrive at 'representation.' (Cassirer, III 307)

So represented characters will be defined by a removal from context and presence. If, according to Iser, what is represented in fiction is not empirical reality but ordinary speech, then in terms of character what is represented is not actual beings but the situational context by which actual beings get to know each other. That is, knowing is represented, not being.

In this sense, the most telling counter-argument to the Chatman/Hochman assertion is that as we spend time with real people we get to know more about them and, even if still a mystery finally, they grow more understandable. With a fictional character, time may give us insight into formal elements of the narrative, but we do not really come to understand the main character any better after the initial two or three readings. This fact is so because authors can only represent knowing, they cannot get us to know the character. To be married to Elizabeth Bennet in the world of reader/character relations would amount to being trapped in a Dantesque circle of hell in which only the same information could be presented over and over.

As Hochman points out, 'if the characters in literature are like people at all, in the ordinary sense, they are like dead people . . . once they are "written," [they] are finished like the dead' (60). Perhaps the real objection to such discussions of character is that such analyses are abstract and universalized. The overarching question is not so much whether characters are just signs or separable from the text, but why did we, as humans, arrive at this particular literary form of the novel that is designed to represent knowing and to provide for us instructions (or 'response-inviting structures' as Iser calls them (34)) that induce us to identify with these kinds of characters in place of or in addition to real people? What need is answered and why did this special technique arise largely during the eighteenth century?

To make my own points clearer, let me make the distinction between personality and character. Personality is what living beings have. Our personalities may not be coherent; they may not be readily understood by us; they may be misinterpreted or not even accessible to others; but they are what we refer to when we refer to ourselves. 'Character' on the other hand is what people in novels have. They are characters with characteristics. The biggest ideological presupposition that novel readers are encouraged to make is to think that characters in novels have personalities. That distinction, or in my view misconception, is the essence of novel reading. In believing in characters, readers are engaged in what Karlheinz Stierle calls 'quasi-pragmatic reception' in which 'the boundaries of the fictional text are transcended through an illusion created by the reader.' Quasi-pragmatic reading is opposed to pragmatic reception in which the reader 'is always overstepping the boundaries of the text in an attempt to fill the gap between word and world' (84). Stierle says that quasi-pragmatic reception is what distinguishes fictional texts from non-fictional ones.

What then is the distinction between personality and character? Personality, as I have been saying, is complex. Who could easily describe their own personality and feel that they have done justice to it? Personality is difficult to fathom, and it is possible to live with someone (or oneself) for quite a long time and feel that that person is still a mystery – not completely knowable. Also, personality is without purpose. Someone is not depressed for a purpose (although they may be depressed for a reason). And, in a post-Freudian age, we may say that personality has a large component which is hidden from consciousness and even in most cases from explanation.

One could argue that Freud gave people a way of thinking about their own lives in novelistic terms – that is, making an organized series of events out of what had previously been seen as random details of life. As Steven Marcus first pointed out in 'The case of Dora,' Freud's conceptualization of the case history as a form was heavily influenced by the formal elements of the Victorian novel (*Representations*). Freud analyzes the development of personality by placing cumulative details into narrative form and searching for momentous narrative incidents or revelations. In psychoanalysis, people become characters in their own novels, finding meaning in events and re-embedding those events in a larger system of explanation and causality. Psychoanalysis is novelistic in the sense that it tries to find continuities and consistencies in personality. In this sense, it would be correct to say that we form paradigms of others and even ourselves in the same way we do with fictional characters. As I will show, part of the problem here is that the ideology of literary forms can often be part of a larger ideological system. Human relations in the early modern and modern world clearly shares features with readerly relations.

Without the intervention of psychoanalysis, though, personality is in and of itself not necessarily consistent. On a daily basis, the many details of life do not always fall into patterns. Personality, as a concept, then becomes a warehouse, in effect, to contain all of our own behavior. Anything one does, no matter how inconsistent, still must be attributed to oneself. The classic case of this necessity arises in accounts of assassins or mass murderers who are described by neighbors as 'quiet' or 'nice.' Only after the murder is the quiet behavior seen as covering up the mass-murdering behavior. Personalities must be the sum of all the erratic parts of their behavior even if the behavior does not make sense. But character must be consistent to be understood by readers as a unity and not simply a random collection of attributes. If a character commits a murder on the 250th page of a novel, then on the first page the reader must be prepared for it.

Not only must characters be consistent, but they must fit into a pattern within the novel to make sense. In life, a variety of patterns clash and syncopate with each other. As Stierle points out:

What basically distinguishes fiction from the experience of real life is the fact that in everyday life the 'theme' is perceived against a horizon of outer contingencies that have to be coped with, whereas in the fictional world . . . the relationship between theme and horizon is predetermined by the relevant textual structure.' (97)

So characters in novels, and readers who inhabit those novels for a while, live in a 'world of relevancy,' and even when the irrelevant occurs in the novel it serves 'the interest of provoking secondary illusions' (98).

Character, therefore, is usually fairly simple and consistent. Even the most complex character in a novel is fantastically simplified when compared with the most boringly simple personality. The reason for this simplification is obvious. Since characters do not exist anywhere outside of the linguistic sign, they must have, in order to 'be,' fairly definite limits or borders to distinguish them from other characters. You may be *like* your brother, but it is unlikely that anyone will have trouble in distinguishing you from him even if the resemblance is very strong, because in life we do not expect two people to have to establish that they are separate individuals. Biological individuality is defined by the fact that you each have different bodies. But novelists have to create characters out of their difference – otherwise they will fail to exist as discrete concepts. If one thinks of a musical theme the point may be clearer. A musical theme must be something simple enough to be recognized by the ear and repeated enough to keep the theme in existence over a period of time. Without this rather structured prerequisite, you will simply have noise. Without the predictable and consistent qualities of a character, a novelist can only produce words or rather spaces marked by proper names.

Character provides form through the biographical predisposition of the novel. Since the novel is usually structured around the life of some character, the form will come from the shape of a life in general. Form, for Lukács in his *Theory of the Novel*, has the Hegelian sense of a philosophical order – something towards which consciousness is evolving both psychologically and historically. In this sense, form is absent in the world. And giving the early Lukács a Marxist slant, J. M. Bernstein interprets form – towards which consciousness is evolving – as the organization of society along rational and scientific lines. Since aesthetic form gives meaning to the formlessness of the post-epic world, 'form founders against life because life is not yet form' (87). Patricia Meyer Spacks puts this point in another way,

113

saying 'real life . . . seldom manifests such orderly and revealing patterns as one finds in its literary renditions. . . . Putting a life into words rescues it from confusion' (21). So the coherence of character can be a kind of substitute for the formlessness or irrational nature of modern consciousness and culture. However, as I will discuss later in this chapter, the biographical form in literature always represents an objectification of personality, because to represent a life in a novel the author must perform all kinds of truncations and distortions of a life.

Take Emma Bovary as an example of consistency and simplification. Though she is capricious, she must be consistent. That is, her capriciousness must be consistent. She must be someone who thinks of life as a novel or romance. She must be sexual and rebellious. She must be self-indulgent. That is who she is. If Flaubert had begun to add more qualities to her, her character would have become diluted. She would have lost meaning, ceasing to be the character we know so well. Suppose Flaubert had her develop an interest in neoclassical architecture, or suppose he made her more ambivalent about sexuality. These minor changes would begin to *un*define her – she would begin to become less strongly etched. In essence, the feeling that we get that we are watching a complex character is largely an illusion created by the opposite – the relatively small number of traits that make up a character.

In fact, as we all intuitively realize, novelists do not create characters but only provide instructions to readers who, in turn, must create a character in their minds. According to Wolfgang Iser, 'we may say that fictional language provides instructions for the building of a situation and so for the production of an imaginary object' (64). What an author does is to provide the instruction: 'Create a conceptual space, give it a name, and let it be identified by a relatively few, consistent linguistic signs.' Character can first of all be delineated in a bold stroke or two. Take Jane Austen's opening account of Mr and Mrs Bennet in *Pride and Prejudice*:

'My dear Mr Bennet,' said his lady to him one day, 'have you heard that Netherfield Park is let at last?'
Mr Bennet replied that he had not.

The first thing to note is the simplicity of the development. At this point in the opening of the novel, all we know is that there is a Mr and a Mrs Bennet. Mrs Bennet's theme of conformity and stupidity is opened and will not be complicated much more at any point. Mr Bennet's sarcasm, superiority to his wife, and pretense to intelligence is also opened and will not vary overmuch. The chapter is closed with Austen's summary:

> Mr Bennet was so odd a mixture of quick parts, sarcastic humour, reserve, and caprice, that the experience of three and twenty years had been insufficient to make his wife understand his character. *Her* mind was less difficult to develop. She was a woman of mean understanding, little information, and uncertain temper. When she was discontented she fancied herself nervous. The business of her life was to get her daughters married; its solace was visiting and news. (53)

Worth noting here is the faith that Austen shares with her reader about the possibility of encapsulating a character. The narrator is almost relieved that Mrs Bennet's mind was not difficult to develop. Chatman talks about character as a 'paradigm of traits,' that is, 'trait' is a minimal unit of character (121ff.). For Austen, here, character is initiated by a series of traits. Roland Barthes presents an even more simplified notion of character saying that 'when identical semes [units of meaning] traverse the same proper name several times and appear to settle on it, a character is created' (*S/Z* 67). That is, character is literally the attaching of several traits or semes to a proper name. In life we may actually hear about someone in this same fashion (proper name + traits), but that kind of encounter is only the most superficial. At some subsequent point our attempt to attach adjectives to a person begins to fall quite short of our personal sense of that person. Even the most superficial personality could not possibly be laid out with the regularity of, say, Mrs Bennet's character. And although Mrs Bennet does not understand her husband, we are thought to be capable of doing so rather quickly.

The next thing to notice is the comfort that Austen herself finds with the idea of giving the instructions. Unlike earlier novels of the eighteenth century in which narrators must either pretend that they are real and introduce themselves in the first person, usually in journal or letter form, or else the novelist must explain his or her role in creating a character and justifying such an extravagance, Austen just assumes a preordained relationship with the reader in which no explanation is necessary. It is simply accepted that these characters are fictional and that the practice of novel reading is so established that no one needs to justify the existence of fictional characters. George Levine is correct in reminding us that, although they seem smug, Victorian novelists were still wrestling with some of the problems inherent in realism, but he seems to be overlooking the extent to which society had become very comfortable with the idea of reading fiction (20ff.). And as Patricia Meyer Spacks has noted, earlier eighteenth-century philosophical problems of identity associated with Locke, Berkeley, and Hume were in effect diffused by the novel's confidence in the idea of creating an identity or character in fiction (22). In other words, the ideology of character is in place in Austen's work, whereas earlier authors like Defoe, Richardson, Fielding, or Sterne had to explain or actively avoid this bizarre notion of creating a character and pretending that it was a personality.

The task of novel reading is in large part made up of getting characters right and then getting to know them. Not uncoincidentally, characters within novels spend most of their time trying to understand who other characters really are – whether in clearing up issues of mistaken identity, revealing the true circumstances of birth, or understanding that someone really loves someone else. Also much literary criticism of the eighteenth and nineteenth centuries revolved around the delineation of character. For example, John Dunlop, who in 1814 claimed to have written the first history of fiction in English, praises Richardson for being the best of the modern novelists and says that 'the chief merit of Richardson consists in his delineation of character.' But Lovelace is condemned as 'an outrage on verisimilitude. Such a character as Lovelace not only never existed, but seems incompatible with human nature.' Smollett is singled out for attempting in *Humphrey Clinker* 'what had scarcely ever been before attempted – a representation of the different effects which the same scenes, and persons, and transactions, have on different dispositions and tempers.' In fact, the whole point of novels is to create a situation in which 'the rude are refined by an introduction, as it were, to the higher orders of mankind, and even the dissipated and selfish are, in some degree, corrected by those paintings of virtue and simple nature, which must ever be employed by the novelist if he wish to awaken emotion or delight' (347, 375, 379, xi).

Reading through such early criticism, one is struck by the extent to which the depiction of character was almost the only criterion for criticism until the twentieth century, and character had the function of reforming the reader by exposure to the virtuous and by witnessing the downfall of the evil. One explanation for this, by our standards, limited focus is that the novel was recognized intuitively as *the* form for the extended description of character and subjectivity that I am claiming it was. It is pretty clear that no other forms, except for some kinds of drama, were currently exploring the creation and representation of character in this new way. Further, the very idea of character is inseparable from the moral and civilizing lesson to be learned. By this point in the nineteenth century, the novel was seen as important for the furthering of civilization and culture – particularly as the base of readership began to spread to the lower classes. The ideological role of character was certainly part of the civilizing or, if you will, the socially indoctrinating aspect of the novel.

To understand the ideological nature of character, one might attempt to account for one recurring complaint in early novel criticism. It is the charge made against novelistic heroes or heroines that they do not develop – that they are stick figures or one-dimensional. But if we understand that all characters in novels are in some profound sense 'one-dimensional,' then we can penetrate the mythology surrounding these characters. Take Mr Bennet who is presented as complex. One could, however, list the rules, as it were, by which he is constructed. In any situation with his wife he will be sarcastic and superior. He will be given the opportunity of turning the occasional smart phrase. He will like Elizabeth and be superior to his other daughters, and he will spend most of his time in his study or alone. The rest of his character will be outside the scope of the novel. Those are simple rules that any living human would find pretty restrictive to live by on a daily basis. So the complexity of a character turns out to be an illusion that, for a variety of reasons to be explored, readers need and want to accept.

Why characters are so simple is a question of great complexity. First, one might speculate that in a literary relationship we actually only want to know a few things in order to establish a friendship, as it were. If we know too much, we may not be able to organize the signs into a being – and further we may not be able to simplify the role of that character in the novel. After all, few of us have roles in life. But characters must fulfil a function, and the more we know about them, the less able they are in a sense to fill the strait-jacket of their function. Second, novels organize experience along ideological lines. One of the aims of the novel is to make personality explicable as early modern society makes life more inexplicable. Characters therefore need to be organized in ways in which their developments and changes make sense.

Since complex characters are defined as characters who must develop, there comes a point in the novel when such characters realize something about themselves or their lives and then change their attitude or actions at that point. This is a long way of summarizing what Aristotle in his *Poetics* called 'recognition.' Mr Bennet's moment comes when Lydia elopes with Wickham. Austen prepares us for this 'recognition' fairly late in the novel when she allows Elizabeth to know what she has never yet known before chapter 42:

> Elizabeth, however, had never been blind to the impropriety of her father's behaviour as a husband. She had always seen it with pain; but respecting his abilities, and grateful for his affectionate treatment of herself, she endeavoured to forget what she could not overlook, and to banish from her thoughts that continual breach of conjugal obligation and decorum which, in exposing his wife to the contempt of her own children, was so highly reprehensible. But she had never felt so strongly as now the disadvantages which must attend the children of so unsuitable a marriage, nor ever been so fully aware of the evils arising from so ill-judged a direction of talents; talents, which rightly used, might at least have preserved the respectability of his daughters, even if incapable of enlarging the mind of his wife. (262)

Just to indicate how 'easy' in a way it is to make a set of themes or rules about a character appear complex, let us remember that Austen has not – until this point – indicated that Elizabeth either knew or felt bad about her father's rather serious faults. Just before she provides Mr Bennet with his moment of recognition, Austen needs to establish which aspect of his character will change. Ironically, it is this one paragraph alone that will add a considerable 'depth' to the character. Finally his moment arrives. After going to seek Lydia, Bennet returns and says:

> 'Who should suffer but myself? It has been my own doing, and I ought to feel it. . . . No, Lizzy, let me once in my life feel how much I have been to blame.' (314)

With this moment of recognition, Mr Bennet will become a better father, a better husband, a better person, and most of all a complex character. Very few narratives of the modern period – even the most sophisticated – are without this switching of themes in a character. Because character is so much a simplification of personality, it only takes one switch of the parameters to make a character seem to have changed profoundly.

Ideologically speaking, then, character gives readers faith that personality is, first, understandable and, second, capable of rational change. As part of the general ideology of middle-class individualism, the idea that the subject might be formed from social forces and that change might have to come about through social change is by and large absent from novels. Change is always seen as effected by the individual. In a novel like *Hard Times* only personal moral changes will bring about the amelioration of factory conditions. The family problems of Louisa and Tom will bring about the change in their father that will help solve the problems of the working class in Manchester. Likewise, Elizabeth Bennet's marriage to Darcy or Pamela's to Mr B. will somehow improve upper-class values a bit.

Because of its reliance on personal biography, one thing the novel finds almost impossible to describe is collective action – and where collective action appears, as in *Les Misérables* or *A Tale of Two Cities*, it is doomed to failure and compromise. When a novelist does include such collective action or solution, the novel quickly falls apart or becomes boring as in Morris's *News From Nowhere* or in Chernyshevsky's *What is To Be Done*. It is as if the novel's reliance on the biographical mode must always oppose the individual to the collective. Given the requirements of creating a recognizable and easily distinguished character in novels, individuality is clearly going to be given a very high priority. The group in novels is almost impossible to portray since it is by and large outside the bounds of this individuality. And if groups are shown, they must be made up of highly individuated characters – as in the work of Balzac or Flaubert. In essence, the collective or the group represents the threat of the dissolution of character. As such, a powerful ideological structure is built into the demand of character development which excludes any but the most individual solution. Zola's *Germinal* contains one of the more successful visions of the group. The culminating scene envisions a rampaging group that castrates one of its enemies and tosses the severed organ from hand to hand – giving us one of the more profound images of the dissolution of individual identity. The community can usually step into the novel mainly in the depiction of rituals – marriage, birth, and death most notably. By contrast, one should note, filmmakers have little trouble representing the group. Sergei Eisenstein is a case in point.

Personal change is made simple in novels. But anyone who has ever tried to fathom or change even the most superficial feature of his or her own personality knows how difficult if not impossible such change is. The novelistic critique of ideology is usually most dramatically manifested in this feature. If a novelist like Dickens opposes a specific constellation of thinking, he will incorporate that whole constellation into a single, unlikeable character such as the utilitarian Mr Gradgrind in *Hard Times* or the business-dominated, unfeeling Mr Dombey in *Dombey and Son*. Such characters will finally 'come to see' through the logic of the plot – usually through domestic disappointment and tragedy – that the way they were thinking led to the failure. The critique of ideology implies that a particular set of public beliefs will shape the contour of a private life. Characters then change their beliefs – their particular ideologies – and their lives improve, they begin to 'feel' and they are morally improved.

It might be worth considering the normative ways in which characters in novels change. Usually the change is from unfeeling to feeling (Gradgrind, Casaubon, Dombey), from crime to moral realization (Moll Flanders, Fanny Hill, Magwitch), from naïveté to world weariness (Jude Fawley, Dorothea Brooke, Raskolnikov), from repression to mature sexuality (Lucy Snowe, Jane Eyre, Emma Bovary). Thus the consummate composite character used to be an unfeeling, repressed, naïve outcast who becomes an integrated, feeling, moral, world-weary, sexually mature being. Obviously, I am fooling around with categories a bit, but in a way the pattern of change is to transform the character from one of them to one of us. Again, the movement is normative, creating humans in the image of an idealized, middle-class image of themselves.

Aside from the overt ideological intention of a work like *Hard Times*, the very idea of character is essentially an ideological construct. That personality can be reduced and summarized into an orderly and coherent set of known features and that a fairly simple and understandable change in thought can produce a completely new set of social relations and outcomes is part of the rather dramatic intention inherent in character. On a simple level, the novel fosters the idea that self-understanding – whether one happens to be in Victorian England or in medieval Florence – is the key to change. The universality of this rule is part of a larger ideological set of beliefs about individualism, middle-class industry and self-reliance, and what Macpherson has called 'possessive individualism' (3). Also, if one follows the lead of people like Paul Delaney, the assertion that the novel develops out of seventeenth-century Puritan spiritual autobiographies seems to point to a very stereotyped vision of character, particularly susceptible to the moment of moral conversion so typical in that born-again variety of writing. Puritans recorded their lives because they could be 'read' and interpreted along certain religious lines, and the great moment of confirmation was always the point at which they came to see the error of their ways, changed the shape of their belief, and therefore permanently changed the world.

One might note that this kind of belief is referred to in psychoanalysis as 'omnipotence of thought' – an essentially psychotic ideation that sees thoughts as so powerful that simply thinking something is enough to cause them to happen. Novels, like psychotics, incorporate the belief that thoughts do have this independent and powerful form and that simply having bad thoughts – or a bad ideology – can make families disintegrate, spouses and children die, and so on. And all this chaos could come to an end by a change of thought and heart. That this state of affairs is common to novels is not surprising since novels are particular instances of thoughts becoming more than just thoughts. Novelists are people whose thoughts become 'true' in a very powerful way.

If one turns to the more definite subject of physical description, other differences between character and personality appear. There is a limit to the physical traits attributable to a character. If one tried to describe the physicality of a human in great detail the task could be almost impossible – and in fact it is almost impossible to describe a human face, for example, beyond the cultural code of skin color, hair color, eye color, height, weight, and eccentric features (limp, glasses, etc.). If we stop and ask ourselves what color hair Elizabeth Bennet has we may have to think twice, whereas we are usually familiar with the hair color of even a minor personal acquaintance. What we are made to remember about Miss Bennet is her sensuous eyes and her

121

wild temperament – since these are singled out by Austen for the reader to recall. But her other features are largely ignored.

As with moral character, physical features must be simplified to be effective. For example, it is almost impossible for the average person to see in the mind's eye a figure that is more than nine-sided – that is, one can posit the possibility of a decagon, but one cannot visualize it mentally. Similarly, in creating a character an author cannot actually go beyond a few descriptive attributes and perhaps a few physical gestures that repeat. We all remember vividly characters like Uriah Heep in *David Copperfield*, but what we are told about him is that he is tall, gaunt, with hands that are cold and which he rubs together repeating his tag line 'I'm so 'umble.' If that is all one could know of a real person, such an acquaintance would be rather superficial, but in the case of a novelistic character it makes this collection of instructions 'live forever.'

As with other simplifications, the 'universality' of characters – the immortality of their form in our consciousness – is produced by eliminating the quotidien details of life. They become *ur*-humans, simulacra, representations who are in effect removed from life. That removal permits characters to live forever in the same way that the Struldbruggs in *Gulliver's Travels* cease to be human at the moment of their immortality. Characters become more subject to the rules and requirements of the novel by simplification. Thus they demonstrate to readers the rationality of the world, the comprehensibility of life and behavior, or in the case of modernist fiction the ability of art to comprehend and incorporate the incomprehensibility of the world.

Unlike the traits of real people, a novelistic character's traits – psychological and physical – are there for a reason. When someone in a novel has dark hair and someone else has blonde hair a certain system of meaning and intention is in operation. These systems have been explicated by critics like Roland Barthes, for example, who in *S/Z* establishes four levels of semiological code in a short story by Balzac and painstakingly moves through tiny units of meaning unravelling them. In real life, however, hair color is (chemical help aside) not intentional. Likewise, if a character in a novel is crippled, the author is probably using that physical trait for a purpose, whereas a handicap in real life may have psychological consequences but has no 'purpose.' In short, character is intentional, personality is not. Of course, one can argue that we make our own personalities, that we for example dress in a particular manner to indicate who we are or want to be. But if four people in a novel are wearing dungarees and a fifth is wearing a seersucker summer suit a system of meaning and intention is put into practice that goes above and beyond the same situation in a room full of friends. Each friend has chosen his or her own wardrobe, but no one has chosen the entire group's arrangement.

One of the most noteworthy deviations from life in the physical description of novelistic characters falls into the category of beauty. In the classic novel, that is, well through the nineteenth century, the convention demands a hero or heroine who is physically attractive. Novels like *Jane Eyre, Villette,* or *Bleak House* go against that convention – but in so doing they only verify the existence of the convention. During the twentieth century, characters in novels do not have to be physically attractive. However, film has taken over the popular function of novels and continues with that prerequisite.

If characters in classic novels must be beautiful, what does beauty signify? First and foremost it implies a correspondence between the psychological, the moral, and the physical. Usually beauty is a sign that such characters are admirable, worthy of imitation, and cultural paragons. The men are brave, rebellious within limits, and romantic, the women are virtuous, rebellious within limits, and desirable. And their physical beauty is often a sign of their social status, or in the case of lower-class women of their future social status. For example, in *Tom Jones* people keep remarking on the attractiveness of the hero – implying that he must be a gentleman, and of course it turns out that his genetic nobility has shown through his physical features after all. A stroll through the National Portrait Gallery in London might reveal what most people know anyway – that the British nobility was singularly unattractive. But when people equated beauty with nobility they were actually equating the life of leisure with the kind of physical difference it emphasized from the life of labor. Freedom from outdoor work or grueling apprenticeship along with plenty of sleep and physical exercise unrelated to manual labor can make twins look different. The privilege of the gentleman or woman is the concealed message of physical beauty. Physical beauty is a sign of being select, chosen, elevated in society. It is almost always a class-related mark. And in the case of physical beauty among the poor – usually poor virgins – this is a sign that they can or should transcend class lines, as does the virtuous maid Pamela in Richardson's novel.

The point is that the physical beauty of characters in novels is also part of a system of meaning, whereas the physical beauty of real people may participate in some cultural system of meanings but was not given for an ulterior motive – unless one is discussing the genetic or evolutionary value of physical beauty. The very valence of beauty or ugliness in novels, then, is not neutral but is predicated on ideological considerations. In nineteenth-century novels, physical beauty becomes not a mark so much of actual class lines as of moral class lines. The beautiful of spirit are beautiful of feature. Dickens' female heroines are always innocently beautiful – with the exception of Esther who becomes disfigured halfway through *Bleak House* – in accord with their moral elevation, and in their often-required moment of death they always become positively angelic in appearance. In novels of the twentieth century, characters can be ugly or repulsive since beauty is no longer related to class, and the lack of beauty in a character signals to the reader the distance the novelist wants to create between reader and protagonist, as part of a larger project of celebrating alienation and meaninglessness. Also, as Lukács has pointed out, the move from realism to modernism abandons the centrality of the subject and overly focuses on form. In this sense, then, the ugliness of modernist characters serves to keep readers from closely allying themselves with a utopian or hopeful cultural model and therefore with the mimetic quality of the classical novel, and displaces the reader's interest to the dazzling display of form and style in, for example, the work of James Joyce or Henry James.

However, the question remains why moral worth needed to be tied to physical beauty in the classic novel. Why must central characters by physically attractive? There is a sense in which in order for a novel to work readers must be powerfully attracted to the central character. Let me approach this issue in a slightly roundabout way. The word that frequently comes up in any discussion of the relationship of readers to characters is 'identification.' Scratch any reader and the first thing they will say is that they 'identified' with one character or another. It is my sense that this word is tremendously misunderstood and misleading. By 'identification' readers usually mean that they 'liked' a character and therefore came to put themselves in the place of that character, experiencing the world through his or her consciousness. Like Flaubert, we say 'Madame Bovary, *c'est moi!*' But often we may read novels in which the central character is not likeable or is inferior to the reader. Few people who read about Robinson Crusoe like him; and readers of *Pride and Prejudice*, even though they may admire Elizabeth Bennet, always feel as though they know more in certain senses than she does during most of the novel. If identification were only the process it is touted to be, we would just 'be' those people without the critical edge I am describing.

The point here is that in life when we identify with a person we usually like that person and in some ways want to be like that person. In novels, I would argue the process of identification is quite different. I want to make a distinction between *psychological* identification and *novelistic* identification. In the first place, the word 'identification' as it is popularly used is a term whose use arose from psychoanalytic thought. Particularly in 'Mourning and melancholia' (1917), *Group Psychology and the Analysis of the Ego* (1921), and *The Ego and The Id* (1923), Freud elaborated his notion of identification. More interestingly, he tied up the idea of identification with the development of what he called 'character' and character formation. For Freud, identification as a psychological process was a key step in the formation of personality, and as such it should help us understand the formation of characters in novels.

Character is based on a series of relations to objects. As Freud wrote, 'At the very beginning, in the individual's primitive oral phase, object-cathexis and identification are no doubt indistinguishable from each other' (*Ego* 19). Objects present themselves at this stage as sources of pleasure to the id, the ego being virtually nonexistent then, and are engulfed or, to use a term coined by Ferenczi, 'introjected.' So identification is almost literally the taking in of the desired object so that the object can be let go. As Freud says, 'it may be that this identification is the sole condition under which the id can give up its objects.' And the *character* of the ego, then, is 'a precipitate of abandoned object-cathexes and contains the history of those object choices' (19). What is being said is that when the id, or the instincts, desires a thing it cannot have, the ego, to please the id, as it were, tries to become *like* that object through identification. As Freud writes:

When the ego assumes the features of the object, it is forcing itself, so to speak, upon the id as a love-object and is trying to make good the id's loss by saying: 'Look, you can love me too – I am so like the object.' (20)

Through this process, humans develop their sense of identity or their character. Cathy Wein puts the point succinctly: 'The concept of identification attempts to account for the construction of a sense of identity through the affective ties to others' (29). Such identifications are not always expressed in terms of love, but can be the result of highly ambivalent feelings towards the object. So, for example, one can identify with an aggressor or rival.

In life the strongest and most lasting identifications occur during the resolution of the Oedipal conflict when the child, learning the hard way that one cannot defeat the rival parent, modulates the problem by identification with the aggressor. As Wein summarizes:

> In the classic oedipal situation, under the pressure of object-libidinal drives toward the opposite-sexed parent and the aggressive drives toward the same-sexed parent . . . the child is forced to 'give up' the object-choice in order to retain the love of the parents. The child resolves this conflict by identifying with the parental prohibitions and thereby increases internal control over incestuous and hostile impulses. (61)

The rival parent then becomes the ego ideal through the process of introjection, and the super ego is formed as 'heir' to the Oedipal conflict, as Freud puts it. In short, the process of identification requires rivalry and admiration, defeat, and internalization of the object. And all future identifications are to some degree reminiscent of this primordial one. As Freud indicated, 'the effects of the first identifications made in earliest childhood will be general and lasting. This leads us back to the origin of the ego ideal; for behind it there lies hidden an individual's first and most important identification, his identification with the father in his own personal prehistory' (*Ego* 21).

Now, when readers say that they identified with a character they usually mean that they 'put themselves into the place' of that character. But the important thing to realize about novelistic identification, as opposed to Freudian identification, is that the desire to identify with a character *precedes* the actual encounter on the first page of the novel. That is, one sets out in a novel *to* identify with a character – even before meeting that character or any character. Novelistic characters exist *because* they are designed to entice us to identify with them. Readers do identify with characters as diverse as Jude Fawley, Tom Jones, Verloc, or Maggie Verver. In novel reading, the desire to identify precedes the particularity of the characters. In other words, it is not a question of liking a character, or finding reminders of our own early relationships in that character, but simply the fact that the form of the novel itself evokes identification. While Freudian identification is largely dependent on the particular personality of the object with whom we will identify, novelistic identification is indiscriminate and promiscuous, if you will, since all objects, all protagonists, have been or will be objects of desire.

Now the issue of physical beauty becomes more understandable. Since the physical beauty of most protagonists is not accidental but taken as a functioning requirement of the classic novel, I would suggest its function is that it encourages the element of desire to enter the reading process. In making a character attractive, the author can draw the reader towards that set of signs much as advertisers can draw consumers toward a product by associating it with a physically attractive model. In effect, it is not so much that we identify with a character, but that we desire that character in some non-specific but erotic way. In this sense, part of novel reading is the process of falling in love with characters or making friends with signs.

This desire for novelistic characters provides a way in which the defensive nature of ideological constructs can be understood. The novel as an ideological form requires attraction as much as pornography requires attraction to succeed. By the connection through identification, ideologies can ebb and flow through a populace. The mechanism is not mysterious or global in this explanation but is an offshoot of a well-known human defense.

Desire here is not necessarily directed only towards people. As I pointed out in the previous chapter, the desire for controlled property turns space into ideological space. So desire has its political component. As Fredric Jameson points out, 'the desire for a particular object [in the novel] is at one and the same time allegorical of all desire in general and of Desire as such, in which the pretext or theme of such desire has not yet been relativized and privatized by the ego-barriers that jealously confirm the personal and purely subjective' (*The Political Unconscious* 156). And as Piaget and his followers have suggested, all relations are ultimately object relations. For Piaget, the only difference between a child's relation to his parents and to a building block is that his parents are more cognitively interesting. In this context, the novel works not only by transforming space into controlled property but by turning personality into controlled character. In effect, personality is rendered a form of property – quite literally if you consider the author's ownership of his or her creation through copyright laws – and a commodity in the sense that readers buy novels in some sense to have access to these controlled personalities. By placing so much emphasis on the process of desire, and the feeling that this activity of novel reading is so dependent on Eros to solve personal problems and reshape character, the novel in effect becomes a social form that changes the complexity of personality into a rather simplified commodity of desire. Like a desirable commodity that seems to offer the promise of an improved life, or like an objectified fashion model who beckons the user of the targeted product into the frame of an advertisement, character holds out the possibility of personal fulfillment in a world that is increasingly making such fulfillment inconceivable.

If 'erotic' is too strong a word for such an attenuated situation as reading, let us say that the process of getting to know the signs and themes of a character is made to seem like the process of meeting and getting to know a desired object. The aim of this erotic transfer is to create what Freud calls a cathexis, a kind of almost electronic charge associated with a particular mental image. The main character is cathected or charged with an erotic valence. This process allows a reader simply to identify or in effect occupy the perceptual space of the character.

Obviously, I cannot develop an entire psychoanalytic model of reading here. So what follows is only a brief sketch and suggestion for further study. The point I want to make is that some very powerful psychological mechanism – operating in conjunction with social factors – must be at work to permit so many humans to read so many words in so many places over so much time. Why *would* we identify with a simulacrum of linguistic signs? What could conceivably be the reason that a sane human being would choose to form a sexualized relation with a set of signs?

As Freud has pointed out, the attachment to the breast and the mother constitutes our earliest connection to objects. In this oral phase we learn to distinguish ourselves from the external world and we learn to believe in and make attachments to objects. Reading, though a skill that is acquired usually during or after the Oedipal phase, is tied up at least thematically with this oral phase since in reading we have to endow signs with a kind of reality and make them objects. Novel reading is in effect wrapped up with object relations and with the primary issue of the oral phase – trust and reality testing. While location and character (that is, the objects within a novel) seem to be related to the oral phase and object relations, plot, as has been argued by such as Otto Rank and Marthe Robert, seems to be more intimately related to the machinations of the Oedipal moment, with searches for lost parents, the family romance, and a general obsession with sexuality and murder.

The Oedipal phase changes certain features of object relations. In this phase one struggles with the renunciation of the primary object and displaces interest to a secondary one. Freud says that 'a human being's first choice of an object is regularly an incestuous one' which must be curtailed by 'the severest prohibitions to deter this persistent infantile tendency from realizaton' (*Introductory Lectures* 335). Or, as W. W. Meisner puts it, 'As ego development proceeds . . . the incorporative desire for total union with objects is gradually relinquished in favor of striving to become like the object' (249). In other words, one has to disengage or decathect from the desired parent, and learn to substitute through the process of identification. Now, in reading novels, as we noted, the process of identification is different because of the rather promiscuous nature of seeking to attach to any central character whatever. The indiscriminate way that readers displace their attachment to the idea of character – aside from any *specific* character – indicates that some kind of repetition is in operation whereby the trauma of that primary, first displacement from love object to rival can be re-enacted and reworked in an attempt to discharge it of its powerfully painful associations. Like primitive puberty rites, the novel acts in a way, I would argue, to release 'the boy [or girl] from the incestuous bond with his mother [or for the girl her father] and of reconciling' the child with the rival parent (*Introductory Lectures* 335). My claim is that novels perform this function by endlessly creating displacing erotic objects (that is, characters) with whom we can form cathexes or bonds without much fear or danger, thus 'proving' to ourselves over and over again that the primary displacement from mother or father was not so bad after all. If, as I quoted Freud saying earlier, the 'character of the ego is a precipitate of abandoned object-cathexes,' then characters in novels provide the occasion to dispel the emotion of all our own abandoned object choices.

What I am saying is that the indiscriminate nature of our desire to identify in novels places that desire in the forefront of the dynamics between reader and character. We read to experience in a fairly painless and riskless way a strong and unique attachment that is like our attachment to a desired parent, but which is able to be put aside with the ease and brief sadness with which we put aside a novel we have finished. In effect, such kinds of quick and easy identifications are characteristic of pre-Oedipal, early magical attempts to link ourselves to powerful objects. As Edith Jacobson has noted, such attachments are 'magic in nature; they represent only a temporary – partial or total – blending of magic self and object images, founded on fantasies or even the temporary belief of being one with or of becoming the object, regardless of reality' (Meisner 250). In effect, what we have been calling novelistic identification is much closer to this regressive process in its indiscriminate and transitory nature than Freudian identification which is more lasting and permanently a part of the psychic make-up.

So indiscriminate is novelistic identification that even the particularity of gender is ignored in this process. That is, readers usually identify with either male or female characters regardless of their own gender. Like the sexlessness of narrators, the polymorphous and indiscriminate nature of sexual lines and our willingness to identify indicates a desire to overcome the duality of gender division – that mark of separation of the Oedipal moment where for the first time sexual awareness draws new lines in the family territorial markings. Castration anxiety, gender envy, and the host of anxiety producing realizations that are bound up with the Oedipal moment are somehow elided in the ambisexual world of the novel, which encourages readers and novelists to cross gender lines, experience sexuality from both sides, to be both parent and child, lover and beloved, sadist and masochist, voyeur and voyee. All of this is true, one might add, even in the traditional male-centered novel which in many ways is about the male author becoming in effect female.

The argument can be made that what I have observed is universal, that people have been forming object relations and going through the Oedipal crisis for centuries. So why should I claim that this process has any special relevance to the novel? Another way of posing this question, more to my own liking, is why does a new cultural artifact suddenly pick up on a pre-existing psychological mechanism? The question can be expanded to ask how do ideological constructs employ defensive structures in the psyche to work? Rather than turning to Freud here, one might turn to Marx's discussion of bourgeois character in *Grundrisse*:

> The universally developed individuals, whose social relations are their collective relations and as such are subject to their own collective control are the product not of nature, but of history. The degree and the universality to which the capacities are developed which make this individuality possible presuppose a mode of production based on exchange values. This mode of production brings about the general alienation of the individual from himself [or herself] and from others, but at the same time it actually creates that universality and diversity with which his relations and abilities are endowed. At earlier stages of history the single individual appears more complete precisely because he [or she] has not yet elaborated this wealth of relationships and opposed them to himself as autonomous social forces. (41)

What Marx is discussing here is of course the subject of alienation in which human relations are changed in the early modern period by the emphasis on a mode of production based on exchange value. Marx's point is that, in a modern economy, human beings appear to be more universal and complete precisely because the notion of individuality is one that sets the individual against the complexity of social forces that make up the lived world. This opposition requires the *appearance* of a completeness to fight the fragmentary quality of modern life. Here I would add that the self that appears capable of fighting alienation is the aesthetic self – particularly the novelistic self. The novel comes at precisely the historical moment that needs it to help overcome 'the general alienation of the individual from himself and from others.' Novelistic characters offer the hope of being the units of complete personality that seem to be missing from life since the early modern period. Consistently, they have to appear in commodified form as products of technological processes since those processes cannot produce complete human beings. And the novel is a form which offers, through the process of displaced object desires, a complete and unalienated relationship to individuals and to a community. This relationship was thwarted in the first place by unattainable objects of desire – whether parents on a personal level or the difficult to obtain 'rewards' of a specialized, industrialized society on a public level. In the simplest terms, the novel promises on a personal level the overcoming of alienation and loneliness.

The psychological and the social come together in the idea that the Oedipal moment can represent a permanent exile or alienation. In the classical Oedipal phase, children must detach themselves from the desired object and identify with the rival parent. The child must shift his or her own desire from within the family to without. The search must then be for a love object who is 'like' the lost mother or father. The child, nestled in the bosom of the family, comes to the realization that he or she is not actually part of the family at all – and in fact is a kind of outcast, criminal, or pariah.[2] It is not a coincidence that Oedipus himself is exiled. That exile is the type for the domestic exile of this developmental period. And the idea of the family romance, the notion held by many children that they are adopted – their real parents being kings, queens, or of some other glorified status – is a way of saying that they are not really part of the family. From a Marxist perspective, alienation, through a series of over-determinations, can be perceived as a variation on this Oedipal exile. That is, the larger social form of alienation can be experienced as a personal extension of the domestic exile. This is one of the major senses in which the novel as a social form provides a collective defense. Here the public ideology of community achieved through such concepts as nationalism is confirmed by the defense of identification which works on both the personal as well as the collective level. In this sense, the novel provides one of the powerful mechanisms that support this perception since the subject of alienation in the novel must always be treated through the personal, biographical history of a character. The domestic explanation in the novel is always the strongest and most available one. Hence, according to my definition of ideology as a public idea linked to personal defenses, the novel can act in this ideological manner.

Moreover, one of the strongest messages of ideology is that alienation can be overcome through art – and that novelists, particularly, are capable of opposing certain destructive forces in society by simply representing them in fiction. The historical moment of the novel with its mechanism for overcoming the distance between self and other coincides with a general trend in art and culture. As Lionel Trilling put it in the preface to *The Opposing Self*:

> whoever has read any European history at all knows that the self emerges (as the historians say) at pretty frequent intervals. Yet the self that makes itself manifest at the end of the eighteenth century is different in kind, and in effect from any self that had ever before emerged [that is in] . . . its intense and adverse imagination of the culture in which it has its being. (i)

Trilling's point is that novelists like Jane Austen, Charles Dickens, Leo Tolstoy, Gustave Flaubert, Henry James, George Orwell, and poets like Wordsworth and Keats, were able through 'certain powers of indignant perception' to turn upon an 'unconscious portion of culture' and make it 'accessible to conscious thought' (ii). Novelists somehow intuitively appear to fight alienation and bad ideologies through their mimetic form. Particularly, love in the novel as a social phenomenon and reading of the novel as the literary equivalent of erotic attachment become important in overcoming separation or alienation. And it is no accident that during the formative period of the novel the theme of loneliness becomes dominant in a variety of literary modes, as John Sitter has noted. The novel provides a form that allows for a feeling of community amongst its readers, a powerful bond between the narrator and the reader that replaces the weakening bonds of family and society.

But the process of reading novels while seeming to satisfy loneliness and overcome alienation is also a process of 'reification,' to use the word in Lukács' sense. Novels rely on the fact that realism acts as a technique by conceptualizing the world as delineated objects that are autonomous and separate from ourselves. The sensuous and immediate relationship with nature that Marx posits as a quality of unalienated life is dramatically cut off in the novel twice over – as Plato in *The Republic* remarked about art – since mimetic art is merely a copy of a copy. The objects in Robinson Crusoe's cave are doubly unavailable to us, once by being on an island and once by being in a book. It is Jameson's point that the novel's special relationship with objects and objectification becomes in authors like Dreiser a 'commodity lust' in which readers and writers share in a voyeuristic desire to see (and possess) the things enumerated in novels (*The Political Unconscious* 159). The line between commodity lust and character lust, in this sense, is a thin one.

The unique ability of novels to reproduce a sensual and sexual world that can be perceived almost directly encourages readers to bind themselves through attraction and fantasy to a fictional society as a substitute for a world of more anomic social relations. Novelistic identification is the special development in human defenses that makes the novel uniquely able to perform its social function – just as the introduction of oil pigment with its capacity for sensuous, almost photographic reproduction allowed for the glorification of wealth and valued objects, as John Berger has pointed out (*Ways of Seeing* 87). However, unlike oil painting, which shows us only a reified version of the object, the comfort of overcoming loneliness through reading is fraught with the tension inherent in the loneliness of reading, the isolation of the act, and the inaccessibility of the fictional characters. Reification, paradoxically, is at one and the same time both lessened *and* intensified in novel reading since the object of our desires is not a member of the human race but a cluster of signs that have been made not only into an object but – through the economics of the booktrade – into a commodity.

The novel's obsession with love and marriage brings in the issue of loneliness in another way. Novels of the eighteenth and nineteenth centuries tend to focus largely on the doings of young people and their choice of a mate. From an almost anthropological view, then, novels are partially a cultural attempt through collective fantasy to overcome the problems presented by the institution of marriage and the diadic relationship. The central point of such novels is how a man or woman who feels outside of the social process can be integrated through marriage without losing a sense of individuality. The focus on marriage in the classic novel constitutes a discussion of this same problem of overcoming the loneliness and isolation of a problematic character through the social institution of romantic love. The solution is highly individualistic – focusing on the moment of choice and the uniqueness of the object.

Given this obsession, it is not remarkable that the reading process itself should mirror the same issue – that is, that reading should resemble the process of falling in love. There is a good deal of sociological and historical information to suggest that attitudes toward marriage and sexuality were changing rapidly in the early modern period. As Lawrence Stone has pointed out, the move from the arranged marriages of earlier times towards erotic marriage was aided by the novel and its celebration of the value of erotic marriage. The point I am making is that the built-in ability of character to arouse desire makes readers feel as if they were integrated into some kind of human community. For example, among the most popular early novels were Samuel Richardson's epistolary ones *Pamela* and *Clarissa*. These novels, constructed as letters written between characters, offer the possibility of overcoming separation since the epistolary novel in particular must always be structured so that two friends or lovers are separated by some obstruction that keeps them apart so they are forced to resort to letters. Their writing then is designed to overcome loneliness and separation – and one could argue that reading their letters gave readers a way of participating in overcoming their own sense of isolation and in reduplicating the primal act of identification (Perry 93ff.).

If it is true that many readers, as my students routinely testify about their own motives, believe that they read novels to learn about life, then reading novels helps them learn about life by 'meeting' characters whose lives – though not real – seem to promise the possibility of some kind of understanding about life. But if one stops to think of the nature of that proposition, things become a bit bizarre. A novel reader retires to the privacy of his or her room (because novel reading is by and large a solitary activity, except in the rare case of group reading, that can only occur in a relatively leisured society), plunges into the solipsistic world of the imagination in which signs are turned into images, reads about the exploits of people who never existed and who on closer examination do not even remotely resemble people who are alive, and does all this to 'learn about life.'

Thus, by a strange twist of fate, novel reading becomes the ultimate in alienated activity. John Dunlop in 1814 described this very phenomenon of the novel:

> By its means, the recluse is placed in the midst of society; and he who is harrassed and agitated in the city is transported to rural tranquility and repose. The rude are refined by an introduction, as it were, to the higher orders of mankind. (xi)

In effect, reading novels is a solitary activity in which readers define themselves by what they are not, put themselves into locations they have never been, and celebrate values that often they would never endorse. The activity is also the ultimate in reification. Rather than actually seeing and perceiving the sensual reality of human life, a patent simulacrum of a human being made up purely of linguistic symbols with certain rules of recurrence is presented as if it were human. And what is more to the point, it is conceived as an object of desire. We seek to locate ourselves in the character and to merge with the character. We read to make friends with signs. Through the seclusion of reading, we seek to overcome loneliness.

Of course, the objection could be made that such alienation might be characteristic of any kind of story-telling. What is the difference between telling any story and the issues I have been raising about story-telling in the novel? As Patricia Meyer Spacks might object to my argument:

> To tell a story of the self is ... to create a fiction. We know this even from day-to-day experience. Even as we form an anecdote to relate in company, we are deliberately or reluctantly sacrificing some part of the actual experience for the sake of its telling. (311)

But to make such an argument is to overlook the ideological particularity of specific narrative forms and to universalize (as novelists would like us to do) the novelistic experience. Novelists must select, as must bardic poets, but the basis of their selection will differ. When I tell a story to my friends, the nature of the encounter (I am 'there'), the limited nature of the involvement of the audience, the simple way that characters are presented in a spoken tale – all are quite different from the prerequisites of the novel. Also, the social function of the novel is more or less discounted in generalizing it as simply story-telling. One wants to keep a close eye on the idea that the novel is a discourse with its own specific limits and not simply blur the boundaries between fiction and fact on all accounts.

As an illustrative parallel to the idea I have been presenting, I want to mention that strangest of characters who links the worlds of art, economics, alienation, and character. I am speaking of what most people in the eighteenth century would have known quite well – the fashion doll. This doll was a life-size or smaller representation of a woman in the latest Parisian fashions. It arrived promptly once a year from France and made a tour of London and the provinces. Since there were no fashion magazines at the time, the fashion doll was the only way that fashions could be popularized. The dolls were known as 'pandoras,' and 'mannequins,' and Addison himself referred to 'the wooden Madamoiselle' (McKendrick, *et al.* 44). The doll even came across the Channel while England and France were at war, so great was the general interest in this attractive figure. At the end of the century, she was transformed into a cardboard cut-out that could be cheaply purchased and was printed in the thousands as opposed to the singularity of the life-size fashion dolls. A contemporary description of the flat doll includes the following:

> Hat or bonnet can be adjusted freely to be pulled over the face or set back. They can be put straight or at an angle, suiting the hairstyle in a tasteful manner or otherwise. In short: dress and coiffure can be varied, and by trying, each given its particular 'air.'
> (McKendrick, *et al.* 45)

The point is that the fashion doll was part of the development in the eighteenth century of a consumer society in which 'fashion was being deliberately designed to encourage social imitation, social emulation and emulative spending' (43).

For our purposes it is enough to note that the fashion doll was a kind of character in a sense who encouraged emulation and even identification. She was a totally fictitious being who existed in a real way for English women. She provided a sense of community and a style to imitate. She was in fact character as commodity. One of the dominant notions of fashion is that in order to 'be' one must 'be in the right style.' Mass-market fashion of course is a dominant feature of a consumer society, and it too represents an extreme of alienation since consumers define their personalities in terms of what is not themselves. If character in novels represents the commodification of the self, the fashion doll serves as an icon on the road to the commodification of the self. Novels, then, are one aspect of that phenomenon.

The character with whom readers most seek to connect is the narrator. Narrators, whether overtly within the novel as first-person informants or outside the structure of the novel as 'author,' wield a powerful control – or 'authority' as Edward Said has called it

(*Beginnings*). Recent work in narrative theory distinguishes between several types of narrators. Wallace Martin distinguishes between author, implied author, and narrator (first or third person) (135). The first is the living writer, the second what Wayne Booth has called the constructed author who may be quite different in our minds from the flesh and blood person, and the third is the voice within the novel that speaks the story. Gérard Genette's typologies are even more complex and include the 'extradiegetic' narrator who either remains loftily above the story, or if in his or her own story then is an 'interdiegetic' narrator (255–6). For my purposes, I am assuming that the divisions between narrators and implied narrators are not as important as the relation between the reader and any narrator at all. What interests me in this chapter is the reader's relation to the organizer of the material being laid out for scrutiny – not the degree of presence or absence such a narrator has.

The aim of the classical narrator, as Fredric Jameson has noted, is 'to restore the coordinates of a face-to-face storytelling institution which has been effectively disintegrated by the printed book and even more definitively by the commodification of literature and culture' (*The Political Unconscious* 155). The presence of the narrator is comforting and mature, and authorizes the restoration of order, community, and communication by his or her very presence. This authority is made even more dramatic in the nineteenth century by the fiction that almost all narrators are male. But even though the narrator might be male, his personal sexual involvement is always muted. Henry Fielding might have been the only author to have allowed his narrator the right to be in love with the heroine when he avows his own attraction to Sophia. The narrator's asexuality, lack of physical features, and general lack of specific, temporal qualities only increases the reader's trust and submission to the writer's universal authority.

Take the narrator in *Pride and Prejudice* who begins her relationship with the reader by writing the following words in gender-neutral terms: 'It is a truth universally acknowledged, that a single man with a fortune must be in want of a wife.' If a strange woman approached a passerby on the street and uttered these words as an opening line to a conversation – what would be the response? Awkward confusion, the desire to flee, a sense of the violation of privacy, and perhaps the judgment that this female was extremely pompous and full of herself. Yet readers for two centuries have been allowing Jane Austen to pitch that opening line at them without batting an eye. What other features does this voice have?

First, one would have to say that the voice implies that the relation between author and reader is one between superior and inferior. Readers willingly accede to being lectured to, pontificated at, deluded, manipulated, and finally enthralled by narrators. Put the problem another way: what person living or dead would you agree to sit with in an attic for twenty hours and listen to almost anything they had to say about anything as long as they sort of kept a story going about someone marrying someone else? Very few indeed, but most of us willingly spend that much time reading any sort of middling novel. What makes us stick with novelists as opposed to ordinary people?

When we begin to read a novel like *Pride and Prejudice* we are doing a few things. First we are trying to isolate the characters, to 'get to know them,' and to figure out what is the problem facing them. We are also in the midst of establishing a relationship with the narrator, even if the narrator – implied, absent, extradiegetic, or whatever – is not directly in the novel. Usually we know that we are reading a novel by Charles Dickens, Virginia Woolf, or Norman Mailer and we want to know more about that author. And in a strange way we want to be liked by the novelist, we want to be, as we are, his or her confidant. But our role can only be secondary and passive. We cannot talk back to the novelist, we cannot suggest alternative courses of action for characters in a work, we cannot do anything to merit the attention of the novelist except to read the novel. In fact, our only source of merit is the fact that we are novel readers – people surely special to a novel writer.

If the relationship between reader and character is one based on the desire of the reader for the main character, the relationship between reader and narrator, as I will explain in the following pages, is one in which readers wish the narrator in part to desire *them*. The reader seeks the approval and the desire of the author. This phenomenon is confirmed through such minor contemporary rituals as book-signing parties in which the author is seen as bestowing a favor on the anonymous readers who deserve the token simply because they bought the book. While readers actually do the author a favor by buying the book, recognizing it as a commodity, the author appears to be favoring the reader with a gift of his or her *oeuvre*. Louis Hyde has demonstrated that cultural objects like books and academic articles are not permitted overtly to be seen as commodities, but rather are presented as gifts or, in the parlance of literary and academic journals, as 'contributions.' And as Natalie Zemon Davis has pointed out, the book, in general, is a commodity that has only been reluctantly seen by consumers as such. During the sixteenth century, a time

> in which the book was being produced by one of the most capitalistic industries in Europe, it continued to be perceived as an object of mixed not absolute property, of collective not private enterprise . . . something not just created by us, but inherited, given by God, given by others . . . a privileged object that resisted permanent appropriation. (87)

Authors' dedications 'establish a context for the subject of the book, the kind of circle where and the spirit with which the book should be read and its contents discussed. The book must seem to come not only to the dedicatee but also to the buyer as a gift, a service' (79). So in buying a novel, even in our time, the sense is that we are in the author's favor.

At the same time as readers seek the approval of the author, readers allow authors to dominate and master them. Indeed, the experience of reading demands this domination and submission. Ruth Perry has noted that the origins of the novel are tied up with plots in which women have 'seductive relationships to authority figures, either fathers or guardians . . . [an appropriate fantasy] for women with so little power over their own lives and so little experience with any but the all-powerful males of their own families' (52). Though the source of this domination may derive partly from the early female readership of the novel, submission to a narrator crosses gender lines and would seem to be part of the very ideological predetermination of the novel as a form.

Another way of looking at this issue of passivity and domination is to consider what kind of a central character is usually the focus of novelistic identification. As George Levine points out:

> it is one of the curious facts about the most virtuous heroes and heroines of nineteenth-century English realist fiction that they are inefficacious, inactive people. Their fullest energies are expended only (if at all) in response to external threat, in the preservation of familial and communal ties. Like Dorothea Brooke and Daniel

Deronda, they are somehow incapable of imagining a satisfying action, a way of life which will allow them seriously to act at all. (33)

Even the industrious Robinson Crusoe is curiously passive since it is only after fifteen years or so of island life that he discovers the fact that natives have been shuttling back and forth from his island prison to their island on small dugout canoes in what is essentially a short and easy commute. It is hard to see Pamela and Clarissa as actually any more than passive victims protesting their fate. Even Tom Jones is more acted against than acting. Scott's heroes are, according to Alexander Welsch, essentially passive, and Dickens' characters are notoriously so. Even fiery characters like Elizabeth Bennet or Jane Eyre are more tossed about by circumstances, reserving for themselves a very compromised kind of nay-saying. Someone like Becky Sharpe in *Vanity Fair* is active but conniving and, as with the picaresque hero of early Spanish fiction, our identification is only partially with her; ultimately it is Dobbin who becomes refurbished from the comic center to the romantic hero of the novel. One could run through many novels, but if one stops and considers, the weight of evidence lies with the passive hero. The main character of modernist fiction is even more evidently passive and alienated – for example, Nick in *The Great Gatsby*, Bloom in *Ulysses*, Holden Caulfield in *The Catcher in the Rye*, and so on.

Levine explains this passivity as part of the novel's attempt to find an accommodation for the individual in relation to the power of society. Ambition and rebelliousness against injustice in realist characters is eventually killed by respect for the established 'civilized community' and by 'the irrational need to escape the consequences of adulthood, to retreat to the innocence and helplessness of the womb where the heroic expression of selfhood is denied' (34).

I would argue that, in addition, the passivity of the main character reflects the reader's own passivity in relation to the narrator. While novels seek characters who appear rebellious (Robinson Crusoe, Tom Jones, Clarissa, Elizabeth Bennet, Jean Valjean, Lucien de Rubempre, Frederic Moreau, Jude Fawley, etc.), these characters often turn out to be rebellious in very limited and compromised ways. Their moment of rebellion, not uncharacteristically, is usually verbal – a moment of sharp, judgmental attack on someone or some institution. This is the moment when the novelist sets up his or her specific ideological attack, such as Sleary's speech to Mr Gradgrind in *Hard Times* or Jane Eyre's plea for a wider role in society for women. As with the reader and the narrator, it is at last mainly the linguistic mode that is available to the main character of the novel.

The linguistic mode is raised in the novel to the highest form of expression and moral justification. Narrators, after all, exist by virtue of the linguistic and from it comes their authority. Take for example Jane Austen, a provincial with a fairly narrow set of experiences. She begins *Pride and Prejudice* with a particular statement that rises to universal terms: 'It is a truth universally acknowledged, that a single man in possession of a good fortune must be in want of a wife' (1). The social reality of publication automatically conveys with it the expectation that a novelist is and must be a kind of authority on all subjects. One of the ideological functions of the novel was to appear to be a storehouse of society's collective knowledge about itself and novelists would be the archivists of such knowledge. As characters, then, narrators may not have physical beauty, but they are required to 'know the world.' The central myth here, as with the myth of beauty, is that if one is able to write a novel – to manipulate words into things – then one must be able to understand things and thoughts better than most other people. But if readers were able to meet Jane Austen before she had ever written a novel, or if she had some manuscripts in the drawer but had never published them, the chances are that they might be passingly interested in her opinions about life but would not regard them overly. People might disagree with these opinions in a way that readers generally do not when in the midst of reading a novel.

For example, here is how one critic performs this kind of overlooking in defense of Austen because she is a novelist. Bear in mind, the same defense would be impossible had she not written novels. Raymond Southall takes up arms on Austen's side against the kind of criticism that she generally receives for being of 'limited scope.' Southall makes the case that 'such criticisms of Jane Austen can usually be dismissed as irrelevant since, by and large, they are not grounded in any close consideration of the character of actual writing of the novels and are mere expressions of prejudice' (107). The fact is that Austen *is* a writer of limited scope – that is simply a descriptive term for her work, her two inches of ivory. But what is worth noting is the implication that if a novelist does not 'know everything' such a weakness constitutes an attack on the very idea of being a novelist. Southall's response is to say that this injury against Austen can be corrected by pointing to Austen's ability to use words. The implicit connection made is that if she can write well, then she cannot have a 'limited scope.'

Consider the importance of the contradiction we have agreed to accept in relation to novelists. A person who spends a good deal of his or her life making up stories, creating out of fantasy elaborate structures of words, is then looked on as an expert, not just in fantasy or simply wordsmanship but in real life, the sum of communal knowledge, and knowledge of general philosophical and moral issues. Why do we not accord this honor to other wordsmiths like advertising copywriters or technical manual writers? Or put the problem in another way: in earlier or more 'primitive' societies in which storytellers were not professionals but were mere amateurs who picked up a pipe after dinner and spun a yarn, or one of many who traded tales of the hunt around a fire, the freight that went with telling a story was of quite a different order. No inferences would necessarily be made about their worldliness, knowledge, and so on. John Berger, in an illuminating discussion of the difference between 'primitives' and 'professionals' in painting points out that

> the craftsman survives so long as the standards for judging his work are shared by different classes. The professional appears when it is necessary for the craftsman to leave his class and 'emigrate' to the ruling class, whose standards of judgement are different. (*About Looking* 65)

The shift from storyteller to novelist carries with it the move from craftsperson or primitive to professional. Instead of being a normal human being who just happens to be telling a story, the novelist becomes the kind of cultural paragon I have been discussing. By becoming novelists, novelists themselves become characters and cease to be personalities, in the sense that they are detached from their context and become objectified. The further point is that this character of the narrator presented as universal is part of this professionalization. As Berger continues:

> The relationship of the professional artist to the class that ruled or aspired to rule was complicated, various and should not be simplified. His training however – and it was his training which

made him a professional – taught him a set of conventional skills. That is to say, he became skilled in using a set of conventions . . . and these conventions corresponded so closely to the social experience – or anyway to the social manners – of the class he was serving, that they were not even seen as conventions but were thought of as the only way of recording and preserving eternal truths. (65)

Berger is not saying that one cannot surmount this problem of professionalism, and his description of the painter Courbet, who acquired his skills without 'taking over the traditional values which those skills had been designed to serve,' is of an artist who 'stole his professionalism' without being in the thrall of the values of certain conventions (139).

The irony, as far as fiction is concerned anyway, is that the novel reaches the height of its universality and power along with the triumph of professionalism. Dickens was one of the first novelists to professionalize the form and to make a respectable living from his own work. But the success, financially and culturally, changes narrative into professionalized novel form – breaking the story away in objectified form – as opposed to the lived and contextualized folktale or story-tellers's tale. In the newer form, character becomes established as the ideological representation of personality, plot plows the disorder of modern life into orderly lines, the natural flow of time is broken up into commodified units which appear serially in magazines or individual numbers to maximize sales. The novelist, as professional, gains with this the 'universal' authority of a cultural, financial, and creative paragon.

What I have been saying about character is central to this argument. If the reader desires the character, access to that object of desire must come through the agency of the culturally approved, professionally endorsed novelist who created that character. In turn novelists gain a special status in exchange for the remarkable act of creating characters – in effect creating life. Copywriters, on the other hand, only create copy. As George Levine points out, this focus on creativity is one reason that the novel *Frankenstein* has such resonance for the study of the novel. This is so because the novel is essentially about the act of fashioning a character from bits and pieces of other things.

In this sense, the author is like an all-powerful parent who can create life, while readers, like children, are for their duration infertile and immature. They can only admire the act of creation and the possession over the character that such creation implies. Even an author is not exempt from such a position since the act of reading levels us all to what is on the page. Such admiration constitutes a kind of narrative envy reminiscent of penis or womb envy. This situation, combining with the problem of novelistic identification, is strongly Oedipal because readers cannot 'have' the character the way the author can. So they have to submit to the parental figure and hope that they will be 'allowed' without being punished to have the desired object. Ultimately, as in the Oedipal conflict, the reader must identify not so much with the object of desire but with the controlling parent. In that move, one is then very clearly wishing for the approval of the narrator and is thus willing to listen, learn, submit, and be passive. Novelistic identification helps readers repeat fairly painlessly the original displacement from the desired object to other substitutes. When we identify with a character, we substitute the character for the originally desired parent. On the other hand, narrative envy places us under the tutelage of the rival parent whom we hope to be like but can never equal. In that sense, the former is identification, the latter is idealization.

If I, as a person standing before you rather than as a typographical line in a book, tell you that it is a truth universally acknowledged that women who work are bad mothers, you might, depending on your views, disagree with me quite vigorously or you might slap me on the back and buy me a beer. But when Jane Austen makes a similar remark involving sexual stereotypes, one lets the statement go by. One may agree or disagree but the statement has a different kind of authority. For one thing, we want to get on with the story, so why stop and quibble about a single opening line? For another, part of the deal we make with novelists is that we not only let them, but want them to know about life. We agree to create a role for ourselves as novel readers in which we are made to accept the 'fact' of our own inexperience and cede authority to a parental figure. The process of allowing a novel to work, allowing it to tell a story, is inseparable from the desire to have each element of the story infused with another kind of meaning – a meaning which controls the 'reality' of the novel and our reaction to it. It is in this very special sense that novels are ideological – not so much because a novelist tells us to vote for a poor law reform or condemn the Vietnam war but because the very presupposition of the novel is that a coherent and rationalizing authority creates an order to which the reader must passively assent in order to allow the novel to work. Even in modern and contemporary novels in which the possibility of order or coherence is denied, there is still the order of the aesthetic or the hermeneutic. The ideological message of the novel's structure here is one of submission, passivity, permanent apprenticeship and childhood, and a profound emphasis on the linguistic mode over any other.

Having been 'selected' by the narrator as a 'dear' reader, certain things are implied. Let us return to Austen's opening to *Pride and Prejudice*: 'It is a truth universally acknowledged, that a single man in possession of a good fortune must be in want of a wife.' This statement exists outside of time and space, as it were. It hangs as a universal banner, and contains within it one of the central contradictions of novels in general – the problem of universality. That is, novels take place in very particular settings – Netherfield, Longbourne, Meryton – but what happens there amongst the particular characters – Elizabeth Bennet, Darcy, Wickham – is thought of as universal. The story that transpires in *Pride and Prejudice* is presented in this opening moment not as if it were part of this time and that place, but about the 'human condition.' That movement towards totality and the generalizing tone of the novel, along with the emphasis on passivity and submission, is one of the most deeply ideological implications of the novel. We can see this universalizing tendency particularly in the reader's relationship to the narrator, who in this type of novel especially must live in a timeless world of observation and recording although the novel's financial success is very much dependent on the specific moment of time.[3]

What is the motive for the narrator's interest in transcribing domestic relations? The ideological message is that narrators of the universal or 'extradiegetic' type are interested in the primarily domestic and local features of life because such features are interesting, worth recording, worth discussing. The realistic effect as it manifests itself in the classic novel has usually to do with representing the very minute and particular problems of daily life – a preoccupation that perhaps can be seen as a result of the nuclear family's withdrawal into itself as a feature of the early modern period. Even when novelists like Victor Hugo or Elizabeth Gaskell attempt a wide sweep of society, the focus of novels must be on domestic arrangements – birth, death, marriage, and money. From the point of view of the novel, such a focus is self-evident and self-justifying. The universal voice of narrator only confirms the intrinsic value of the retreat of the family within itself and the personal arrangements that result.

Although Austen's statement is said to be 'universally acknow-ledged,' the point Austen really wishes to make is that most people are quite foolish and that their views on marriage are equally contempti-ble. And the reader is immediately included in a circle of people who do not really believe what is universally acknowledged. The primary belief of the new possessive individualism of the middle class is that their individuality is sacrosanct and guaranteed. Ironically, that individuality is gained at the expense of being part of a class that held its beliefs to be universal, as did the Founding Fathers who wrote phrases like 'We hold these truths to be self-evident.' So the reader is part of a discerning élite who shares the author's inside knowledge about the 'real' values in life. Wayne Booth is essentially correct when he points out that our beliefs must by and large coincide with the author's while we are reading the novel. Of Arnold Bennett, the novelist, he writes, 'Whenever I find myself disagreeing with him [a novelist] . . . the book suffers in my eyes' (147). To read novels then is to belong to a group of believers – in effect an ideological group.

And what makes the reader so special and select? Simply the fact that he or she is reading this particular novel and more extensively is part of the novel-reading public. Readers are singled out as being part of a general literary community. When Werther and Lotte first discover their attraction for each other it is through the mediation of literature. Werther sees Lotte with novels in hand, and when he asks her what they are he is 'astonished.' She notes:

When I was younger . . . all I liked to read was novels. I can't tell you how happy it used to make me when I could curl up in a corner on a Sunday and participate heart and soul in the joys and sorrows of some Miss Jenny or other. . . . And I like those writers best who help me find my world again, where the sort of things happen that happen all around me, and the story is as interesting and sympathetic as my own life at home, which may not be paradise but is, on the whole, a source of quite inexplicable joy to me. (35)

Werther writes that 'I did my best to hide the emotions her words aroused in me. I didn't succeed very well because, when I heard her speak casually and very candidly about *The Vicar of Wakefield* and about —— I was quite beside myself.' (35–6)

In this moment, for Werther, learning about Lotte's admiration for Goldsmith is tantamount to falling in love. And worth noting is that Lotte sees novels as recording her life. Werther and Lotte each recognize each other as part of the literary élite whose interests and issues are incorporated into the novel. Novelists are forever slipping other novels into the pockets of their characters. In *Tom Jones*, Partridge carries his copy of *Robinson Crusoe*, Frankenstein's monster keeps his copy of *Werther*, and Bouvard and Pécuchet catalogue the entire literary experience.

It is more or less assumed that novel readers share a certain set of beliefs. These implied or 'informed' readers, to use either Wolfgang Iser's or Stanley Fish's notions, have a particularly strong belief in romantic love and a certain contempt on the one hand for unworthy aristocrats and on the other for those in the middle class who are only interested in money. Dickens relies on his reader to be compassionate, Christian, and prone to tears. Henry James, Ford Maddox Ford, or James Joyce all assume that their readers will be part of a group that is aesthetic, highly educated, and minutely interested in the subtleties of language and gesture. Indeed, the assumption of a community with shared values implies the strength of the ideological nexus. Think of these contradictions: we all share these beliefs, they are self-evident, any reader is therefore interchangeable with any other reader; however, at the same time, each reader is an individual who balks at the repressiveness of certain features of society. This *ur*-community, this ideological gathering, is false specifically because it is not based on individual or class interest but simply on the implied community of interests of novel readers. In reality readers will vary widely. Patricia Meyer Spacks has spotted in the works of Fielding and Sterne a certain 'anxiety' that readers will not be so homogeneous but might 'remain unpredictable, individual beings . . . not firmly under their control or that readers may not work hard enough at the task of participation to receive what the writer has to give' (304). But the rebelliousness of readers must be a deep secret to the novel, as the rebelliousness of the working classes must not appear too publicly in the speeches of politicians. The reality of the novel is that passivity, conformity, and the comfort of being under the thumb of the narrator are the operative ideological restraints on the institution of novel reading. Inherent in these assumptions is the notion that people in novels who read novels are by and large the best people – unless of course they read bad novels as does Emma Bovary. In other words, the value of the project of reading itself is almost never put into doubt in the classic and modernist novel. On the contrary the project is raised to incredible importance.

That novelists should tout literature as the road to a certain kind of understanding and salvation is only to be expected. If all novelists were basketball players, then the qualities and ideologies of basketball would be promoted and fostered in their particular art form. Or if drawbridge oilers were the exclusive creators of a particular art form with mass appeal then their art would focus praise on, say, particular kinds of industrial lubricants and the people who use them. This state of affairs is perhaps most obvious in the film and popular music industry today which treats the project of film-making, Hollywood, or music-making with a centrally directed focus – even if the big motion picture corporations are occasionally depicted as corrupt, the idea of making the valuable and popular picture is a frequent theme. Or in the musical film the whole idea of dancing or singing can never be put into question – what Fred Astaire, Jimmy Cagney, or the members of *A Chorus Line* do must *ipso facto* be good and worthwhile. What rock and roll or country and western singer ever composed lyrics about the worthlessness of their own music? This is not the place to explain this general phenomenon, but it is a fairly consistent quality of social institutions that they do not by and large try to undermine themselves and their own goals.

If music or the image are celebrated in their respective art forms, the novel is a form that places an incredibly high value on language and the proper use of language – particularly spoken language. Wolfgang Iser goes so far as to say that fiction is the representation not of reality but of language or signification (64ff.). In chapter 5 I will look at dialogue and the development of language in the novel, but here I just want to point in the direction of the centrality of language. In a novel like *Pride and Prejudice* the whole point of conversation is to turn a good phrase. Banter becomes the focus of courtship, and silence is outside the realm of possibility. Sexuality appears totally at the level of the linguistic and cannot appear elsewhere – except in the exchange of glances which is an acceptable form of non-verbal contact and does not involve touch.

The myth of linguistic competence along with that of physical beauty reinforces one of the cherished ideological points of the classic novel – that social class is arbitrary and that lower- and middle-class characters are somehow above and beyond class distinctions. Further, upper-class characters are routinely shown as corrupt or inadequate without the beneficial leavening of middle-class virtues – restraint, repression, and industriousness. The universality of novelistic identification – the idea that *all* readers will willingly desire and link themselves to the main character and in turn allow themselves to be mastered by the universal narrator – underlines one of the central ideological presuppositions of the novel that overcoming class distinctions is largely an individual matter, that class disagreements are able to be solved on the erotic level by having lower-class people (usually women) marry into the upper-class, and that all classes are capable of being virtuous while remaining separate. In terms of character, this means that all approved central characters, from whatever class, will speak (and write) English with the competence of a novelist and say things that will strike us periodically as profound or significant. It is true that in modernist novels one may find incoherent or even linguistically incompetent central characters, like the idiot in *The Sound and the Fury*, but their incoherence becomes on the one hand a metaphor for artistic expression divorced from the non-artistic world of bourgeois literalness and on the other a justification for the profundity of madness or *naïveté*. Ironically, these linguistically inept characters are used to celebrate the novelist's own ability to write.

Moreover, there was a dramatic change taking place between the late seventeenth and early eighteenth century – precisely during the period of the beginning of the novel – in English attitudes toward language and language acquisition. As I will show in the next chapter, this change in attitudes created in effect a kind of social élite, seeming at first to be related not to class but to the proper use of language and the ability to do things like read novels.

The novelist who revealed the most about the ideological workings of the novel was not a working-class agitator but a man of leisure and a Yorkshire curate. Rather than appearing at the end of the novel's development and looking back, he was one of the first 'novelists.' I am, of course, referring to Lawrence Sterne and his irrepressible and hard-to-read *The Life and Opinions of Tristram Shandy*. For some reason, probably because Sterne was living through the earliest days of the development of the novel, he was perhaps less swayed by the ideology of the novel. In this sense, he could see the conventions of the novel without having come to the point that Austen reached some fifty years later of assuming that those conventions were virtually universal forms.

Sterne (unlike most novelists) was painfully aware, even if this pain was the pain of humor, that to write a novel one had to perpetrate all kinds of distortions upon reality in the name of reality. His work reflects a permanent reluctance to create an 'objectified' character and his realization of the ultimate impossibility of turning personality into character. Of course, Sterne was no modern critic or nascent James Joyce, and his consciousness was purely eighteenth-century. It is precisely my point that only at the beginning of the development of the novel could an observer be far enough outside what was going on to notice the change. As Marshall McLuhan is reputed to have noted – whoever discovered water, it could not have been the fish.

Sterne resists the objectification of character initially by blurring the lines between himself and his character Shandy to remind us that the narrator is not purely a character severed from the context of the lived world. Of course we know that Shandy is not Sterne, but there are many moments when the two merge. Most significant is Sterne's promise

> not to be in a hurry – but to go on leisurely, writing and publishing two volumes of my life every year; – which, if I am suffered to go on quietly, and can make a tolerable bargain with my bookseller, I shall continue to do as long as I live. (65)

This was a promise he carried out, dying after volume 11 and leaving the entire work unfinished as he intended.

One cannot read this book without being aware of the lived experience inherent in the writing of the work and of the death inherent in the incomplete ending. Of course, Sterne did not plan to die before he finished the work, but his plan to write two books a year is a project without an ending – except the natural contour presented by the prospect of death. Rather than using the typical, objectifying, biographical mode – which presents a life schematically and intentionally – Sterne's choice is to give the work the more natural and less organized shape of his own life with the unpredictable and unprepared ending of his own death. Also, Sterne's leisurely way of writing 'not to be in a hurry' indicates his non-professional relationship to the task. That is, Sterne regards his work more as a kind of process and activity, almost a performance rather than a commodity; and when he talks of it as a commodity, he is more honest than most in specifying his financial relations with his publisher. In this sense, he is an 'amateur,' and here one recalls Roland Barthes' use of the word with its Latin root in mind to signify a 'lover' of a process rather than a professional (*Roland Barthes* 52). Sterne resists the move to become an author and authority, in the sense that Edward Said gives that word (*Beginnings*). Sterne will not artificially shape reality into a falsifying simulacrum without reminding us constantly of that action.

Sterne as narrator continually draws attention to the fact that he has a life separate from that of the text – that the text is not a universal object but is being written by a specific person over a certain period of time. As the narrator says in one place, 'I have been at it [writing] this six weeks, making all the speed I possibly could' (65). Or at another place Sterne puts down the date of the moment he is writing:

> it is no more than a week from this very day, in which I am now writing this book for the edification of the world, – which is March 9, 1759, – that, my dear Jenny, observing I looked a little grave, as she stood cheapening a silk of five-and-twenty shillings a yard, – told the mercer, she was sorry she had given him so much trouble. (73)

One feels at such moments that Sterne just felt like including a bit of his own reality in the text. His reference to his own life and his own Jenny deepens the effect. Later he plays with the reader by asking us to guess Jenny's identity – is she his wife or his mistress? At such moments we are forced to abandon the idea that the narrator is a universal being. Of course so much of what Sterne does is meant to be comic, nor is he the first or the last self-conscious narrator. But in this comedy there is a thoroughgoing critique of the novel.

Sterne stresses, over and over again, the impossibility of actually recording a life in a novel. It is in this sense that he is pointing out the ideological nature of the categories I have been discussing throughout this chapter. For example, Sterne focuses on the impossibility of beginning to talk about a character. Where does one find the origin of character? At the moment of birth? At the moment of conception? At the moment of naming? Or perhaps even before birth, as the discussion of interuterine baptism suggests. What about the moment of marriage? With an exploration of the details of the marriage contract? Uncle Toby is Sterne's real joke about origins of character. Sterne traces all of Toby's personality to his wound at the Battle of Namur. When asked in which place he was wounded, Toby's response, rather than point to his groin, is to recreate the town and environs of Namur. Is not such a recreation the essence of novel writing? The novel was to account for origins by mimesis, tracing character back to some initiating place and moment – like the moment that Walter Shandy forgot to wind the clock or misnamed his son. But as with Toby's huge model, explanations of this sort are futile since they ultimately never establish a true causality.

Because character is a simplification of personality, one must leave out something to create a character. But since simplification in effect becomes a falsification, Sterne through satire points out the impossibility of really including everything that makes a human human. The novel creates the illusion that somehow readers are inside the minds of characters, following their thought processes. In that way, the novel gives us the opportunity 'to learn about life.' But Sterne questions the notion that to secure a person's mind on paper properly you have to trace their thoughts. Since there are so many thoughts in a moment, which thoughts must we include and not include? If novels just follow a few focused and coherent thought streams, that action must lead to a parody of the complexity of any – even the most leaden – human mind. But if one chooses to include a good deal of what goes on in consciousness, then it becomes impossible to write a novel. As Sterne wails frequently 'there is no end of it; – for my own part, I declare I have been at it these six weeks, making all the speed I possibly could, – and am not yet born: – I have just been able, and that's all, to tell you *when* it happened, but not *how* – so that you see the thing is yet far from being accomplished' (65).

This frustration leads Sterne to the best description of the impossibility of ever writing a novel:

153

> I am this month one whole year older than I was this time
> twelve-month; and having got, as you perceive, almost into the
> middle of my fourth volume – and no farther than to my first day's
> life – 'tis demonstrative that I have three hundred and sixty-four
> days more life to write just now, than when I first set out; so that
> instead of advancing, as a common writer, in my work with what I
> have been doing at it – on the contrary, I am just thrown so many
> volumes back – was every day of my life to be as busy a day as this
> – And why not? – and the transactions and opinions of it to take up
> as much description – And for what reason should they be cut
> short? as at this rate I should just live 364 times faster than I should
> write – It must follow, an' please your worships, that the more I
> write, the more I shall have to write. (286)

No novelist, I believe, has ever really addressed the problem that
Sterne puts forward here. The ideology of the novel *has* to
make readers forget about the fullness and sensuousness of lived
experience.

Rather, the idea of character in a novel becomes subsumed to
another system – in a way not so dissimilar to the way the culture that
produced the novel subsumed individuals and groups to a dominant
system of production and meaning. As the domination of ideology
over politics becomes a rule in western Europe, character becomes in
effect a personal way of forgetting about the increasing contradictions in daily life. As human experience becomes more and more
commodified, the very commodifying process of buying and selling
novels becomes paradoxically a way out of readers' feelings of being
marginalized and objectified; it is in the objectified unit of character
that people come to believe that they can find their true selves – or
their better selves. Avoiding the quality of experience that comes
from living in time – with millions of individual moments in an
ordinary day – readers can posit beings who are not of the moment,
or the sum of the moments, but who transcend moments. As Sterne
reminds us, to include all moments – the itchy foot, the casual gesture
of checking for one's wallet on the subway, searching with the
tongue for the raspberry seed between the canine and the molar – is
impossible in the novel. The novel depends on the fact that characters
usually do not itch at the moment they have a major realization
about life – and if they do, there is a reason for it. The universal
quality of characters and narrators always derives from their objec-

tified status. The main point here is that character is always isolated from life – whether in the plot itself as outsider, disinherited, orphan, or criminal – or even from the details of lived experience. Whereas lived experience and personality is formed amorphously and cumulatively, characters in novels are formed from a series of discrete and isolated moments designed by the author for their impact. So, the isolation of the character from any deep involvement in the quotidien renders character the ultimate in alienated consciousness. And, ironically, if we read to escape loneliness we do so by observing the life of a character who is centrally isolated.

Narrators are isolated too by their lofty perspective atop the prospect of their words. Sterne's aim is to show that when Henry Fielding speaks familiarly to his readers he is participating in a false notion that the relation between reader and narrator is one of intimacy and attachment. Sterne points out that 'you and I are in a manner perfect strangers to each other' although he does hope that the relationship will 'terminate in friendship' (41). And at one point he mocks the intimation of intimacy by saying to the reader 'I need not tell your worship, that all this is spoke in confidence' (64). Ironically, the intimate confidence is the result of the disseminating act of publication. We are thus intimate by being impersonally part of a public.

Another blow to the ideology of character is dealt in the dialectical way that Sterne treats Tristram. Since Tristram is not only the infant being described but also the person writing the novel – which Tristram is the one at the center of the novel? Sterne's message is that both the child and the conscious adult must be. At which point is Tristram really Tristram? Fielding, for example, has no trouble with the continuity between little Tom and big Tom. They are the same character. But for Sterne the continuity is put into question. The continual game that Sterne plays with relative time (as when Obadiah goes out to get Dr Slop) reveals the novel's use of discontinuous time in relation to character. Why should that set of signs designating the infant Shandy have anything to do with the set of signs supposed to be writing the text? Why do we even have a sense that time is passing when a character 'ages'? How can there be a continuity at all in terms of character and time? The writing-Tristram is attempting to draw a picture of his life and opinions by positing a beginning in the infant-Tristram. But his project is hopeless since, in effect, the two Tristrams can never be linked.

The problem with what I might call 'character time' – that is, the illusion that somewhere there *is* time during which a character has had a chance to grow and develop – is that such a duration is outside of history and memory. In this sense, character time is deeply ideological, as I believe Sterne felt, because novelists want to place characters into the real flow of time when characters can only be of particular moments in an idealized and universal time. As with the other features of character I have noted, this ideological presupposition gives priority to ordered and controlled personalities over and above the development of actual personality anchored in social experience and history. John Berger has suggested that the illusion a photograph creates is the effect of being suspended outside of time. He recommends that photographs be viewed in their context to time so that we can 'put a photograph back into the context of experience, social experience, social memory.' His solution is to put the photograph back in 'narrated time.' 'Narrated time becomes historic time when it is assumed by social memory and social action' (*About Looking* 61). For the novel, narrated time is usually blocked from becoming historic time by the novel's commitment to the individual biographical mode. Novelists want us to feel that explanations are available for character on a particular, case-by-case basis. But these explanations are not anchored to history or memory. They exist between the spaces of linguistic signs. Character time is negative time because it has not occurred, being merely posited. In reality, there is no time before the 'now' of the reading moment except other earlier reading moments, just as there is no time before the original divine moment of creation, according to Augustinian logic. As Sterne points out, only the experience of reading involves any true duration:

> It is about an hour and a half's tolerable good reading since my uncle Toby rung the bell, when Obadiah was ordered to saddle a horse, and go for Dr. Slop, the man-midwife; – so that no one can say, with reason, that I have not allowed Obadiah time enough, poetically speaking, and considering the emergency too, both to go and come; – though, morally and truly speaking, the man, perhaps, has scarce had time to get on his boots.

Constitutively, then, narrated time or character time can never be historic time. The social experience of time and memory is permanently blocked from connection to the sense of character – although the novel would have us think otherwise.[4]

Since I have used Sterne as an example here of the ultimate critique of the novel's ideology, one might stop and ask why novelists have not heeded his critique? First, his mode was comic. Therefore, the implied message of such a work is that even though his work may be to the point, trenchant, and so on, there is no call to action. Sterne, though he became quite popular through his writings, always remained the outsider, the provincial, the minister on the sidelines of life. As Fredric Jameson points out, the comic mode is essentially 'salvational or redemptive [in] perspective of some secure future' (*The Political Unconscious* 103). Since, as Jameson goes on, literary genres are essentially 'institutions, or social contracts between a writer and a specific public, whose function is to specify the proper use of a particular cultural artifact' (106), the comic mode will guarantee that its own use will aim towards some ideal world never to be reached. Sterne's goal is utopian, in that sense, since one can never overcome the problems inherent in the novel through the novel. All attempts to reveal the ideology of the novel through the novel form have been mainly in comic or parodic form. There has never been a novel, to my knowledge, that actually seriously addresses this issue and presents a narrator who allows himself or herself to be a real person in the real world.[5] In addition, Sterne never gave his readers any choice other than amusement. After all, why should he have? It would have been pretty much of a folly for someone in the eighteenth century to have understood that the incipient novel would become the dominant cultural narrative form of the nineteenth and part of the twentieth century. Sterne had, given his limitations, to respond finally that his work was only 'A COCK and a BULL . . . and one of the best of its kind, I ever heard' (615). In that dismissal, Sterne did himself and his work a disservice that later critics have sufficiently corrected.

There is one contemporary novel, not particularly well received and not at all accepted into the canon of literary study, that I believe does in the modern period what Sterne had attempted in the eighteenth century. Most often, *Tristram Shandy* is compared with James Joyce's *Ulysses*, in the sense that both works explode conventions of the novel, play with time, and so on. Such comparisons are on solid ground, but while Sterne always puts his own project into doubt, Joyce never overtly questions his own role. Indeed, the point of

Joyce's opus *is* the glorification of his own project and his role as author. The novel that might be more aptly compared with Sterne's is *If on a Winter's Night a Traveler* by Italo Calvino. Most of my students who have read the book cannot get through it and do not like it. The reason for this, I would maintain, is that the book defies the conventions of novel reading so much as to make it impossible to do the kinds of things I have been suggesting are necessary to the novel – and it goes against these conventions explaining that it is doing so all along.

The main character of Calvino's book is The Reader – that is, you, the reader. In this sense, it is a novel adjusted towards the reader-response direction. The book begins with a direct address that places the reader into the context of the book:

> You are about to begin reading Italo Calvino's new novel, *If on a Winter's Night a Traveler*. Relax. Concentrate. Dispel every other thought. Let the world around you fade. . . . Find the most comfortable position: seated, stretched out, curled up, or lying flat. Flat on your back, on your side, on your stomach. (3)

Of course, in doing this, Calvino has to mock the idea that there is only one ideal reader. As readers, we are forced into facing the ideological nature of the reader-narrator relationship. Since readers are each people who are not settling into a chair, etc., that postulate immediately seems false. Yet insofar as we exist only by being a reader, the designation must be correct. The myth of the community of informed readers with shared values is also exposed: 'You derive a special pleasure from a just-published book, and it isn't only a book you are taking with you but its novelty as well, which could also be merely that of an object fresh from the factory' (6). And the notion that the reader had a special relationship with the author and is special because of that relationship is also exploded: 'You are the sort of reader who is sensitive to such refinements; you are quick to catch the author's intentions and nothing escapes you' (25).

Even the identity of the author as a being with a recognizable existence goes out of the door. Calvino writes:

> So here you are now, ready to attack the first lines of the first page. You prepare to recognize the unmistakable tone of the author. No. You don't recognize it at all. But now that you think about it, who

ever said this author had an unmistakable tone? On the contrary, he is known as an author who changes greatly from one book to the next. And in these very changes you recognize him as himself. (9)

If the novelist only exists in language, then style is identity. Without it Pamela or Dickens is just a bunch of marks on a page. So an author characterized by the absence of a recognizable style is like a song without a tune or words.

Character is even more elusive. The first chapter begins with a scene in railway station. The first character is the narrator:

I am the man who comes and goes between the bar and the telephone booth. Or, rather: that man is called 'I' and you know nothing else about him, just as this station is called only 'station' and beyond it there exists nothing. . . . I am an anonymous presence against an even more anonymous background. If you, reader, couldn't help picking me out among the people getting off the train . . . this is simply because I am called 'I' and this is the only thing you know about me, but this alone is reason enough for you to invest a part of yourself in the stranger 'I.' (11, 14–15)

Here Calvino, echoing Barthes, reveals the starkly linguistic fact of the existence of characters in the novel, and intuitively understands the indiscriminate nature of novelistic identification.

In the next chapter, the 'I' disappears as The Reader becomes the central character. In reading the first chapter the reader discovers that, through an error at the bindery, part of the edition of Calvino's book has been mixed up with signatures from a polish novel *Outside the Town of Malbork* by Tazio Bazakbal. So that the first chapter is actually from another book. The Reader then goes back to the bookstore to replace the defective copy – but gets involved in an attempt to find the novel by Bazakbal. The following chapter seems to be that novel, only it turns out not to be the Polish work but an unfinished Cimmerian novel called *Leaning from the Steep Slope* . . . and so on.

By focusing on The Reader, Calvino reminds us of the extent to which the reader's consciousness is involved in the transaction between narrator, character, and reader. So in a sense Calvino correctly understands Henry James when he says that what the author does is to 'make his reader very much as he makes his characters' ('Novels of Eliot' 485). Calvino frustrates the basic ideological devices of the novel by never allowing us to find an object of desire except for the character called The Other Reader – whom The Reader will end up marrying since, as Calvino points out, 'In ancient times a story could end only in two ways: having passed all the tests, the hero and the heroine married, or else they died' (259). Having dispensed with plot, Calvino can frustrate any attempt to place characters in a life or plotline by arranging the work so that each chapter will be the first chapter of a new novel. In short, there is no 'life' in Calvino's work, only our presence as the reader.

I am not claiming that Calvino's book is great literature. In fact, for many the work is unreadable. Its unreadability is exactly what interests me. The ideology of character is such that if we are constantly foiled in novelistic identification, we cannot make objects and create characters. If we cannot do that, then we cannot read novels since novel reading is largely charged by the displacement of early identifications. As Freud points out, the ego either incorporates objects through identification and introjection, and thereby 'loves' or casts them out through projection. In effect, 'the world is divided into a part that is pleasurable, which it has incorporated into itself, and a remainder that is alien to it' (*General Psychological Theory* 99). By frustrating novelistic identification, Calvino has made his novel difficult for ordinary readers to get through, as he had desired. His success is his failure. If the only character is The Reader, then The Reader cannot truly be a reader since novel reading will not work. As The Reader says at the very end in a discussion with five other readers, 'For a while now, everything has been going wrong for me: it seems to me that in the world there now exist only stories that remain suspended or get lost along the way' (257). The book has provided nothing to attach to identity, no place for setting, no plot or continuous action, only an unrelieved series of self-conscious revelations. The fact that *If on a Winter's Night a Traveler* is so annoying is a sign that the reading process in the novel involves fairly rigid conventions with which one cannot tamper lest the entire project be dissolved.

Such is the strength of the ideological structures in novels. Far from being accidental or universal, character, as I hope I have shown, is particular, historically and socially determined, and serves to shape and color the way we perceive ourselves and our role in the world. Resisting novels, then, means resisting the normative shaping of personality by character. We tend to think of the novel as a form that takes personality and converts it into character. But the secondary process occurs on the reverse loop. Identification with characters in novels become part of the mechanism by which ideology penetrates defenses and becomes introjected, as it were, into the personality of the subject. In making friends with signs we are weakening the bond that anchors us to the social world, the world of action, and binding ourselves to the ideological. It may seem unfair to attach such an onerous burden to the simple fun of reading a novel, but we do little for ourselves and the world by avoiding the complex implications of simple pleasures.

5

Conversation and dialogue

One must speak a little, you know. It would look odd to be entirely silent for half an hour together.

Elizabeth to Darcy in Jane Austen, *Pride and Prejudice*

If the written language codifies the estrangement of classes, redress cannot lie in regression to the spoken, but only in the consistent exercise of strictest linguistic objectivity. Only a speaking that transcends writing by absorbing it, can deliver human speech from the lie that it is already human.

Theodor Adorno, *Minima Moralia*

Why must characters in novels speak? We take for granted that people in novels will engage in dialogue, and that such dialogue is a rough equivalent to the kind of conversations we have in life. We usually assume that writers include conversations in novels because conversations take place in life. The writer is merely trying to reproduce, using a realistic effect, a naturally occurring event. Dialogue is also one of the major ways that authors develop their characters by allowing them to interact verbally. I want to claim something quite different. To put the argument in its most extreme form, I would claim that novelists invented conversation and that novelistic conversation too is a defensive, ideological structure. The point is that after novelists invented conversation, readers strove to include conversation in their own lives. In other words, first came the literary conversation and then came the striving for real conversation.

I do not mean to say that people did not have conversations before 1700. Obviously people talked to each other then as now. But conversation in its inscribed form as a literary phenomenon had to grow to acceptance during the seventeenth and eighteenth centuries. The point that interests me here is how these sets of signs and arrangements on the page, which actually look and sound almost nothing like real conversations, got to be accepted as the rule for conversation rather than the exception. The other correlate to this set of circumstances is how did readers then tend to think of their own natural speech as a replica of that printed form.

The shift from the oral paradigm of conversation to the printed paradigm, as it were, seems to have occurred between 1650 and 1750 – as I will show in detail later in this chapter. As Leland Warren has pointed out, the eighteenth century initially mistrusted the printed word over the spoken word. 'Practiced correctly, conversation should assure the continuing usefulness of language by keeping it always within the social contexts from which writing threatens to remove it' (67). But writing is dangerous particularly because 'it emerges from an isolated, private act and shapes permanent structures of language' (66). So the spoken conversation was held in great esteem in the eighteenth century, and hundreds of handbooks to encourage and spell out the rules for good conversations were published. The feeling was that 'only in conversation does language find its proper role' (67) and as Fielding put it, by 'the reciprocal interchange of ideas, by which truth is examined, things are, in a manner, *turned round*, and sifted, and all our knowledge communicated with each other' ('An Essay' 120). However, the written clearly came to prevail over the spoken, and by the end of the eighteenth century it would have been hard to imagine anyone objecting to the writing down of conversation, for example.

In this chapter, I am arguing that conversation is not a neutral requirement for the novel but, like location and character, is an ideological construct that serves defensive purposes to society at large. Of course, there are some novels of the modern experimental type that may eschew dialogue in favor of lyrical monologue – but even these are not possible without some kind of representation of speech. If not direct conversation, then some kind of free indirect discourse might be used (Rimmon-Kenan 110ff.). My reason for making this argument rests heavily on a single observable fact. If you show a transcript of a conversation to the participants in that discussion, most people will be shocked at the disparity between their perception of the conversation and the transcript. If what we call conversation is to most conversationalists unrecognizable, then what we are actually doing when we talk to each other cannot be conversation. Another point is that people who participate in conversations, and we all do, by and large are unable to reproduce those conversations accurately either verbally or in writing, and when shown transcripts of those conversations will experience them as 'wrong' or most commonly 'illiterate.'

If what we do when we chat with a friend, meet someone on the street, or buy a pound of potatoes does not at all resemble what we think we are doing, then the student of narrative forms must ask how such a disparity arose. Why do we think that characters in novels engage in conversations, but that we ourselves when confronted with transcripts of conversations do not appear to be having 'literate' conversations?

In novels, conversation is essentially a literary form. It signifies – completely aside from the topics being discussed – that the speakers are literate, civilized, and cultured and particularly that they are part of a reading culture that knows the rules of its own language. In addition to intuitively knowing the rules, these 'civilized' speakers are aware that there *is* a body of rules to be mastered. If speakers in novels are not literate and civilized, then their speech will be signified in ways that appear non-literary – that is, paradoxically closer to actual speech, as for example is Francis Phelan's speech in William Kennedy's *Ironweed*:

> Pig's ass. And he won't feed you till you listen to him preach. I watch the old bums sittin' there and I wonder about them. What are you all doin', sittin' through his bullshit? But they's all tired and old, they's all drunks. They don't believe in nothin'. They's just hungry. (22)

The irony, as I will show, is that representing speech that is 'non-standard' by the use of abbreviation, contraction, and vulgarity is a way of disguising the fact that the actual language of narrative is in effect 'non-standard.' As Ann Banfield notes: 'if, from the point of view of its structure, the language of the novel is a classless one, it is really certain socially preferred dialects which masquerade in the guise of this classless, abstract and universal language' (252). While not all of us speak like Francis, not all of us speak like the typical admirable novel hero or heroine either. We probably speak closer to Francis than we do to Elizabeth Archer, Elizabeth Bennet, or even Oliver Twist.

The reason I am stressing this point is that conversation constitutes far and away the single most widespread and central use of language, or, according to anthropology, conversation is the central institution of language use (Moerman and Sacks). We may read once a week, write occasionally, listen to a newscaster or watch a sitcom, but the majority of time when we use language it is in the natural and social use of conversation. From our earliest moments of consciousness, we aim to talk, to engage in conversation. The rules and structures for the social interaction of spoken language are complex. Humans learn and internalize with great facility these rules. There are even bio-logical responses to conversation that are beyond socialization and almost beyond perception (such as increased iris size as an indicator of interest). In other words, one could well expand Aristotle's definition of man as a political animal by saying that humans are conversational animals. So the fact that conversation is centrally located in the novel, while not a structural requirement of the novel, is perhaps not so strange after all. What is strange, though, is with all this expertise in creating and engaging in conversation why are most readers of novels willing to accept a very distorted representation of conversation as the real thing?

That is, why do critics and readers respond to the dialogue in novels as if it were very close to conversation? Mikhail Bakhtin, for example, says that 'characteristic, even canonic, for the genre [of the novel] is the spoken dialogue framed by a dialogized story. Charac-teristic also is the proximity of its language to popular spoken language' (251). It is clear to any reader that speech in the novel is closer to the popular spoken word than is the language of the epic or the lyric. However, dialogue is still quite far from conversation. Bakhtin jumps too quickly from the novel's reliance on dialogicity and heteroglossia to everyday speech. That is, Bakhtin says that the novel was shaped by 'decentralizing, centrifugal forces' of the 'lower levels' of ordinary language usage best demonstrated 'on the stages of local fairs and at buffoon spectacles, the heteroglossia of the clown . . . the *fabliau* and *Schwanke* of street songs, folksayings, anecdotes.' So, he implies that this kind of language somehow just went directly into the novel's heteroglossia. But what is of substantial interest is how much difference there is between conversational language and literary language. Bakhtin is not blind to this aspect, but he plays it down:

> As they [dialects] enter literature and are appropriated to literary language, dialects in this new context lose, of course, the quality of closed socio-linguistic systems; they are deformed and in fact cease to be that which they had been simply as dialects. On the other hand, these dialects, on entering the literary language and preserving within it their own dialectological elasticity, their other-languageness, have the effect of deforming the literary language; it, too, ceases to be that which it had been, a closed socio-linguistic phenomenon, as is the linguistic consciousness of the educated person who is its agent . . . what results is not a single language but a dialogue of languages. (294)

Bakhtin has his own agenda, and his aim is to include the diversity of human life and human speech in the novel – since he sees the novel as inherently democratic and not demagogic. By telling us that actual practices, like conversation, folk stories and songs, and other non-élite activities like the celebration of the grotesque among peasants, infiltrate and create the novel, Bakhtin hopes to claim the novel – particularly the work of non-Marxist writers – for his own camp.

Bakhtin's aim is aided by the fact that most readers will perceive conversation in the novel as simply a kind of transplantation – with changes to be sure – of ordinary speech. But, as was noted, dialogue in novels looks actually nothing at all like conversations in real life. Take for example the two following conversations. The first is from Robertson Davies' novel *Unfinished Business* and the second is a transcription of a real conversation:

> 'Liesl, I am fifty, and I have a wooden leg, and only part of one arm. Is that interesting for Faustina?'
> 'Yes, anything is for Faustina. You don't know her, but far

worse you don't know yourself. You are not so very bad, Ramsay.'
    'Thank you.'
    'Oooh, what dignity! Is that a way to accept a compliment from a lady? I tell him he is not so very bad, and he ruffles up like an old maid and makes a sour face. I must do better; you are a fascinating old fellow. How's that?'
    'If you have said what you came to say, I should like to go to bed now.'
    'Yes, I see you have taken off your wooden leg and stood it in the corner. Well, I should like to go to bed now too. Shall we go to bed together?'
    I looked at her with astonishment. She seemed to mean it.
    'Well, do not look as if it were out of the question. You are fifty and not all there: I am as grotesque a woman as you are likely to meet. Wouldn't it have an unusual savour?' (Davies 222)

*   *   *

A: I mean b'cause I – eh you're going to this meeting at twelve thirty, en I don't want to inconvenience *you*.

B: Well, even if you get here et abayout eh ten thirty, or eleven uh'clock, we still have en hour en a hahf.

A: OK. *Al*right.

B: Fine. We'd have a bite, en // (talk).

A: Yeh. Weh – *No!* No, *don't* prepare any//thing.

B: And un – I'm not gunnah prep*are*, we'll juz whatever it'll be, we'll (   ).

A: *NO!* No. I don't mean that. I min – because uh, *she* en I'll prob'ly uh be spending the day togethuh, so uh:::we'll go out tuh lunch, or something like that. So I mean if you::have a cuppa cawfee or something, I mean//thatuh that'll be fine. But//uh –

B: Yeah.

B: Fine.

A: *Oth*uh th'n that don't//uh.

B: Fine.

A: Don't bothuh with anything else. I – uh:::

(1.2)

A: I – uh:::I *did* wanna tell you, en I didn' wanna tell you uh::last night. Uh because you had entert – uh, company. I-I-I had something – *ter*rible t'tell you. So//uh.

B: How terrible *is* it?
A: Uh, tuh – as worse it could *be*.
   (0.8)
B: W–y' mean Ada ?
A: Uh yah.
B: Whad'she do, die?
A: Mm::hm. (Schegloff and Sacks 259–60)

[The method of transcription is one devised by sociolinguists to account for held syllables (:::), overlapping dialogue, pauses (0.2 seconds), emphases (OK.), upward intonation (/), interruption (//), and aspirations (hh).]

Both these conversations are ones in which a surprise subject is brought up at the end. The first's surprise is a calculated literary effect while the second's is a naturally occurring surprise in a real conversation. But, what strikes us about the second transcription is how illiterate it seems. There is an uncouth feeling about the transcribed conversation as compared with the literary conversation. A and B slur their words, fail to finish sentences, talk at the same time, overlap their comments, fill in space with 'uh' and respond by saying 'yah.' They repeat themselves and ramble, delaying the most important piece of information until the end. By contrast, the dialogue in the first is coherent, orderly, directed in its topic and logically developed. The turns taken in speaking are longer and both interchanges develop an idea consistently. It is important to point out that the second conversation here is hardly between two illiterates. Any conversation, even one between two highly educated conversationalists, will tend to look like the one I have included here. And even the fact that the conversation is mediated by the telephone is largely irrelevant, since other tape-recorded conversations resemble all the features of this one.

Our confusion (and one might even add disbelief) arises from the significant fact that our mental method for imagining conversation derives largely from reading the texts of novels or plays. But what we are actually reading in those cases is what is called 'spoken prose.' When we listen to a play, when we read a conversation in a novel, when we listen to dialogue in a scripted film, when we listen to a news announcer or a presidential speech – we experience the speaking of prose. One can intuitively tell when a speaker departs from a written text to make 'comments' because the quality of the spoken utterance is so different. Anyone who has ever read a paper in public will also know that no matter how natural they try to sound, what is produced always sounds as if it were read.

This phenomenon is so, according to David Abercrombie, since prose is essentially language arranged for visual presentation. As for spoken prose, no one speaks it and 'no one *can*, or at least not for very long at a time.' More bluntly put: 'the truth is that nobody speaks at all like the characters in any novel, play, or film' (3–4). So when we see the transcription of actual conversation, the whole thing strikes us as very strange. As Abercrombie puts it:

> Although we are well accustomed to hearing *spoken* prose, we are certainly not accustomed to seeing *written* conversation. . . . However, when you look at the written text of a genuine spontaneous conversation, it is pretty horrifying – particularly when it is a conversation in which you yourself have taken part. It is sometimes unintelligible, and it is always illogical, disorganized, repetitious, and ungrammatical. (6)

In some sense, as I pointed out in the case of character as opposed to personality, the essence of spoken prose is that it represents an alienation and objectification of language. By a strange process, the real seems unreal and the unreal becomes real. We feel when we are speaking that our best speech acts achieve greatness the closer they come to literary speech, that is the less they sound like actual speech. The material nature of speech, its production in oral form, is transformed or reproduced into the material of the written or printed sign. Only then does it become recognizable to us as acceptable conversation. In continuation of the commodification of experience that I have been tracing insofar as it concerns the development of the novel, the notion of a correct and civilized language which can only be acquired through education and – until the mid-nineteenth century – wealth makes a certain amount of sense. And the novel becomes a form which is the showcase for such a language. The defensive nature of this development is fairly obvious. The linguistic becomes the dominant mode for representing thought, and as Hans Aarslef has shown, debates about the priority of language over thought take up a good deal of eighteenth-century philosophical wrangling. Readers can then pride themselves on being part of that group in society which demonstrates its social success through its linguistic abilities.

Obviously, language becomes that thing which has to be acquired through education of various sorts. Even the process of social presentation through conversation becomes an acquired skill, and good conversation becomes a commodity, an acquirement, like a good suit of clothing by which a person's character is expressed and ornamented.

It may be objected that dialogue in novels is simply the fictive representation of speech and as such it will of course only vaguely resemble speech. What is interesting in this case, though, is not the resemblance – which is obvious – but how *different* dialogue is from conversation. Far from representing conversation, dialogue actually transforms the object so that conversation becomes another entity entirely. The fact that most readers fail to notice this difference – that most readers would assume that conversation and dialogue are similar if not identical – tells us that our very mode of perceiving conversation is deeply contaminated through ideological conditioning. Even quite educated people can probably recall a time as children when literary conversations seemed stilted to us. When Hamlet or Ophelia spoke, what they said was barely intelligible and certainly ludicrous, and Jane Austen's characters seemed to be reading from the dictionary. That too was a time when our own conversations were not analyzed but only produced. That is, we had a natural and easy sense that we were speaking – not trying to turn a phrase or make conversation into spoken prose. Even people educated mainly by television will have to shape their conversation to conform to some pre-written notion of how admired characters banter or boast. In effect, readers of all types have to be conditioned to accept the literary conventions of speech in its recorded form. And, historically speaking, readers during the seventeenth and eighteenth centuries had to come to accept these conventions as well, though those readers may indeed have found such a notion strange.

Let me perform an experiment here to make a point. I have taken a conversation from *Pride and Prejudice* and turned it from prose speech into normal speech. Darcy and Elizabeth are dancing at a ball. Look how odd it seems:

[Two minutes of silence]
Elizabeth: It's your turn to uh say uh something . . .

Darcy   (interrupting): What?
Elizabeth: . . . now, Mr Darcy. (.09). Er, well, I talked about the
    dance, and uh hh *you*, you ought to make some kind . . . some
    sort of uh remark . . . er . . . on the size o' the room . . . er or on
    the number of you know couples.
Darcy: O.K. I'll say wh . . . whatever you uh like.
[Silence: 2 seconds]
Elizabeth: Very goo . . . well. Umm that reply will be OK . . . will
    do [.09] for er now . . . uh for the present.

I hope that Austen will not displace too much topsoil in reacting to
the above travesty. The point I want to make is that now when we
make Elizabeth and Darcy speak the way they actually might have,
we have quite a different feeling about the conversation. First, the
characters seem less worthy of admiration. They seem less literary
and more illiterate. But they are actually doing what we all do
without knowing we are doing it. Yet as a middle-class reading
public, the level of our resistance to the simple disparity between
spoken prose and actual speech is so strong that we do not wish to
distinguish the two. Why?

In terms of ideology as linked to defenses, we perhaps have to ask a
larger question – what role does the desire to have ourselves speak in
what I might call a 'commodified mode' serve for ourselves and
society at large?

The development of the novel might give us a clue since the novel
had to develop both this elaborated literary speech and the technology to record it. As many linguists have already pointed out, narrative
fiction is distinguished from other forms by the diversity of representations of speech available to it (Banfield, Rimmon-Kenan). I
doubt that Shakespeare prided himself on realistic speech, but the
aim of early novelists was to find a way of recording conversation
that was not obtrusive and that was unlike the dramatic script form –
which was of course never intended to be read.

One clue to this interest was the development of a technology
for recording speech – that is, shorthand. The first treatise on
shorthand appeared in 1558, but the most intense development of
shorthand was during the eighteenth century. Readers of *Clarissa*
may recall that among his other abilities, Lovelace knew how to
write in shorthand – a convenient skill, given the tough writing job
Richardson doled out to his character. And, as I have shown,

recentness and the attempt to capture language virtually as it was happening are characteristics of the early novel (*Factual Fictions* 183ff.).

Eighteenth-century writers eventually developed a fairly conventional method of transcribing conversation, or what linguists call 'direct discourse' – that is, a method to indicate the opening and closing of direct speech with quotation marks (or in the continental tradition only the opening of the conversation with a dash), and to indicate the speaker by tagging or interrupting the speech with 'he said' or 'John replied.' Seymour Chatman notes that 'in the nineteenth century there arose in most European languages another distinction which crosscuts that between direct and indirect speech and thought, namely that between 'tagged' and 'free' style (*style indirect libre, erlebte Rede*)' (201). This form is also referred to as 'represented speech' (Banfield), 'free indirect discourse,' or for the acronymically minded 'FID.' Thus tagged direct discourse would be evident in the following example: '"I have to go," she said.' Tagged indirect discourse would be: 'She said that she had to go.' Free direct discourse is: 'I have to go;' and free indirect discourse (FID): 'She had to go' (Chatman 201). Tone is indicated by the further step of telling how the speaker spoke, as in 'John replied warmly' or 'Sarah quipped.' There are of course many other degrees of representing speech which are not particularly relevant to this discussion (Rimmon-Kenan 106ff.).

The set of conventions for direct discourse was more or less fixed by the 1780s in England and France, but it was not so easily arrived at (Mylne). In epics or the Bible, certainly conversations do occur, but there is clearly little attempt to achieve dialogue in the sense of a realistic approximation of speech. More often than not, characters like Job's comforters break into speeches rather than engage in speech. In *The Iliad*, each character is given the occasion to make a speech, but conversation as such does not seem to occur with any regularity. One has the feeling that when each character speaks he or she stands up and holds forth – as does Achilles who 'stood up among them and spoke forth' and finishes in the same way since 'he spoke thus and sat down again' (I, 58, 68).

For European novelists of the eighteenth century, the dominant previous model for transcribing extended conversation seems to have been, of course, the theatrical script. Scripts were by and large not meant to be read, so that they stood in relation to conversation as a musical score stands in relation to the heard symphony. But early writers like John Bunyan in *The Pilgrim's Progress* or *The Life and Death of Mr Badman* could clearly figure out no other way of recording conversation than simply borrowing from the form of the theatrical script. In *Robinson Crusoe* and his other works, Defoe has to experiment a bit with various ways of writing down what people say. At various points he uses paraphrase, as in the opening speech with his father, italics to indicate direct speech with a boringly unvarying 'says I / says he' format, and also theatrical dialogue markings in his discussions with Friday. Richardson in *Pamela* and *Clarissa* rarely uses quotation marks and when he has the letter-writers indicate speakers 'he said / she said' is invariably the rule. It is with Fielding that we tend to see the conventions of recording conversation established in the way we now know it. So, in effect, it took novelists about one hundred years to fix on the conventions of recording spoken prose.

The inadequacy of such a system of transcription was recognized by quite a few people. Many of the universal language schemes of the seventeenth and eighteenth centuries were in effect attempts to make orthography, the visual recording of words, more phonetic and more like speech. It was appropriately James Boswell, the Hercules of conversation recording whose efforts to capture a life in language have seen no equal, who complained that he could not capture Dr Johnson's speech adequately using both the theatrical script form and the 'novelistic' form. After describing an incident in which the actor David Garrick mimicked Johnson quite perfectly, Boswell wrote:

> I cannot too frequently request of my readers, while they peruse my account of Johnson's conversation, to endeavour to keep in mind his deliberate and strong utterance. His mode of speaking was indeed very impressive; and I wish it could be preserved as musick is written, according to the very ingenious method of Mr. [Joshua] Steele, who has shewn how the recitation of Mr. Garrick, and other eminent speakers, might be transmitted to posterity *in [a kind of musical] score.* (599–600)

Boswell was referring to Joshua Steele's book *Prosodia Rationalis; or, an Essay towards establishing the Melody and Measure of Speech, to be expressed and perpetuated by peculiar Symbols* published in 1779. Steele wrote his book to find a way to transcribe 'the melody and measure' of speech, that is the non-phonetic parts of speech – tone, intonation, and so on. As Abercrombie notes,

> the aim of writing is not, usually, to represent actual spoken utterances which have occurred. But if we should want to get down on paper the precise way in which a particular person said a particular thing, then it is at once clear that ordinary writing, as Boswell complained, will leave all-important features out. (36)

This point may lead us into a discussion of some of the concrete differences between conversation and dialogue. Here we have seen that conversation is always the product of the immediate context. It occurs as an historical event and is bound to the face-to-face interaction of the moment. Dialogue in novels is freed from context. Of course it should always be relevant to the logical sense of the story in progress. It may be tied rationally or unconsciously to themes being embedded in the text by the author. Dialogue will be tagged with linguistic signs identifying the 'speaker.' But, in effect, such conversations are not contextual. They exist outside of the inter-activity of conversation and they are not in and of themselves historical events. They are of course representations – but as such they are missing the crucial identifiable features of conversations.

I make this point because it is important to remember, as I will emphasize, that natural conversation is social, interactive, and communal by nature, whereas dialogue in novels is not. It is monolithic, non-negotiable and, in that sense, not egalitarian and democratic since it proceeds from the absolute authority and unity of the novelist. Thus, as I will argue, dialogue stands for a departure from a more social and communal existence as have other features of the novel as a commodified experience. In this sense, the defense provided by our desire to engage in dialogue and read dialogues is an extension of the growth of what Macpherson calls 'possessive individualism.' That is, it defends against the isolated nature of the speaker, the non-interactive society that is emerging during the early modern period, and the growth of alienation and reification.

Another cautionary point: I am not saying that the difference here is between the real and the imaginary. Such a distinction would be obvious if not commonplace. What I am pointing to are the conditions in actual social interactions that determine what conversation is. The problem is not just that dialogue is spoken by imaginary creations but that even if that problem were somehow reparable, what those characters do not participate in are the bare requirements for an adequate description of conversation.

To understand this point better, look at one of the remarkable features of conversation – its multi-stranded nature. Most of us are only aware of the tip of this interactional iceberg, but the verbal part of conversation is only one limited feature of this interaction. As Harris and Rubinstein point out, 'In any conversational encounter, often the flashpoint is the *way* things are said, not the things *themselves*' (252–3). In fact, 'paralanguage' – that is, gesture, posture, nuance, and so on – may be the central action and the conversation may be the epiphenomenon to it.

When we talk, then, our paralanguage is constantly making information available about our social class, identity, city and country of birth, relative interest, and intentions among other things. In other words these crucial features of language are essentially non-verbal, although always filled with meaning. 'Thus, man has built up, through cultural evolution, a complex network of co-systems or sub-assemblies within the symbolic process which enables him to engage predictably in patterned relationships, to be able to "read" his partner and be "read" by him' (255). Other researchers who have studied subjects recorded on film note:

> Language, in its natural occurrence as speech, is never disembodied but is always manifested through behavior. For example, what does the lowering of the voice, 'while' the eyes widen, 'while' the brows raise, 'while' an arm and fingers move, 'while' the face flushes, have to do with what was said or left unsaid? (Condon and Ogston 338–47)

In other words, human conversation is not just the verbal part of our interchange but the totality of the interaction. To separate the two is to make an artificial division between affect and cognition – between our emotion and what we say. Certainly this prejudice is part of a general tendency in the west towards 'enlightenment,' to use Adorno and Horkheimer's term, which places an overvaluation on the rational. The work of Jacques Derrida also serves as a critique of this tendency, emphasizing western culture's tendency to valorize the written sign over the spoken utterance.

I am spending a bit of time here to show that when novelists reproduce only the verbal signs of conversation they are changing dramatically the nature of the act. They are universalizing the particular moment and, more important, robbing it of its interactive, face-to-face quality. Of course, it is true that a novelist can indicate some of the non-verbal parts of conversation in saying 'her eyes widened,' or some such equivalent. But the extent to which gesture can be indicated is severely limited.

The defense here serves to allieviate the separation of the reader from the community, thus emphasizing the ideology of individualism. Further, the individual is characterized as one who values language and uses it easily. Therefore language is given priority over action and affect. With the exception of adventure novels, characters who do things often come off worse than characters who reflect and react to things. Naturally, since novelists are predisposed to language and the skilled use of words, their 'best' characters will be the ones who are able to express themselves most like a novelist. Shy, taciturn, silent characters are rarely likeable – or, in the case of a character like Fanny Price in *Mansfield Park*, her silence is balanced by authorial intrusion, partially through the use of free indirect discourse (FID), which makes her taciturn exterior open generously to our readerly gaze. Further, since novelists are people who work alone with language, the recreation of a kind of conversation that does not require interactivity is of course desirable – even if only unconsciously as a means of reproducing the occasion of production.

As much as humans like conversation, there is a good deal of anxiety that goes into speaking to each other. In fact, some linguists would claim that conversation is held largely to avoid silence, which is almost always considered hostile. John Laver explains why we engage in chitchat or 'phatic' conversation when we first meet. This type of conversation reduces some of the tension of speaking and helps to negotiate how the conversation will go. Phatic conversation also serves as a way of lowering the anxiety of entering into conversation by acknowledging the speaker's awareness that he or she has aggressively entered the listener's territory (226).

The procedure by which humans in our culture enter into conversation is also highly regulated to reduce the initial anxieties of talk. Our aim is to enter a 'working consensus' so that the main topic of conversation can be introduced. Laver details the steps involved in entering conversation in a public place:

1 making eye contact
2 distant greetings
3 cordial facial expressions
4 proximity
5 contact greetings
6 body orientation
7 phatic conversation
8 initiation of main business (219)

I mention all this to show how intricate and important is the full range of behaviors that initiate and govern conversation. In other words, I have taken you on this long route to dramatize that conversation is not simply the activity of talking about something. Much of the work of conversation involves the difficulty of starting and the difficulty of ending. This difficulty in the situation of talking is largely avoided and vitiated by novelists who rely on the fact that characters will simply slip into dialogue. This ease in entering and leaving conversations in novels serves to display for us that there is really no problem in social organization. The difficulty of fitting into a non-traditional society is vitiated by the defensive structuring of dialogue. Rather than experiencing anxiety about our lack of place in the modern world, we can simply imagine the ease of penetrating linguistically into pre-accepting and hospitable surroundings.

Further, novelists create and shape conversations so that there is a theme or an overall design. That is, each unit of dialogue has an aesthetic or structural mission to accomplish within the novel. But actual conversation works on an utterance-by-utterance basis so that there is no overall design. In actual conversations, all participants are engaged in a competitive and co-operative activity of turntaking in which there are no gaps in conversation and no overlaps. Turntaking is an interactive, highly social process that is 'characterized by a division of labor' (Sacks, *et al.* 42). We all have things that we want to say in conversations – those things are called 'mentionables' – but we have to wait until the conversation makes possible a transition to those subjects. We therefore have to negotiate our way through a conversation and use the rules of the form to get our turn to speak. The process is co-operative and social to say the least.

Thus, conversation is truly 'dialogic,' to use Bakhtin's phrase – that is, including all voices. However, and here I would disagree with

Bakhtin, dialogue in novels lacks this crucial and democratic strand – everything that comes from the author is autocratically determined. The very basis of conversation – mutually negotiated turntaking – is replaced by order determined unilaterally by the author. This feature is something I will make more of later in this chapter. Bakhtin insists that it is precisely the idea of dialogue, conversation, the imitation of the diversity of spoken languages that characterizes the novelistic discourse. Indeed, one of Bakhtin's 'basic types of compositional-stylistic unities' of the novel is 'the stylistically individualized speech of characters' (262). The fact that the novel substitutes a simulacrum of conversation does not mean that the truly dialogic is being represented. Quite the opposite, I believe, is the case. As is the case with the oversized cuckoo's egg duplicitously placed in the nest of the hapless and smaller mother bird, the disguised conversation is hardly the real thing. By being fooled into reading and accepting the wrong thing for the right thing, readers are, to a degree, being transmitted and accepting ideological messages.

In disagreeing with Bakhtin, I am not disagreeing with all that he says. In fact, one might want to stress that 'dialogic' and 'dialogue' are quite different terms. Dialogicity in novels is a quality that incorporates many levels of language and dialects. 'Heteroglossia' is another way that Bakhtin refers to 'the diversity of social speech types . . . and a diversity of individual voices, artistically organized' that define the novel as a form (262). Yet the fact remains that for Bakhtin, who did not have the benefit of recent work in ethnomethodology and sociolinguistics, dialogue in and of itself – with its diversity and dialectical nature – was sufficiently strong an indicator of the political nature of the novel's form and its origin in popular culture. For me, the crucial distinction must be made between conversation as it occurs in society and dialogue in novels, which are actually denuded of most of the heteroglossia and popular strength of actual conversation.

Let me apologize for dragging the literary reader through this body of socio-scientific literature. The point I want to make here is that dialogue in novels is so completely denuded of the essential qualities of conversation that we might want to ask ourselves why it is that crucial features of conversation are missing. Of course, we all recognize that any representation will be only that – a copy with all kinds of distortions which permit the medium to mime the reality. My point throughout this book is not to dispute such an observation, but to assert that what is left out is not arbitrary or random but, like omissions from any narrative, a constitutive statement about the ideological nature of the production. In this sense, the argument coincides with the psychoanalytic assertion that absence is presence.

What is absent in dialogue? First, the obvious point is that any occasion for social interaction is absent for characters within the dialogue as well as for the reader who is to some extent an observer of the conversation. Unlike real participants in conversations, characters cannot influence the production of speech, and cannot signal disapproval or indicate the desire for their turn to speak. The complex rituals of beginning, continuing, and ending are eliminated by the constraints of the form. In other words, the contentious and anxiety-producing aspect of being in a conversation is eliminated, rendering what might be considered a somewhat stressful, though necessary, social interaction pleasant, easy, and unconflicted. In this sense, dialogue is to conversation as Valium is to stress.

Dialogues in novels are controlled, manageable units, lacking the wild-card nature of conversations in which there is no overall plan or design. The purpose of conversations is not to work out an economy of turntaking, but to explicate in fairly linear ways the point-of-view of character and to reveal conflict or simply provide information. Therefore, the linear nature of the exposition really points to the reality that, rather than Bakhtin's notions of heteroglossia or dialogicity in novels, control descends from the author who may label linguistic signs as two voices but ultimately controls the essence of conversation – its form. Rather than many voices, on this formal level, the novel contains one voice – that of the author.

This lack of sociability, of dialogicity, in the novel is furthered on several levels. First, in actual conversations, there are limits to the amount of time one speaker can speak. We say that someone who talks for too long is 'hogging' the conversation or is self-centered (Sacks, *et al.* 12). Interchanges are always patrolled by listeners who can indicate boredom, can interrupt, or can end the conversation. Novels, on the other hand, tend to promote excessively long (by real-time standards) turns. Pick up any Dostoevsky novel and you will find speeches that number several pages. The rule in novels is for characters to 'hog' the page. This phenomenon indicates to the reader, again, the single-voiced, anti-social quality of literary conversation.

Second, dialogues in novels tend to be weighted against group discussions – a feature which emphasizes the novel's constitutive difficulty in portraying the group or group action in general. It is rare in novels to find a lot of talking by a lot of people at one time. Dialogues tend to be best held between two characters. This bias against group talk holds to a degree in real-life conversations where, for example, it is difficult to sustain turntaking in large groups without a group leader. In that case, conversations will frequently split into smaller groups speaking at the same time, a phenomenon we find taking place at the typical dinner party. In novels, such simultaneous groups speaking at the same time are technically impossible to show. So the novel tends, in effect, to have a very poor range of mimetic possibilities to handle group linguistic behavior. In this sense, we can see a bias against the larger social group in favor of the individual voice – or two individual voices controlled by the author's single voice. And where the voice of the community is heard it is often in the form of rumour, gossip, paraphrase, or some less than admirable form. This prejudice against the group is part and parcel of the defensive structure of the novel that rationalizes individualism while defending against the stress of being alone and without the group.

Third, since in real conversations we are called upon to display our understanding of the previous speaker's statement, listeners are bound into the process of group comprehension. The novel does not make such a demand on a reader, who in effect is the silent member of a literary conversation. Readers can be quite comfortable in the knowledge that they will not be called to account if they miss a point or skip a phrase in a novel. Only literature classes and detective stories require readers to be extremely aware of what is going on in a story.

Fourth, since phatic conversation and all the negotiatory qualities of conversation are removed in dialogue, so is the anxiety of entering or leaving conversation. Novel reading then can offer the reader, as silent conversationalist, the illusion of a social relation without the attendant anxiety and responsibility of that relation. There is no reason to ignore this feature as being part of a trend toward specialization during the early modern period. Readers become specialized receivers of commodified conversations. Their specialization relieves them of being in the complex wholeness of language for those periods in which they are reading. This fragmented existence is at once satisfying in its limited demands and great gains, and at the same time obviously a feature of social alienation since readers are separated from the means of language production and from the linguistic marketplace of free interaction.

So one could say, at least formally, that what is offered readers is the possibility for an unconflicted, individual, passive activity that appears to be social, interactive, and so on – but is not. The truth is that this activity is denuded of its more dangerous and threatening aspects, giving the illusion of a group practice and a multiplicity of voices without the attendant obligations and responsibilities of membership in a group.

Now, let me move from the openings, closings, and negotiatings, to return to the actual quality of spoken prose as opposed to natural conversation. Let me rehearse, borrowing from Abercrombie and adding a few that have been observed earlier, some of the features of spoken prose as opposed to speech.

1 In spoken prose the intonation is standardized.
2 The tempo is even.
3 Pauses are related to grammatical structures.
4 Silences are largely invisible.
5 Sentences are usually complete and grammatical.
6 Stammers, errors, and normal 'non-fluency' are absent.
7 Repetition is avoided.
8 Meaningless words and phrases ('sort of,' 'kind of') or 'silence fillers' are kept to a minimum.
9 Intimacy signals ('you know,' 'you see') that are meant to make the hearer feel at ease are minimized.
10 Most aspects of body language are invisible.
11 Turntaking does not have to be negotiated.
12 Phatic conversation is absent.
13 There is no negotiation over openings and closings. (43)

This list reveals the fact that what we have routinely called conversation in novels is anything but that. The difference is so evident, formally speaking, that it seems astounding that anyone would consider dialogue to be a rough mimesis of speech. One might as well consider singing to be talking. If I say that a character in a novel sang a song, we would expect that roughly what that character did would correspond to what we in real life experience as singing. When characters in novels are said to talk, and then talk with the above features, how is it that most experienced readers think that such spoken prose even resembles speech?

Let us break down a few of the features of spoken prose to attempt to analyze some of the unspoken assumptions in the form – that is, to arrive at the ideological implications of form. The first four features, standard tone and tempo, absence of silence, and grammatical coherence are all attempts to give dialogue the shape of regularity, harmony, and artistic form. The attempt might be said to eliminate the disharmonious elements from speech – the stammers, the silence, the manifestations of anxiety that occur when a speaker 'takes the floor.' Speech thus becomes not an occasion for *what* is said, but for *how* it is said. Speech becomes display – but a display of education and civilization.

In order to explain the transformation of speech into prose, I think it is necessary to consider how popular attitudes toward English changed during the seventeenth and eighteenth centuries. I take this step because the ideology behind the desire to record conversation in novel form, and the hidden agenda in transforming speech into its written 'equivalent,' seems to be linked to a more general ideological view of the function of English. Having first immersed the reader in sociolinguistics, I must apologize now for delving into the history of language. (For more information see Aarsleff or Cohen.)

Before the eighteenth century, by and large, all speakers of English were thought of as competent in language, although some were obviously more competent than others. This was so because English, unlike the dead languages of Latin, Greek, and Hebrew, was a language without a grammar or a dictionary. Poets, scholars, and aristocrats all had to learn English the same way – on the laps of their mothers. Of course Shakespeare could use English with greater control than could a peasant in Northumberland, but it was a matter of style more than of competence. The analogy here is to say that a bad tennis player and a Wimbledon star can both play by the rules of the game – but one simply plays better than another. Angel Day expressed this early view of universal linguistic competence in 1595 when he wrote *The English Secretarie* as an advice book to people who would be secretaries to wealthy or great men. The book implies that secretaries are people particularly good at writing letters, but that anyone can speak English. As he says:

although pregnant wit ensuing by nature was the foremost cause that first used the invention of Letters, and that every one naturally can speake, or in some sort or other let down their meaning: Yet Art prevayling in the cause, and by cunning skill marshalling everything in his due order, place and proportion, how much more the same is beautified, adorned, and as it were into a new shape transmuted by such kind of knowledge, the difference that dayly appeareth may yield proof sufficient. (introduction)

At this point at the end of the sixteenth century, 'wit' and 'art' seem to be the focuses of a beautified and adorned use of language, but there is no doubt that 'every one . . . [can] let down their meaning.' There is no special sense that the literary experience is unique since letters are simply an extension of thinking 'no more than what the mind willeth in all occasions to be performed, and according to such indications wherewith at that instant men are fed when they write' (introduction).

From the middle of the seventeenth century through the middle of the eighteenth century there began to be a kind of revolution in language. This movement really began with schoolmasters whose job it was to teach Latin and Greek to young boys. Along with a growth in nationalism, these schoolmasters expressed the idea that English should not be without a grammar – and began to formulate various language schemes for creating grammars, systematizing spelling, and generally trying to make language structures appear to be rational. Within a hundred years, grammarians had made such a mark that some felt one could not learn English unless one was taught it at school. Joseph Aickins wrote in 1693 that English cannot be learned by imitation. 'Imitation will never do it, under 20 years; I have known some foreigners who have been longer in learning to speak English and yet are far from it: the not learning by Grammar is the true cause.' Aickins adds, 'for how can Boys make good English, if they do not know the parts of speech, the rules of joyning words together, and the true manner of accenting words?' Directly address-ing his student reader he notes, 'My child: your parents have desired me, to teach you the English-tongue. For though you can speak English already; yet you are not an English scholar, till you can read, write, and speak English truly' (A3, A7, 1).

So, now, learning and writing correct English intimately involves education. One cannot then speak 'truly' unless one has attended school. *Ipso facto*, lower-class speakers are excluded from the 'true' language – and anyone without a private education cannot be said to be a competant speaker. This change in one swoop creates, in effect, the groundwork for the universal and specially chosen, linguistically competent hero or heroine of the novel – a form itself in turn dependent on the raising in value of English itself, a language that Aickins now claims is, like Latin, 'copious enough of itself, to express every thing and notion' (A3).

If it seems logical that English should have a grammar and that it should be taught in school, one needs to remind oneself of the disagreements occurring during this period. In 1669, William Holder, attempting to make phonetic sense of English orthography with the aim of teaching deaf people to speak, wrote that although

> we are apt very unjustly to laugh at the uncouth spelling in the writings of unlearned persons, who writing as they please, that is, using such letters, as justly express the power or sound of their speech; yet, forsooth, we say write no *true English*, or *true French*, &c. Whereas the Grammarians themselves, ought rather to be blamed and, derided for accommodating words so ill with letters, and letters with so faulty alphabets, that it requires almost as much pains to learn how to pronounce what is written, and to write what is spoken as would serve to learn language itself, if characters or signs written were exactly accommodated to speech. (107–8)

One notes here Holder's adherence to an older notion of universal competence, and his praise of the 'unlearned' because they intuitively use whatever letters seem to express the 'sound' of their speech, whereas grammarians arbitrarily assign spellings that do not conform phonetically to English. Grammarians are making English difficult to learn, whereas Holder proposes a way to make signs conform more naturally to sounds.

Like Holder, John Locke tried to stop the tide of scholars and grammarians. In *Some Thoughts Concerning Education* Locke made some recommendations which he himself realized were against current trends. He opposes the idea that languages need to be learned through grammars. His proof is that women do not learn grammar at school yet can speak with 'a great degree of elegancy and politeness ... without knowing what tenses and participles, adverbs and prepositions are' (304). He recommends teaching foreign and classical languages as well as English by 'the original way of learning a language by conversation . . . the most expedite, proper, and natural [method]' (304). Locke's attitude is that all people speak languages naturally and need not study them as such: 'Men learn languages for the ordinary intercourse of society and communication of thoughts in common life without any farther design in their use of them' (304). And he adds:

> I grant the Grammar of a Language is sometimes very carefully to be studied; but it is only to be studied by a grown man, when he applies himself to the understanding of any language critically, which is seldom the business of any but profess'd scholars. (295)

People like Locke and Holder were trying to put their foot in the way of a march that could not be tripped up. Freshman composition courses and grammar books are the heirs to that movement. The consequences for literature and the novel are that 'true English' becomes the privileged language of the few, learned at school, with rules, regulations, and so on. The development of a universal grammar in England and Europe also led to a universality of performance. Regionalism and diversity in language gave way to a 'national' language. The fact that in conversation Dr Johnson might have had a strong Midland accent becomes irrelevant in his measured, national prose.

National English is a language that is not necessarily the privilege of the upper classes but of the humanistic elect. The novel as a form helps to create a kind of cult of the written word, a predisposition toward rationality and reason that Adorno and Horkheimer have traced to this period. Characters in novels who write and speak this true language are therefore immediately part of a cultural elect. In this sense, the limits of character and of the novel in general meet up against this growing ideology of the civilizing and saving grace of language.

Regional and class difference can only be represented in dialogue as 'difference'. The implication is that unaccented speech – or actual pronunciation – is the norm. As Banfield notes:

> the language of narrative has no accent; it is written but never spoken . . . even in a first person narration, the narrator's telling – a David Copperfield's or a Marcel's – is never a voice with the tones or accents of real speech. Or if it is thought of metaphorically

as a voice, it is the disembodied, impersonal voice that in 'Heart of Darkness,' Marlow's becomes to his listeners. (247)

The implicit argument of the novel that its own narration is accentless or transparent is false. As Banfield asserts, 'all speech has an accent. It is only in writing that this transparency really exists' (249). And the hidden agenda is that all readers should be transparent, accentless, commodified users of this nationalized language – a stance which equates knowledge, status, and power (as well as marriageability) with linguistic usage. This overdetermination has an historical moment: as Banfield points out, 'the spontaneous appearance of narrative style, and in particular, of represented speech and thought [i.e. free indirect discourse], in western literature, is the result then, of the transformation of western culture into a literate culture [with the development of a universal grammar]' (254).

So by 1784 one grammarian could write:

> During the last thirty or forty years, English literature has been enriched with many valuable compositions in prose and in verse. . . . Yet perhaps it will appear, upon a careful view of these compositions, that whatsoever credit their authors are entitled to, for acuteness of understanding, strength of imagination, delicacy of taste, or energy of passion, there are but few of them that deserve the praise of having expressed themselves in a pure and genuine strain of English. In general they have preferred such a choice and arrangement of words, as an early acquaintance with some other languages, and the neglected study of their own would naturally incline them to. (Fell 10)

By this point, the earlier emphasis on style and eloquence is shifted toward competence. Now only those who have studied English are really capable of writing in a 'pure and genuine strain of English.' Even those who write literature may not be admitted into the elect of proper users of English.

It is true, however, that writers like Jean-Jacques Rousseau, Adam Smith, or Lord Monboddo were emphasizing during the same period that natural language was superior to current language, which in some profound sense had degenerated. However, many of the attempts I have discussed to improve language were exactly efforts in the direction of eliminating the degeneration of the language. And while the romantics, as James Thompson points out, were character-ized by a deep distrust of language's ability to encompass experience, it would nevertheless be hard to imagine Austen, Wordsworth, or any other writer advocating the return to a non-grammatical English.

When characters in novels distinguish themselves linguistically, they are participating historically in the rise of the new, linguistic elect. As much as Wordworth may praise the silent and even inarticulate peasantry, he clearly knows that it is mainly through his use of poetic language that their inarticulate harmony with nature is made available to the rest of the élite world. Dialogue in novels, no matter which novels, was and still must be weighed down by this ideological baggage in inherently structural form. Of course, various writers can try to surmount the built-in prejudice towards the individual, the asocial, the uni-vocal, and so on. But any such struggle will be fought against the enormous odds of form.

A few examples for argument: in *Pride and Prejudice*, Elizabeth divides the world into two – those who are bright in conversation and those who should not speak. Readers of the novel are made to feel, by a kind of pride by association, that they belong to the former, even if in reality they are not facile speakers. In fact, one of things that draws Darcy and Elizabeth together is their facility in conversation. As Elizabeth notes:

I have always seen a great similarity in the turn of our minds. We are each of an unsocial, taciturn disposition, unwilling to speak, unless we expect to say something that will amaze the whole room, and be handed down to posterity with all the éclat of a proverb. (134)

The novelist sets up a series of oppositions by which one is forced to side with the Elizabeths of the world, as opposed to the Mrs Bennets or the Mr Collinses – who are always saying the wrong thing or putting things badly. Mr Collins, after all, does not like reading novels, and Mrs Bennet is forever exposing her daughter to upper-class scorn with her indiscreet speech. There are many moments in which 'it appeared, that had her family made an agreement to expose themselves as much as they could during the evening, it would have been impossible for them to play their parts with more spirit, or finer success' (143). But Bingley and company are described as being particularly successful at lively speech: 'Their powers of conversation were considerable. They could describe an entertainment with accuracy, relate an anecdote with humour, and laugh at their acquaintance with spirit' (99).

What separates and marks out the character of Elizabeth is her ability to rise above her middle-class background through an exceptional liveliness of style to make her worthy of the aristocractic Darcy – just as Pamela became 'worthy' of Mr B. quite differently than she would have if Richardson had accurately portrayed her with a regional accent and a limited ability to write. Fielding honed in on this point in his parody *Shamela*, when his heroine speaks and writes as a female domestic might actually have done. The absolute paucity of sympathetic deaf or mute characters in novels – *The Heart is a Lonely Hunter* and *In This Sign* excepted – points to this bias in the novel form.

The novel's history and its very structure turns sharply on the problem of language. In a completely simple-minded way, one might say that the novel requires the ability and desire to read. In the centuries before the beginning of the novel, the primary forms of entertainment – drama, ballads, epics – were oral and did not require literacy. The success of the novel as a cultural form is obviously dependent on literacy (Banfield 254; Southall 12). Therefore, one would assume that literacy, skilled use of language, and even a kind of 'super' use of language would be required of heroes and heroines. Also, most early novels were written in the first person. This type of journal writing encouraged the feeling that what distinguished the central character was not necessarily an unusual life or adventure but the fact that they could *record* – and did so with facility. It is Robinson Crusoe, not Alexander Selkirk, who is admired because Selkirk remained personally outside of the discourse of publication. Actually, Defoe could have made Crusoe virtually illiterate, or at least devoid of an interesting writing style, but such a thought would have rendered the work unprintable since the convention of novel writing implies a familiarity with language and style. In a work like *Moll Flanders*, the putative editor has to tell us that Moll, although perhaps an interesting writer, still speaks like 'one still in Newgate than one grown penitent and humble' (3), and her language has to be raised to a level of acceptability for print.

In epistolary fiction, the dominant form of narrative during much of the seventeenth and eighteenth century, the writer's personality can only be conveyed by writing style. Further, what distinguishes letter writers is of course their commitment *to* writing. In Richardson's *Pamela* the remarkable thing for all concerned is that Pamela can speak and write so well. Mrs Jewkes notes with annoyance that certain matters 'would better bear talking of, than writing about' (144), and Pamela's constant interest in such writing points to the notion that it is precisely Pamela's linguistic ability that selects her as the heroine. If nature abhors a vacuum, the novel abhors silent, inarticulate characters. (Of course, later novels will capitalize on silence of a sort as a form of rebelling against this trend. But true silence is impossible for the novel – even Henry James, whose silences are filled with observations and implications, has not used silence – but only made the articulations of silence more visible.)

When during the nineteenth century the convention of the beautiful female is dropped occasionally it is usually dropped in favor of the plain but verbally adept woman. Jane Eyre, Lucy Snowe, Esther Sommerson, Maggie Tulliver are just a few of these women who can always be counted on for a snappy reply. The skilled use of language is part of a general trend towards praising the literary experience. Terry Eagleton, Raymond Williams, and Chris Baldick, among others, have pointed to the change during this period in middle-class views about art and the redeeming power of culture. If characters by and large are physically attractive, as has been noted, then their linguistic abilities are their other distinguishing feature. And if beauty seems to represent their being part of a new moral aristocracy, as opposed to the aristocracy of birth, then their ability to speak places them squarely in the center of this qualified nobility. When Werther and Lotte first discover their passion for each other the experience is intermingled with mutual admiration for their reading lists.

The centralization of language must take our attention because it focuses so many of the issues raised by other conventions of the novel. Raising the ability to describe and speak to a special level creates a linguistic elect, and denies class or regional affiliations by insisting on a confederacy of those devoted to reading, but at the same time stresses the class distinction of those who can speak and write from those who cannot. Giving language a priority over action also distracts from involvement in actual social conditions, defends against alienation, and reinforces the individual against the group. Perhaps in a paramount way the connection between money and powers of expression is denied on the level of content (that is, poor Oliver or Pamela may speak) but on the level of ideology it enforces the exclusive nature of those who actually may speak (someone from the class of Oliver or Pamela can never write a novel or speak to a typical novel reader). Even today, the illiterate 'thoughts' of the protagonist in *The Color Purple* or *The Sound and the Fury* only serve to reiterate the impossibility that such a character would ever have the opportunity to speak at length and be listened to by any reader. In both these novels, the dialect used is a sign only that our language is not that of the illiterate. In that distance, the difference between conversation and dialogue, we can measure the separation between our lives and the stories we tell about them.

6

Thick plots: history and fiction

You can put anything you like in a novel. So why do people *always* go on putting the same thing. Why is the *vol-au-vent* always chicken?

D. H. Lawrence, *Reflections on the Death of a Porcupine*

The whole inevitably bears no relation to the details – just like the career of a successful man into which everything is made to fit as an illustration or a proof, whereas it is nothing more than the sum of all those idiotic events. . . . The whole and the parts are alike; there is no antithesis and no connection. Their prearranged harmony is a mockery of what had to be striven after in the great bourgeois works of art.

Theodor Adorno and Max Horkheimer, *The Dialectic of Enlightenment*

What is plot? It is in one sense the most obvious part of the novel, and in another sense the most mysterious. It might even be more proper to say that the clarity of the word 'plot' conceals its utter lack of meaning. Wallace Martin correctly notes that plot is the 'literary term for narrative structure' (81), and if plot is that, then it is probably everything else one can imagine too. In recent years, literary theory has leapt into the question of plot and, as Martin points out, 'modern theories of narrative fall into three groups, depending on whether they treat narrative as a sequence of events, a discourse produced by a narrator, or a verbal artifact that is organized and endowed with meaning by its readers' (82). That is, plot has been considered in at least three ways – formally, rhetorically, or in terms of reader response. In view of this diversity and complexity of analysis, this chapter cannot attempt even remotely to be synoptic or at all inclusive.

Rather, I want to inject into the general discussion of plot a remedy to the particular bias that sees plot or narrative structure as a kind of universal given. Almost all the recent work in narrativity, from the early twentieth century through Frye, Booth, Propp, Lévi-Strauss, Barthes, Genette, Todorov, Chatman, Rimmon-Kenan, Iser, and so on all tend to focus on the similarities and connections in narrative rather than the discontinuities and differences. It is quite true to say that *Oedipus Rex* and *Tom Jones* both have plots, but there seems some profound sense in which those plots are different. In this chapter, I want to argue that the structure of plots in novels is significantly different enough to take notice of – that, in effect, plot in novels is, like character, location, and dialogue, ideological. Further, history enters the scene in the sense that the plot structure of novels (and not necessarily the plot content) is historically determined, to a degree, by the social function of the novel as a form.

In making this argument, I may be accused of taking a deliberately retrograde step in the study of narrative. That is, the whole movement of narratology in the past twenty years has claimed as its liberating goal the erasing of distinctions between genres. As Seymour Chatman notes: 'No individual work is a perfect specimen of a genre. . . . To put it another way, genres are constructs or composites of features' (18). And he adds that 'narratives are indeed structures independent of any medium' (20). This step in the history of narrative away from the artificial confines of imposed literary genres was a terribly important one because it opened up the possibility of including all kinds of writing as narrative. I myself in *Factual Fictions* insisted on understanding the beginning of the novel by opening up the definition of the novelistic discourse to include journalism and history along with prose fiction. But, as with all expansions of knowledge, subsequent limitation is essential if the discipline is not to become so embracing as to be meaningless. It seems to me that having defined the novel form not as a simple received genre, but as a discourse with its own regulations and limits, one must then go on to describe the particularity of that genre. Narratology has for the most part given up on that responsibility by substituting the responsibility of drawing large, general patterns.

Narratology in the last twenty years has treated narrative or plot in a very general sense as a linguistic or semiological structure with a grammar to be analyzed. But a telling point is that such studies are so general that there has been virtually no feminist or politicized reading of narratives on the level of form. Any study which is impervious to these powerful humanizing and historicizing trends in criticism must be, in a sense, artificially armored. The problem arises largely from the fact that narrative has been seen simply as 'language' without any qualifiers. As Wlad Godzich argues, noting the work of the linguist J. Margolis, linguistics needs to move in the direction of literary studies since language can be seen as 'an object, abstract to boot, that offers itself up passively for knowledge to the linguist, but is the complex interplay between institutionalized practices and individualized tactical decisions' (Pavel xvi). This weakness in linguistics that sees language monolithically, rather than dialectically and dialogically, to use Bakhtin's word, has been transferred wholesale to narrative studies. Consequently, there has been very little attempt to see the formal elements of plot as part of a social process.

Like Godzich in relation to language, I want to de-absolutize plot and allow for different types of plots driven by different social and historical motors. In this sense, I find myself in agreement with Ann Banfield who in *Unspeakable Sentences* points out that 'any attempt to construct a literary theory must begin with the assumption that not just anything written is literary. . . . What literary theory must seek at the present to do is define the limits of the literary' (14). Banfield's assumption, which is directly contrary to reader-response theory, is that narrative fiction is a particular category that is completely outside of the 'communications model' of language which sees every kind of utterance as originating with a speaker and destined for a listener. Narrative is defined by Banfield as that type of language which does not involve a speaker and a listener, author and reader, or a you and I. This particular mode she calls 'represented speech and thought' by which she means something rather close to *le style indirect libre* or the 'free indirect style' by which an author can represent speech and thought without saying 'he said' or 'he thought.' Thus 'represented speech and thought . . . falls outside any framework structured by the communicative relation between *I* and *you*. . . . [In] what context is represented speech and thought found? The obvious answer is in "literary contexts"' (141). So Banfield justifies the notion of a discussion of narrative particular to narrative fiction, and from the historical point of view she notes, 'Narrative style as we have defined it, unlike language itself, has a determinable historical origin; no earlier examples are given among the data presented here, because no earlier ones exist' (225). Banfield points to a general sense of agreement among linguists and classical scholars that 'represented speech' only begins historically in Europe in and around the seventeenth century (228). I take the reader through this narrowly academic point to show that, even from a strictly linguistic point of view, the novel can be seen not as a general case of narrative and plot, but as a special and particular instance with rules of its own. As I will argue in this chapter, plot in the novel is not the same as plot in other literary forms.

So to return to the opening question, what is plot? Most of us probably have little trouble conceiving of or discussing what character, location, or dialogue are, but plot always seems to reduce iteself to the story, the events of the story, a sequence of events, or as Aristotle puts it 'the arrangement of the incidents' (13). Having said that, one seems to be able to do little more than 'tell what happened' in the novel. As Wlad Godzich comments:

> Our attitude toward plot today is rather ambiguous: on the one hand studies of plot enjoy a new status in literary scholarship and appear to increase in number and in degree of sophistication; on the other hand, as readers, and particularly as specialist readers, we tend to be wary of discussions of plot and, unless they are couched in the terminology devised by plot analysts, we dismiss them as paraphrase. (Pavel xvi)

Even the most advanced systems of narratology must wind up with a descriptive paradigm or diagram to explain what 'happens.' This is what Godzich calls the 'apparent artlessness of plot' (Pavel xvii).

Plot, as a concept, is particularly confusing because it does not necessarily describe a discrete object. Is the plot only the bare summation of the actions of characters? As Robert Caserio asks 'Is plot the sequential element in narrative? The suggestion is dissatisfying if it means that plot and story are mere successions of events, a meaningless matter of "now this, now this, now this"' (5). For example, is the plot of *Robinson Crusoe* that a man, disobeying his father's injunction against going to sea, is shipwrecked on an island where he spends a long stretch of time taking care of his physical and emotional needs until he saves the life of a native about to be sacrificed and together they stop a mutiny on a ship and are brought back to England? Somehow that summation seems inadequate and participates in what Cleanth Brooks referred to as the 'heresy of paraphrase.' So, we might say that a more minute breakdown of incidents would be more like what we want to call 'plot.' We might focus on one day when Crusoe discovers grain seemingly magically growing in the sand and thinks it is a miracle only to recall that the grain had actually sprung from some husks he had earlier discarded. A string of such incidents would be a paraphrase – but is it the plot?

Recent work in narratology has suggested that we might divide plot into two categories. The Russian Formalists called these two 'fable' (*fabula*) or the basic summation of the story and 'plot' (*sjuzet*) or the story as it is actually told. As Chatman writes, citing Boris Tomashevsky,

> fable is 'the set of events tied together which are communicated to us in the course of the work,' or 'what has in effect happened;' plot is 'how the reader becomes aware of what happened' that is, basically the 'order of the appearance (of the events) in the work itself.' (20)

Structuralists make the same distinction referring to *histoire* and *discours*, or what Chatman translates as 'story' and 'discourse.' And Gérard Genette makes the division threefold, distinguishing between *histoire*, *récit*, and *narration* – in which the second term is equivalent to 'discourse' and the third term introduces the notion of a narrator and a listener. These kinds of distinctions offer a separation between the story in some abstract form and the narrative actually created by the author. As Chatman continues, story becomes

> story-as-discoursed. . . . Its order of presentation need not be the same as that of the natural logic of the story. Its function is to

emphasize or de-emphasize certain story-events, to interpret some and to leave others to inference, to show or to tell, to comment or to remain silent, to focus on this or that aspect of an event or character. (43)

This distinction carries on a structuralist distinction between *langue* and *parole*, that is between the material of the language that may be drawn on and the particular enunciation of a particular speaker. Although such a distinction is important in working with detailed analyses of narrative, its overriding significance is in practice somewhat less than interesting. It divides plot in two but is less helpful, in either case, in telling us what plot is.

Further, at this level of analysis, the plot would have to include motivation which would then sneak over into the category of character. So is character divisible from plot? Would *Tom Jones* make sense if we left out the important detail that Tom is a fellow who is good-hearted but imprudent? Studying the issue carefully, it may seem that character and plot are indivisible – since the plot is the trajectory of a central character. Likewise, a character in a novel can be defined mainly by his or her choices within the plot. Henry James made this point in *The Art of Fiction*, saying:

What is character but the determination of incident? What is incident but the illustration of character? . . . It is an incident for a woman to stand up with her hand resting on a table and look out at you in a certain way; or if it be not an incident I think it will be hard to say what it is. (cited in Martin 116)

Wallace Martin concurs, noting that 'on this point, I find Propp, Tomashevsky, and Barthes in complete agreement with James: functions and characters cannot be separated because they are always in a reciprocal relationship' (116). Chatman says that the character is the 'narrative subject . . . of the narrative predicate' (44). Even in the face of such agreement, there remains something stubbornly *not character* that seems to be plot. Anyone who has tried to write fiction will tell you that it is pretty difficult to avoid having a plot, and that rambling, poorly developed plots are the recipe for bad stories. As William Labov, in his book on inner city language, points out: 'Pointless stories are met in English with the withering rejoinder: "So what?" Every good narrator is continually warding off this question' (366). In effect, one can say that plot might simply be the attempt on the part of authors to avoid the aggressive 'So what?'

Plot is something you need in any story or novel, but it seems to be hard to isolate what a plot is. Indeed, the very act of trying to isolate plot from a narrative may be so artificial that it will change the object under study. The summation of a novel's plot is always a distortion of the object. Think about the task of summarizing *Swann's Way*. If plot is something that should not be isolated, but can only be understood if isolated, where are we?

For the most part, it might be helpful to divide up those who have treated the concept of plot into groups and see where such a study may lead. For practical purposes, one group would be those who believe a text is a series of 'narrative modalities' like 'probability, accident, knowledge (recognition) or ignorance, good and bad' (Martin 101). Such would be likely to be called Aristotelians, and we could include Aristotle himself in this group. It would also include R. S. Crane, Norman Friedman, and several noted members of the English Department at the University of Chicago. The second group comes out of the Russian Formalist movement and includes Vladimir Propp, A. J. Greimas, Claude Bremond, and Tsvetan Todorov. The Aristotelians tend to stress the unity of plot, the harmonious work-ings of the individual elements as they contribute to the whole design. The Formalists have tried to make a grammar of plot elements that in effect can be applied universally to all narrative. Or as Frank Kermode puts it, this group attempted 'to find methods of describing a story or novel as a linguist describes a sentence – without regard, that is, to the meaning it may communicate, only to its structure' (169). The third group is less oriented to the text and more to the reader's response, and in this group would appear Roland Barthes, Wolfgang Iser, and Stanley Fish among others. These critics locate the existence of the plot not in and among units of narrative or modes of presentation, but in the varying and changing expectations of the reader as he or she pursues the windings of the reading process. Every reading produces a slightly different plot, as if each reader were in fact the hero of the novel.

Historically, the Aristotelian definition of plot has tended to be the one that has been applied to dramatic as well as to novelistic plots. For Aristotle, plot is the central issue in drama: 'The Plot is the first essential and the soul of a tragedy; character comes second' (14). Aristotle reasons the centrality of plot by saying that while character is important, it is only through action that character is revealed. 'Men are what they are because of their characters, but it is in action that they find happiness or the reverse' (15).

His other requirements for plot are that it must be the imitation of only one action and that all the parts of the plot must be related to that action. Further the plot must have the famous beginning, middle, and end and be of a sufficient length that will allow 'a sequence of events to result in a change from bad to good fortune or from good fortune to bad in accordance with what is probable or inevitable' (17).

Anyone who has read even four or five novels will have to say that there is a limited usefulness in applying Aristotle's formulations to early modern novels. Aside from saying that plots have beginnings, middles, and ends, and stressing the unity of some plots, there is actually little one can apply. And as for choosing the priority of plot over character, it is almost impossible in the psychological realm of fiction to agree that 'without action there would be no tragedy, whereas a tragedy without characterization is possible' (14). Of course, this was E. M. Forster's well known disagreement with Aristotle in *Aspects of the Novel* in which he emphasized that character was superior to plot. Try to imagine *Clarissa* or *Madame Bovary* without characterization. Also, Aristotle's notion of change of fortunes is central to novels but in novels tends to be usually more of a good-to-bad-to-good variety than the tragic reversal.

In this study the central problem of using Aristotle is twofold. First, Aristotle's system, and this is especially true when it is used by his present-day followers, is outside of history. It is meant to apply to all fictional works, and fails to distinguish between the function of plot in the historical moment that Fielding wrote *Tom Jones* and, say, the moment in which Fitzgerald wrote *The Great Gatsby*. R. S. Crane in his graceful essay 'The concept of plot and the plot in *Tom Jones*' never once considers that the terms he uses, like 'unity,' 'wholeness,' 'harmony,' and so on have totally different meanings in our own cultural moment from that of Fielding. Critics in publications like *The New York Times Book Review* prefer to use those words like 'fragmented,' 'disoriented,' or 'disjointed' as terms of praise nowadays.

The second objection to using Aristotle is that in spite of a certain intuition on our part, it is almost impossible to describe what 'unity' or 'wholeness' is. We may *feel* that a book has a unity, but the chances are that our neighbor may feel the opposite. Such terms are merely disguised ways of talking about cultural norms, expectations of readers, evaluations of traditions. And when one reads through such Aristotelian analyses, the real hidden agenda is evaluation. That is, either a novel has a good, whole, total plot or else fails. So R. S. Crane can say of *Tom Jones* 'there are not many novels of comparable length in which the various parts are conceived and developed with a shrewder eye to what is required for a maximum realization of the form' (89). One knows what this means intuitively, but if one scrutinizes 'maximum realization of form' the term obfuscates. In order to know what form is, one needs a preconception of form – and that preconception is obviously culturally and historically determined. And even with that cultural preconception, one really has only a vague, intuitive sense of what 'the form of a novel' is. David Goldknopf can then write an essay on 'The failure of plot in *Tom Jones*' and have a totally different view of the 'maximum realization of the form.' And, of course, any good artwork will always challenge or break the form. Aristotelian views, then, are usually geared to a norm and are evaluative, claiming to be universal when these judgments are of course linked to a place and a time. I should add that a work like Paul Ricoeur's *Time and Narrative* makes excellent and scholarly use of Aristotle without falling into the evaluative trap. However, such a work remains loftily ahistorical.

The second major analysis of plot centers on the Russian Formalists and their structuralist successors. Their work derives from Vladimir Propp's famous *Morphology of the Folktale* which attempts to categorize the various elements of folktales to come up with that which is universal, and which isolated thirty-one possible actions that take place in folktales along with seven *dramatis personae*. The work of Lévi-Strauss in anthropology furthered the notion that folktales have analyzable structures. A. J. Greimas clearly lays out his aim in *Du Sens*: 'It appears important to us to insist above all on the semio-linguistic character of categories used in the elaboration of these models, and guarantee their universality and means of integration of narrative structures in a general semiotic theory' (157 [trans. mine]). The aim here is avowedly universal and ahistorical, first and foremost, and usually linked not to novels but to simpler narrative structures like folktales. And a critic like Peter Brooks, who recognizes this problem in the work of the Formalists, turns to psychoanalysis to explain reading and in so doing still keeps the analysis relatively ahistorical.

Of the third group of reader-response critics, the same objection may be leveled. Since the reader is a concept more than an actuality, as no one of us is the ideal reader, reader response refers to the generality of readers and how they will interpret data. The relative differences of texts and of their situation and context is largely irrelevant. The particularity of the novel as a form is disregarded in favor of the universality of the reader. If reader-response theory were called 'this reader's response' the entire project would fall apart under the cacophony of voices produced. In order to avoid Babel, reader response constructs its own tower of ideal readership limiting dialogicity to a reducing univalence of reading. This move from the confusing particular to the comfortingly general makes this type of theory much less interesting for the purposes of studying particular forms.

So, to avoid the evaluative features of Aristotelian analysis and the scientistic and universalizing of the Formalists – how is it possible to understand plot in the novel? In order to do that, the question must be asked – is the plot in novels different from the plots of earlier literary forms? Another way to ask this question is – what function did the plots of novels serve for early modern readers? Not particular plots – but simply plot in general – during the eighteenth century?

In the Homeric period, there were clearly plots in both epic and tragedy. In addition to plots, people related stories and folktales, and recounted daily occurrences. But we have to recall that when Aristotle talked about 'plot,' he used the word *mythos* which could translate as 'myth' or 'traditional narration.' He also used the word 'praxis,' that is, action, occasionally for what we would call 'plot.' So it makes a certain amount of sense for Aristotle to say that 'myth' was the soul of tragedy because so much of Greek art is patterned on the Greek myths.

This linguistic usage might give us a clue to the difference between plot in the novel and earlier plottings. In traditional society, such as the pre-novelistic world Georg Lukács describes in his *Theory of the Novel*, the stories were laid out in folklore and legend. The artist rarely if ever 'created' a plot. So plot in these earlier periods was part of the collective, social fabric. The story belonged to the community, whose function was to recount those stories that embodied the values and strains within the community. In fact we should probably note

200

that until the proliferation of print and the total dissemination of the electronic media, the majority of the world lived in the thrall of folkloric plots. The storyteller knows the plot (*mythos*) but must recreate the story each time – unlike the bard of the Homeric poems who stuck with a relatively fixed text. As Italo Calvino points out in his book on Italian folktales, until quite recently in Italy the 'storyteller, [was] a prominent figure in every village or hamlet, who has his or her own style and appeal. And it is through this individual that the timeless folktale is linked with the world of its listeners and with history' (xxii). This figure – in Italy more often than not an old lady – was well known to the community. Walter Benjamin links the storyteller to craftsmanship and communal work, such as weaving or spinning, reminding us that storytelling itself was a craft not an art (91).

Of course, it is a kind of myth to say that no one created or invented plots in the past. Surely Aristophanes or Chaucer invented some elements of their plots. But I think the preponderance of evidence suggests that such original creations did not have the currency that the new and novel had beginning in the early modern period. As usual, we are speaking of broad trends, and although instances can be produced to contradict the point, the weight of numbers is in the favor of this argument.

In English, on the other hand, the word 'plot' has no relation to traditional myths or storytelling. It comes into usage in the sixteenth century, roughly the period that heralds print and early picaresque novels and tales. The origin of the word 'plot' is related first to a plot of land, and subsequently to the describing of that bit of land – that is, plotting its dimensions. So, rather than coming out of myth or pre-established stories, 'plot' in English seems related to property. I should add, by the way, that the sense of evil in the word plot seems to come from an entirely different source – the word 'complot.' Of course, it is always risky trying to establish historical connections through philological ones, but I think the linguistic here leads to several valid observations.

First, at least in some sense, the plot of the novel is property and particularly the property of one person (the author), while the plot of the *Iliad* is the collective property of society which the bard uses, embellishes, but cannot substantially alter. The rather early recognition of literature as property can be seen in the founding of copyright laws in the first quarter of the eighteenth century, a period that coincided with and encouraged the early development of the novel as a form. Indeed, it would be hard to imagine that the novel could survive as a cultural form if not for the existence of copyright laws, since so much of the reason that people write novels is for the ownership of that property – for personal as well as financial reasons. During our own period, this relation is so obvious that in publishing houses and in Hollywood, narratives are simply called 'properties.' In this process of the commodification of narrative the plot becomes central. As Wlad Godzich elaborates:

> Forced to function more autonomously and without the claim to respect and attention that the storyteller could put forward, the story, functioning like a commodity in the market, must take on the aura of art in order to maintain itself. Divorced from the lived experience of the teller who previously stood as its guarantor, it must become part of ours. (Chambers xviii)

In other words, as we move more towards the realistic novel and away from the situation and context of the storyteller, paradoxically, the plot becomes more objectified, commodified, structured, original, and so less related to lived experience and daily life. One could argue that plot, in the process of becoming objectified and commodified, becomes more subject to the constraints of early modern life – particularly to the enlightenment concepts of order and utility. As Adorno and Horkheimer point out, such a development leads to an Enlightenment view of art in which 'whatever does not conform to the rule of computation and utility is suspect' (6). The ideal of Enlightenment thought is 'the system from which all and everything follows. . . . The multiplicity of forms is reduced to position and arrangement, history to fact, things to matter' (7). In the novel, this devotion to system is most manifest in the area of plot. Novel plots are somehow different from tales and *récits* in their devotion to consistency and the subsuming of events under a more totalizing structure. The emergence of plots of self is linked to this notion of system. The self in epic and folktale is not as central as is the overriding social network. But, according to Adorno and Horkheimer, the new 'awakening of the self is paid for by the acknowledgement of power as the principle of all relations' (9). So, power relations get expressed through the systematic enmeshing of the self into the totality of system – which is what plot in the novel amounts to. As Benjamin notes, the decline of storytelling is linked to the rise of the novel. 'What distinguishes the novel from all other forms of prose literature – the fairy tale, the legend, even the novella – is that it neither comes from oral tradition nor goes into it' (87). So novels are so divorced from lived experience that even the *Bildungsroman* is 'in direct opposition to reality' (88).

I want to stress this point because it is so odd to our way of thinking. To most readers, Defoe's work seems much more real, much closer to life, than the epic of Gilgamesh or the Grimms' fairy tales – and yet I am arguing that precisely the opposite is true. The realistic plot mimes the real world to convince us that its existence is more real than the folktale. Indeed, the whole thrust of various early novelists' introductions was to say that by shunning fairy-tale elements – what Fielding called 'the marvelous' – they were closer to the lives of their readers than were these outlandish and improbable tales. Probability became a keyword in defending novels, and an attack on a novel would be made if probability was violated (Patey 175). Fielding spelled out the rules for probability in the famous chapter opening Book VII, but at the same time Richardson attacked *Tom Jones* for being 'a rambling collection of waking dreams, in which probability was not observed' (*Selected Letters* 127). The point is that, while novels are closer in plot to our life plots, the situation – the way the stories are presented in society, what I have called the 'pre-structure' – is more alienated, separated from life and community than are folktales. That is, the situation of the storyteller-told tale is more connected to life and lived experience and the subject matter of such tales evolves directly from a shared experience. As Ross Chambers reiterates:

> But the modern age is one also in which the literary text itself, as a form of communication, undergoes the process of reification, becoming *specialized* as 'artistic' communication and more particularly *autonomized* as 'text,' that is, as a form of communication cut off from the circumstances of 'direct' communication. (11)

The plots of novels, as commodities divorced from life, are designed to make themselves necessary to life, in the way that commodities always do. To illustrate this point I might say that plot is to experience as sexuality is to designer jeans. By this I mean that plot is the commodification of experience just as jeans are the commodification of sexual appeal. Just as consumers define themselves in terms of their commodities – the ultimate act of alienation since they define themselves by that which is by definition exterior to them – so do readers define themselves by the plots of novels, saying, in effect, I am as a reader a person who experiences aspects of life through plot. Not that readers are gullible dupes or Emma Bovarys, but since the advent of the novel a good many people spend a good deal of time following fictional plots. And these plots, unlike folktales, function in a dual sense – on the one hand they are bought in stores for a price while at the same time claiming the status of lived experience with its associations of ethical and moral lessons.

This point was made quite clearly by Fielding, who regarded *Tom Jones* as a kind of 'public Ordinary, at which all Persons are welcome for their Money.' As Robert Weimann notes, Fielding was new in considering his novel as 'his own property. . . . [As] a kind of entertainer who is free to sell his fare, he may quite deliberately approach his narration as the product of his own comprehension of things' (Weimann 256). The strange thing is that we have come to ignore the interpenetration of commodification with ethical teaching, so that few of us would buy a product that would affect our ethical and moral world in unpredictable ways if it were sold in a pharmacy, but have no problem if it is sold in a bookstore.

The point about plot as opposed to *mythos*, and particularly that of *Tom Jones*, is that plots make more money and establish themselves in proportion to their complexity and originality. If I am a novelist, I must prove my excellence through my originality, and such emphasis on newness is one of the most basic features of a consumer society. Neil McKendrick, John Brewer, and J. H. Plumb argue in *The Birth of A Consumer Society* that English life changed drastically in the eighteenth century because it became a consumer society. Plumb goes on to say that:

Novelty, newfangledness, must be matters of excitement for an aggressive commercial and capitalist world: ever-increasing profit is not made in a world of traditional crafts and stable fashions. Appetite for the new and the different, for fresh experience and novel excitements, for the getting and spending of money, for aggressive consumption lies at the heart of successful bourgeois society. (316)

There is no reason to exclude the novel from this development, and ever new and different plots seem to be vehicles for creating the new in fiction. This emphasis on difference is striking in contrast to the folktale which operates not on originality but on collective conformations. People who live in an oral culture do not want the storyteller to be too original in presentation because then they will not keep their favorite stories intact. Anyone who has tried to change an element or even a word in a child's favorite story will get the point. As Benjamin points out 'storytelling is always the art of repeating stories, and this art is lost when the stories are no longer retained' (91). However, rather than repeat a story, the novelist, to be truly acceptable and 'lifelike,' will have to use the artifice of realism combined with an original and complex plot – that is to say one that is so distinct from life experience that it will not be thought of as 'like' everyday life. For example, the plot of *Tom Jones*, as much fun as it is, is so improbable that it could not pass for life – nor should it. The remarkable coincidences, the transformation of Alworthy's judgment in such a short time, the origins of Tom's existence, and so on point to the creation of a highly artificial and artistic structure which is divided into nice divisions of six books per location, as has been pointed out frequently by many and noted in greater detail by Frederick Hilles. We are drawn to the life in *Tom Jones* precisely because of its distance from life. In this sense, plot is the ultimate commodification and reification of life.

If this is the case, one might like to look more closely at one particular development in plot that occurred during the early modern period which seems to amount to a major structural alteration in previous plots. As such, I will argue that novelistic plots tend to have characteristics substantially different from plots in general. First, I would like to try and distinguish between the *mythos*-type plot of the epic and tragedy and the novelistic plot. Epic tends to have plots that are linked in an 'and-then-and-then' fashion or, as Scholes and Kellogg have put it, 'These plots are episodic, and present the deeds (or *gestes*) of a hero in some chronological sequence, possibly beginning with his birth, probably ending with his death' (208). The events unroll with a linear logic, as we can see in this passage typical of Malory: 'And then the king let search all the towns. . . . Then much people drew unto King Arthur. And then they said that Sir Mordred warred upon King Arthur with wrong. And then . . . [etc.]' (XXI, iii). This form of plot I would call 'consecutive' or 'causal' since the elements are arranged in an apparently linear or causal sequence. Shlomith Rimmon-Kenan calls this type of narrative 'temporal succession' and would argue that consecutiveness and causality should be treated as distinct concepts, although causality can be *implied* by 'temporal succession,' as she notes:

> By way of example we may cite the witty account of Milton's life where the humour resides precisely in the cause and effect relation which can be read into the explicit temporal succession. Milton wrote *Paradise Lost*, then his wife died, and then he wrote *Paradise Regained*. (17)

Whether or not causality is implied, we can still say that we are at a very simple level of narration. Typical of consecutiveness would be picaresque tales like *Lazarillo de Tormes* as well as episodic fiction of any kind.

Some would disagree with the notion that any plot is linear. Thomas Pavel argues against Propp's view that all narrative is actually a linear string of events, saying that 'the naive view of a plot as a linear sequence of events proves inadequate when dependencies at a distance must be accounted for' (116). By this he means that even in the case of our description of Malory's work, in which events seem to be strung like beads on a string, there will be dependent relations between elements that cannot be purely linear. In fact, even Propp allowed for the notion that plot functions go in pairs, and this doubling or coupling seems in fact to be a rule for plot in general (Pavel 116). Nevertheless, even by Pavel's standards, simple narratives seem to predominate during period 1300–1600 in European drama and prose composition.

Through the course of the eighteenth century, consecutive plots give way to what I would call 'teleogenic' plots in which the element of 'and-then-and-then' may still exist but is overridden by the various plot points and ultimate ending of the work. Such works are generated by their end (*télos*), hence 'teleogenic.' What I mean is that a consecutive plot may look like:

$$\rightarrow \ \rightarrow \ \rightarrow$$

but a teleogenic plot will look like:

In the latter case, the revelation of information directs the reader to the end which then reshapes the information already read. In most teleogenic plots the reshaping of past information will happen all along at strategic plot points and not just at the end. So the teleogenic elements will be embedded all along as sub-reforming units.

It should be said, at this point, that many literary forms point their readers towards a past within the text, as for example did the French heroic romances, according to Paul Salzman, who notes that 'the narrative is pulled back towards the past, and the reader must concentrate in order to keep track of the complex temporal levels of the proliferating histories' (189). However, as Salzman points out, the relationship of the stories that direct attention to the past is more a function of tales told within the romance, the proliferation of the *récit*, than any teleogenic structure which reforms the entire work. Salzman notes:

> the narrative moves inwards, rather than forwards, and the con-clusion is never a surprise – not so much because it is a stock device, but because we feel we are moving in a circle: the conclu-sion is not the end of a narrative line, but the moment when the stasis suggested by the romance's structure is finally reached. (189)

So even though the romance as a form had arrows pointing to the past, it is clearly not teleogenic.

E. M. Forster, in *Aspects of the Novel*, defines plot as 'a narrative of events, the emphasis falling on causality. "The king died and then the queen died", is a story. "The king died, and then the queen died of grief", is a plot' (93). To this I would add that a particularly novelistic plot is one which reads: 'The king died, and then the queen died of grief, but, as it turned out, the bishop killed them both.' The last version is the one that strikes us intuitively as more novelistic – the other two could quite easily be included in lyric or drama. As Forster writes, 'the plot, then, is the novel in its logical intellectual aspect: it requires mystery, but the mysteries are solved later on' (103).

In describing the teleogenic form, I may be overlapping with Cedric Watts who, in his *The Deceptive Text*, formulates the notion that novels are made up of the overt plot and the covert plot. The covert plot is defined as 'another purposeful sequence but one which is partly hidden, so that it may elude readers . . . at a first reading.'

The purpose of this covert plot is that it 'proves to organise and explain those elements of the text which at first may have seemed odd or anomalous, obscure or redundant; and the whole text is in various ways transformed' (30). Watts calls novels of this type 'janiform' since like the two-faced god Janus these works present two faces to their readers – one hidden and one obvious. For Watts, this quality is not confined to classical novels which resolve mysteries through the covert plot, but even modern ones in which the covert plot subverts the overt plot without necessarily providing a neat closure or resolution. Both Watts' work and this one are calling attention to one quality of the novel which seems different in a sense from earlier more sequential plots.

What then constitutes the teleogenicity of the novel? First, it should be noted that the teleogenic does not simply refer to plots that reveal a secret at the end, as do the classic novels of Dickens like *Oliver Twist* or *Great Expectations*. Teleogenicity can have to do with the other kinds of endings. Let me give some examples. In *Robinson Crusoe*, Crusoe's redemption and financial success at the end reshape the island experience in retrospect. Had Crusoe not been saved and not gotten lots of money, we would view his existence on the island quite differently. Or in the case of Pamela, her successful marriage to Mr B. revises and justifies the entire early part of the novel and her behavior. And in a novel like *Bleak House*, Dickens seems to be deliberately sabotaging the notion that the end will clarify things. However, the uncertain resolution and the dwindling evaporation of the chancery suit, although refusing to tie things up with a satisfying ending, still provides a revision to all the legal disputations that precede the end, casting them in a new light.

These cases are ones in which the ending is less overtly teleogenic. However, in *Tom Jones* there is more emphasis on the transformative power of the ending. The revelation of information unknown to the reader and to Jones reverses much of the pre-existent plot and recreates much of the early novel. And misinformation transforms the middle of the novel, as when one realizes that Tom is making love to his mother – a deliberate transformation of earlier material that itself will have to be transformed by the ending. That is, if you read over the first few chapters with a knowledge of what is to come, you will read them in an entirely different manner than if you are a first-time reader. As Sartre has Roquentin in *La Nausée* point out:

When you narrate you appear to start with a beginning. You say, 'It was a fine autumn evening in 1922. I was a notary's clerk in Morommes.' [But] In reality you have started at the end. It is there, invisible and present, it is what gives these few words the pomp and value of a beginning. . . . The end is there, transforming everything. (59–60)

Of this paragraph, Peter Brooks writes: 'The very possibility of meaning plotted through sequence and through time depends on the anticipated structuring force of the ending' (93).

This relationship of end to beginning is also described by Walter Benjamin who quotes Moritz Heimann as saying: 'A man who dies at the age of thirty-five is at every point in his life a man who dies at the age of thirty-five.' Benjamin quibbles with this observation saying that in real life it is the remembrance, the retrospective vision of this man, that colors our vision. But he notes that Heimann's observation is true in novels since, to use my own terms, that character is teleogenic, that is, by definition created to be determined by his end (100). Thus Tom Jones is a man who will be noble throughout the novel, although the fact is not revealed until the end.

This trend towards the teleogenic plot becomes quite dramatic in the nineteenth century when that specialized and intensified form of teleogeny appears – the detective novel. Sherlock Holmes or Dupin become the ideal readers, in this sense, since they spend all their efforts discovering the teleogenicity of embedded plots. Likewise, the actual reader must be alert to the hidden plots that organize the material. The repeated scene in the Sherlock Holmes story is always the one in which the petitioner enters Holmes' lodgings where the artful detective quickly interprets the stranger to the perpetually amazed Watson. In 'The red-headed league,' Jabez Wilson enters the scene, and Conan Doyle lays out two readings – the sequential reading of Watson's and the teleogenic one of Holmes. Watson says:

Our visitor bore every mark of being an average commonplace British tradesman, obese, pompous, and slow. He wore rather baggy gray shepherd's check trousers, a not over-clean black frock-coat, unbuttoned in the front, and a drab waistcoat with a heavy brassy Albert chain, and a square pierced bit of metal dangling down as an ornament. A frayed top hat and a faded brown overcoat with a wrinkled velvet collar lay upon a chair

beside him. Altogether, look as I would, there was nothing remarkable about the man save his blazing red head and the
expression of extreme chagrin and discontent upon his features.
(49)

Watson is in the realm of inventory here, tinged with a class
haughtiness. The details are laid out in a sequence or line without an
overriding, revising sense of order. Holmes, of course, links the
diverse elements and chains the details together through a teleogenic
revision.

Beyond the obvious facts that he has at some time done manual
labor, that he takes snuff, that he is a Freemason, that he has been
in China, and that he has done a considerable amount of writing
lately, I can deduce nothing else. (49)

Holmes' second reading is the one closest to our hearts as novel
readers, and so Watson will always be the dummy – that naïve reader
who lacks the lore of the knowing novel reader. Of course, like
Watson we too are dupes, equally amazed at Holmes. But, readers
always place themselves carefully between Holmes and Watson.
Jacques Lacan notes in his essay on Poe's 'The purloined letter' that
the essence of the story lies precisely in the doubleness of the reading.
Part of the function of plot is to create the duplicity that we ourselves,
always of course helped silently by the author, explode. Like the
benighted ethnic group in the joke who are described as having flat
foreheads and high shoulders because they shrug their shoulders in
response to all questions and then strike their foreheads when told
the answer, readers of novels revel in plots that puzzle and then
reveal. The simplicity of this bizarre behavior is revealed in Jabez
Wilson's response after Holmes' explanation for his amazing deduc-
tions: '"Well, I never!" said he "I thought at first that you had done
something clever, but I see that there was nothing in it after all"' (49).
These perhaps may be the very words of each reader who, having
reached the threshold of teleogenicity, by which all the previous
material is transformed by the ending matter, suddenly is brought to
the realization that he himself is a good deal cleverer than the author
or the narrative structure. De-plotting then becomes a way to assure
ourselves that order is available for a price (since Holmes always has
his fee, and every book has its price), that success can always be

gained through each journey through narrative, if not in actual life, and that novels at least provide a location in which things can be worked over and changed through intelligence – a telling point, as I will show in the latter part of this chapter.

Although the detective novel focuses the point, ordinary novels of the nineteenth century are firmly rooted in the teleogenicity I am describing. Our sense, as readers, when we meet the plots of eighteenth- and nineteenth-century novels is that the notion of plot is thickening – that is, growing more complex, involuted, and substantially more teleogenic. Defoe's work seems substantially thinner in this regard than does the work of Fielding.

To all this one might object that novels are not the only forms to have teleogenic plots. For example, a good deal of drama – both Restoration and Jacobean – revolves around endings which transform the previous elements. There are two points to be made in reference to this observation. First, in drama – especially in Shakespeare – the revelations are more often than not known to the audience but not to the characters, so the revelation transforms the elements only for those within the play, and not for the observers – as does the ending of any number of comedies including the most Heleodorian ending in *Twelfth Night*. And this would be the case as well with the classic play of reversals, *Oedipus*. No matter how surprising the ending of the play is, the audience clearly knows the ending in advance. The second point is that there is no doubt that many of the refinements of plot that were adopted by the novel did not come out of the void but were developed in burgeoning moments of the theater – and in the case of *Twelfth Night* there seems to have been a deliberate reading and use of Heleodorius' romances. The fact remains, I believe, that the teleogenic plot seems to be a feature of the early modern world, of which the Elizabethan and the Jacobean stage is certainly part. A third qualification is that the theoretical generalization I am proposing will not work in all cases and in all novels. I am pointing towards a broad general trend, but certainly there were teleogenic plots at various times in history. The novel, however, developed as a form that came to use this particular device at this particular time for particular reasons, as I will show.

Finally teleogenic plots are obviously more likely to be features of a commodified era by involving readers more actively in deciphering a story. Thus the use of suspense and a variety of plot techniques, such as the inclusion of delays and gaps in information

(Rimmon-Kenan 125–9) can create such involvement. The story-teller can respond directly to listeners and does not have to entice listeners artificially to keep the story going. In drama, the audience is in a sense captive. Its commitment in terms of time is rather limited, and much of the pleasure of drama is involved in the dramatic irony of knowing what the protagonist does not know and then watching that character go through the world with a limited or truncated knowledge. But the novel is a different story. Novels depend on keeping the reader going by not providing all the information. More often than not it is the reader, not only the central character, who does not have information about all the elements of the plot. The novel's plot, as commodity, must keep the reader interested and motivated in a way more powerful than the 'and-then-and-then' format. Obviously, some of these features had to apply to romances and earlier forms of narrative, but the mass-market basis of the novel makes reader involvement not just interesting or likely but of dire necessity. Novels have to maintain their broad appeal as a commodity or perish.

Therefore, since readers are not involved at all in the process of story-telling – the way a collective audience would be if only on the level of body language and reaction – teleogenic plots appear to involve the reader in an active deciphering of the story (as does the modernist trend to aesthetic and obscure fiction which demands that readers keep on their hermeneutic toes). In other words, precisely to the degree that the novel is reified and alienated from life, it has to create the further illusion, along with its use of the technique of realism, that the reader is actually part of the making or unmaking of the plot.

Now comes the central question. Assuming that what I've said is at least provisionally true, what is the function of teleogenic plots for the historical period we are considering? Plot in narratives, and most particularly novels, helps readers to believe that there is an order in the world. As Peter Brooks writes: 'We live immersed in narrative, recounting and reassessing the meaning of our past actions, anticipating the outcome of our future projects, situating ourselves at the intersection of several stories not yet completed' (3).

Narrativity is not simply confined to novels but, as many writers including Hayden White and Paul Ricoeur have shown, is a feature of history. History, in the view of many structuralists and those in the post-structuralist era, is no more than the stories we tell ourselves about what happened in the past. Such a view has become commonplace. In *Fictional Narrative and Truth*, L. B. Cebik argues that 'extensive probing into historical narrative led to the conclusion that the features of narrative that were epistemically fundamental to that form of discourse were common to both its historical and fictional instances' (9). So we might say that the idea of plot is part of an idea of history – that history and novels share a certain faith in plot. As Brooks puts it, 'Our common sense of plot . . . has been molded by the great nineteenth-century narrative tradition that, in history, philosophy, and a host of other fields as well as literature, conceived certain kinds of knowledge and truth to be inherently narrative, understandable (and expoundable) only by way of sequence, in a temporal unfolding' (xi). And Hayden White has pointed out in his study of nineteenth-century historians, modern history is bound up with shaping chronicle into meaning by using plot so that plot structure 'has its implication for the cognitive operations by which the historian seeks to "explain" what was "really happening" during the process of which it provides an image of its true form' (11). In this sense, when Fielding calls himself an historian, and his book a 'history,' he is simply following this way of organizing experience.

If the Greeks relied on *mythos* and consecutiveness rather than plot and teleogenesis, their histories too reveal a belief in those elements. Herodotus is not terribly bound to a scheme of explanation that is anything but chronological: rather than a plotter he is, according to Walter Benjamin, 'the first storyteller' (89). Much of his organization of material is eccentric, and in no sense is the beginning transformed by the end. Thucydides does have a stronger sense of destiny and movement in his accounts, but his account is still linear. His justification for his work is that the Peloponnesian War was the greatest war ever fought – so history is seen as building in a consecutive way on the past. Thucydides' method focuses on causality, the same way that Greek physicists tried to account for principles of motion in nature (Ricoeur 22n). But a causal structure is quite different from a teleogenic one. This is so because causality implies a consecutive action in which past events accumulate to present causes, whereas the teleogenic model implies the transformation of past events by subsequent ones.

By the time we come to the seventeenth and eighteenth centuries something has begun to change in the European view of history. Previously, for the average European of the Elizabethan period, history had its share of ups and downs of monarchs, but life remained as it had for centuries. I am talking about what the historian Fernand Braudel calls the 'inertia' of history. And reading through a book like his *The Structures of Everyday Life*, one cannot help being amazed at the primitive and unchanging conditions of life in Europe even until very recently. While we tend to stress the intellectual changes and advances of an extremely élite group, the majority of Europeans lived in a dark circle of necessity, repetition, and grinding custom according to Braudel:

> Between the fifteenth and the eighteenth century, these constraints hardly changed at all. And men did not even explore the limits of what was possible. . . . In the end, the only real change, innovation, and revolution along the borderline between the possible and the impossible, came with the nineteenth century and the changed face of the world. (27)

The history of kings, wars, and intrigues probably did not seem like change at all in the secular lives of average Europeans until the tumultuous upheavals of the Glorious Revolution, the American and French Revolutions, and the dramatic redistribution of populations and wealth during the industrialization of Europe. It was with historians like Vico, who noted the end of religious history and the beginning of secular history with his notion that humans make history, that human events began to be seen as having a plot that could be organized through narrative – and a plot in which later events reorganized earlier ones. Writers like Voltaire announced the end of theology and the beginning of history. The American and French revolutions were devoted to the rewriting and re-envisioning of past events through the action of present events.

In effect, we can say that earlier views of events saw history as determined by destiny or fate. Monarchs succeeded monarchs and generations succeeded generations as fate or God willed it. A teleogenic aspect of history's plot could only be on a religious level, as it was when Christ's coming transformed and reconditioned previous events. Thus the Old Testament could now be read in the light of the new, Moses' actions prefiguring those of Christ, according to early Christian hermeneutics. Christ's coming was obviously the most powerful pattern of a teleogenic plot, but it was not until the early modern period that such a plot could be secularized. Only when human history, as made by humans, could be changed and affected, could the novel as a form conveniently participate in such a *Zeitgeist*.

If we look with new eyes perhaps at the opening of the *Declaration of Independence* we can see this aspect of teleogenic plot:

> When in the Course of human events, it becomes necessary for one people to dissolve the political bands which have connected them with another, and to assume among the Powers of the earth, the separate and equal station to which the Laws of Nature and of Nature's God entitle them, a decent respect to the opinions of mankind requires they should declare the causes which impel them to the separation.

What is striking is that the notion of a 'course of human events' practically dovetails with Aristotle's definition of plot as 'a combination of incidents.' Perhaps, as part of their ideology for intervening and changing the past, the writers of the Declaration had to see themselves as acting as characters in a new type of plot that could reverse the past. Indeed, the writers of this remarkable political statement clearly saw the necessity of giving an account or a narrative of the abuses they suffered under the king so that they would be understood by 'the opinion of mankind.' The motive almost implies a readership to whom they must be accountable. Breaking the plot of the past was clearly no easy thing as these writers knew:

> Prudence, indeed, will dictate that Governments long established should not be changed for light and transient causes . . . but when a long train of abuses and usurpations, pursuing invariably the same Object evinces a design to reduce them to absolute Despotism, it is their right, it is their duty, to throw off such Government and to provide new Guards for their future and security.

Thus, 'the course of human events' is distinguished implicitly from divine events which cannot be changed. Here the plot, the course of human events, is made by people and can thus be changed by people – although the attempt must not be imprudently done. But the point is that it *can* be done.

Of course, not all of Europe welcomed such a notion of change. Edmund Burke expressed the conservative view in his *Reflections on the Revolution in France.* He looked on change as an anomaly of nature. Watching Burke react to the revolutions of his time provides a laboratory to see the old and new views of history clash with each other. Burke wrote:

> The very idea of the fabrication of a new government, is enough to fill us with disgust and horror. We wished at the period of the Revolution, and do now wish, to derive all we possess as *an inheritance from our forefathers.* Upon that body and stock of inheritance we have taken care not to inoculate any cyon [sic] alien to the nature of the original plant. (117)

But Burke, as much as he might protest, could not stop the notion that men and women might make their own history.

Later Marx developed views of history that saw a teleogenic process through which later events transformed earlier conditions. History was seen as an ongoing plot with a denouement – evolution – that would in effect abolish history. Cedric Watts notes that Marx 'claimed that what most people understood as history was merely (in effect) its overt plot. . . . He proposed to reveal its covert plot: the long-term economic war of class against class' (177). And Fredric Jameson has pointed out, history becomes collectivized in a kind of unconscious narrative – 'the political unconscious' – which he might as well have called the unconscious plot (*Political Unconscious* 35). On this same subject, Hayden White notes that Marx's plot for explaining history envisions the proletariat as the 'true protagonist' (317) – and in that sense they, like the Founding Fathers, became a group endowed with the ability to change history, alter the story, and transform the past.

If we can agree that the texture of history changes during the historical period of the rise of the novel to a mode in which people feel they can change their plot, their 'course of human events,' then what I am suggesting is that the stories that Europeans tell themselves – both narratives of fiction and history – adopt this new view. Certainly this was the case with the philosophers of the eighteenth century who, Carl Becker noted, 'were not primarily interested in stabilizing society, but in changing it. They did not ask how society had come to be what it was, but how it could be made better than it was' (97). In the case of fiction, we see the teleogenic plot which serves to show the transformative power of people to affect what

216

previously was seen as divine acts or simply unchanging inertial tradition. As Igor Webb in glossing Lukács notes, 'The total involvement of nations in revolution and war, the development of a mass army, destroyed the notion of history as at once fixed and "natural," and revealed it as a process of change affecting each individual and determined by human activity' (19). Frank Kermode too has commented on the shift from a literature that relies on static history to one that focuses on changing order. 'We probably have to accept, though without making too much of it, an historical transition, related to this protraction of time, from a literature which assumed that it was imitating an order to a literature which assumes that it has to create an order, unique and self-dependent' (167).

Another way of discussing this issue, and in effect adding a solution to the general problem of plot, is to see the teleogenic plot as a way of dealing with what Wlad Godzich has identified as the problem of 'agency' in narratology and in history in general. 'The inability to identify a viable social agent of change' (Pavel xxi) has historically been a problem in western thought, and particularly since the proletariat in the west has not fulfilled that role. Likewise in the theory of plot an 'aporia' has been reached in the ability to describe what makes plot progress and change. That is, analysts of plot can describe plot, but they cannot or have not answered the question 'why does plot progress?' Here, using the idea of the teleogenic, we can say that the illusion of change or transformation of the past – providing agency to linear plot – to a certain extent drives plot forward. This notion would further Godzich's use of Margolis' notion that plot is a 'covering institution' (Pavel xxii). Covering institutions are ones which 'afford sufficient regularity, within given social and historical contexts, so that particular behavior and work can be causally explained by reference to them' (Margolis 88). If plot serves this function, the idea of the malleability of the past becomes a dominant part of middle-class ideology during the founding period of the novel. It must be noted that as a covering institution, plot most commonly serves not as an *example* but as a *replacement* for agency and change. This is the way that plot serves as a defensive structure for readers. That is, plot normalizes behavior and naturalizes change so that it appears more a feature of reading and of the individual than it does a social and progressive aspect of history and politics. Hence the novel always gives priority to individual change over and above social transformation. The novel then represents a form that channels the idea of change away from social institutions and towards personal, psychological, and moral transformation.

Another way of looking at this problem can come if we introduce the utterly complex question of time. All narratives are bound by time – both what Rimmon-Kenan, summarizing the work of Gérard Genette and Christian Metz, calls 'story-time' and 'text-time.' The former is the passage of time within the story itself, and the latter the 'real' time it takes for a reader to read a text (45). Text-time is 'one-directional and irreversible, because language prescribes a linear figuration of signs and hence a linear presentation of information about things' (45). The inherent one-directional quality of all texts, which are of course bound through the process of reading in a temporal succession by the use of the continuum of language (or in the case of film by the uni-directionality of the stream of celluloid images), operates as a spatial metaphor for the passage of time in history. As opposed to text-time, the plots (story-time) are not so linear since flash-backs and other deformations of time are the rule rather than the exception. The teleogenic plot is a case in point since it acts as a repudiation of text-time. The linearity of the history of the novel, as with the history of western Europe, can be shaken, upset, and pulled out of time by the revisions and transformation that come with ending. In this case, writers could aid readers by creating fictional worlds in which the present could dramatically alter the past, provoking change at least on the familial and personal level.

At the same time, the commodification of plot creates a demand for greater and greater originality which in turn requires plots that depart from traditional stories – just as revolutions depart from traditional history as Burke knew so well – and move into the area in which not only do people make their own history, but novelists make their own stories.

What I am saying is that changes in notions of history and time have led to the particularly novelistic use of plot. However, the paradox is that while novels participate in a revisionistic view of history in which the past can be changed, that view must be mutated through the ideological or defensive modality. Massive social change is, after all, a disturbing idea to middle-class sensibilities, even if that same class had to get its own power through some such upheaval. That is, even though Samuel Richardson might be considered an 'organic intellectual,' in the way that Terry Eagleton uses Gramsci's term, Richardson and such intellectuals did not find the concept of revolution particularly genial (*Rape of Clarissa*). So, what plot does is refocus these cultural concepts through the lens of the novel into less threatening visions of personal and familial reform. Actually, the teleogenic notion of plot appears in its personal mode rather strongly in seventeenth-century Puritan spiritual autobiographies which rely on a 'once-I-was-lost-but-now-I-am-found' format that transforms the early plot by the later revelation (Delaney). That personalization of reformation is the accepted mode through which novels can bring change to life.

My earlier inclusion of the Declaration was only partly serendipitous, because the very notion of liberty is one that is central to the novel as a form. This is a subject for future detailed study, but in short I might hazard the following. Writers both radical and conservative during the eighteenth century spoke much of liberty in their pamphlets – and each group assigned a meaning to that word that fit their predilections. But whether from the side of Burke or of Rousseau, liberty involved a notion of choice and the freedom to choose within parameters. Clearly, the concept of history I am discussing is based on a notion that choice is inherently part of people's relation to the stream of historical events. This choice is completely dissimilar to the tragic view of choice, which implies that there are two choices open to a character – both of which are in some sense fated and wrong. For Oedipus or Antigone to choose is what is wrong – no matter what they choose. The novel as a form, as is true in this view of history, is all about choosing. Characters must choose, but choice is more positive in nature. Similarly, novels are often centered around characters who must choose – most often sexual partners or financial objectives, and often both. Whereas romance is focused not on choice but on obsession with the beloved, novels hover over the freedom of choice – Emma with Knightly or Frank Church, Lydgate with Dorothea or Rosamond, Jude with Arabella or Sue, and so on. This promotion of choice, the (so to speak) pro-choice position of the novel, is of course paradoxical since readers are bound to the novel by the very fact that the reader is the one who is least able to change anything about the plot. The novelist and the characters at least stand in a different relation to change; readers can only follow along with plot elements. Even with a reader-response orientation, one would have to attribute a certain closed quality to the text, even if it is made differently in each reader.

This paradox is furthered by the obviously static relationship of reader in relation to the novelist as opposed to the more dynamic relation of auditor to story-teller. Readers of novels cannot create change within novels because they are simply followers of the plot, bound helplessly to its twists and turns. The use of realism and reader involvement through suspense and hermeneutic decoding are two ways of compensating for this distance, implying that the reader is somehow observing something he or she knows and is involved in the process of knowing about it.

While I have been concentrating mainly on the early modern period, it is possible to make a few observations about the trajectory of the novel. Clearly, the teleogenic model of plot changes during the nineteenth century. With modernism we encounter a falling away from plots whose endings resolve and reform on the level of plot. Actually, even in Dickens' and Flaubert's final books, and in Hugo's *Les Misérables*, the disillusion with plot becomes in part a sign of the helplessness of individualism when confronted with massive movements of history. In a sense, literary plots fail during the time that political plots seem to fail as well. The passivity of the reader is equated more openly with the passivity of characters. Perhaps the novel that most clearly marks this turning point is Flaubert's *Sentimental Education*. This novel, falling in the middle of the nineteenth century and organized around the failed revolution of 1848, dwindles down into a novel with no plot, with a character with no destiny, and ends on the deflating note that the best time for Frédéric and Deslauriers was the time before the novel began, the time when they attempted to enter a whore house but failed in a moment of cowardice. It was Flaubert's intention to write a 'moral history of the men of my generation: the "sentimental" history would be more accurate' (Nadeau 184). What is odd is the use of the word history here. History has become, rather than the triumph of progress, the progress of failure. There is clearly a plot to *Sentimental Education* but Flaubert's emphasis is on the failure of plots and history to resolve anything – even Frédéric's love for Madame Arnoux. The self-destruction of history is paralleled in the destruction of all the major characters. Contemporary reaction to the book reveals that critics considered it 'not a novel' (Davis, 'Flaubert' 1390). And Flaubert's final works, including *The Temptation of St Anthony* and *Bouvard and Pécuchet*, are brilliant assaults on history, morality, and plot.

What I am suggesting is that a failure of history, at least in the eyes of those of the middle class who were not attracted to socialism, begins to appear in the ideological correlate of plot. Nevertheless, even under the assault of de-plotting, teleogenicity remains in a different form. A work like Conrad's *Heart of Darkness* is constructed like a mobius strip in which the end is the beginning. Sitting out on the *Nellie*, Marlow begins his narration at the end and at the end of the book he is still there on the *Nellie*. The units of the plot move along with only the attraction of finding Kurtz, but the traditional quest plot is inverted when Kurtz turns out to be an absence rather than a presence – marked only by a wasted body and an enigmatic death rattle enunciating the words 'the horror, the horror.' Of course, now we must look back on the beginning in a new light, but the reorganization is not on the level of plot arrangements, but in symbolic or semantic revisions. That is, the movement in the modernist period is for the teleogenic decoding to occur on the level of hermeneutics rather than actions and familial arrangements. Even plot becomes hypersignified so that, in a work like Joyce's *Ulysses*, plot events become significant not simply for their own participation in the story, but for their symbolic and signifying power.

In this sense, change is now removed even from the realm of the personal and psychological, as it had already been from the historical. Change becomes valenced by purely aesthetic categories – an aestheticism approved and promulgated by much of modern criticism. The arrangements of the units of the story become valuable for what they tell us about art and our relation to art. Teleogenicity in the twentieth century thus serves to play down the reviving powers of order and ending in human life and social life, and to replace those with the healing powers of art – which by diligent interpretation can be made to yield order and form, but on a purely formal level. Thus, aestheticized versions of the teleogenic offer the 'work' of decoding art as a compensation for the sentence of hard labor first imposed in the Garden of Eden but then only ratified and enforced in its modern form as a feature of middle-class life. As Adorno and Horkheimer have pointed out, 'Amusement under late capitalism is the prolongation of work. It is sought after as an escape from the mechanized work process, and to recruit strength in order to be able to cope with it again' (137). So it is part of the irony of our own period that the attempt to decode plot and reveal its hidden, sacralized significance has taken what was clearly more of a genuine escape in the early modern period and turned it into a function of work with a some-what religious overtone. Thus the work of reading for the plot, in the sense of aestheticized teleogenicity, becomes an 'after-image . . . of the work process itself' (137).

The order that the classic novel's teleogenicity called for seems to be replaced by an impetus to drive art to chaos. Paradoxically, chaos becomes the organizing principle for art. The modernist teleogenic revision now ends with chaos, with 'the horror,' which then revises the previous work. But chaos is very subtly not entropy but a highly ideologized way of organization. Chaos transfers plot from the level of events to the level of form. If art is unable to express logical meaning, then art is chaotic. But if analysis and study is demanded to bring forth rational discourse from chaos, then the study of such art demands a revision in terms of order. Thus the principles of the Enlightenment are still present in the very form of the teleogenic revision, even if that revision is primarily removed from plot units and sublimated, as it were, to the categories of the aesthetic. And the most modern of novels, the ones that operate on the most formal levels, such as *Finnegans Wake* or the works of Robbe-Grillet, are in effect the most chaotic, since the primacy of form becomes a way of artificially organizing material to its most reified form. The abstract painting, for example, is the ultimate in chaos, since the form is given clearly but the application is not.

Where the classical teleogenic plot remains, unaffected by mo-dernism, is largely in the popular forms of narrative – harlequin-type romances and mass media. Here, the teleogenic is monarch. It rules at each predictable twist and turn of spy thriller, it confounds us at the end of murder mysteries, and it relieves us with success stories. In the realm of totally ideologized audiences, the great themes of progress, triumph, success, and order can reign with the widest hegemony. Here in the kingdom of the dominated, aesthetic objects had better not call attention to themselves. Plots that abandon plots are no plots at all.

It is perhaps a commonplace to note, as Peter Brooks does, that plots belong to low art and ' "point of view," "tone," "symbol," "spatial form," or "psychology" ' (4) belong to high art. Or as he puts it, 'plot is why we read *Jaws*, but not Henry James' (4). Yet perhaps this chapter has suggested, through the use of the idea of the teleogenic and its relation to ideology, that the dominated audience clamoring for new and better variations on standard plots, and the intellectual at work on the hidden meanings, are perhaps both laboring in the vineyards just outside the walls of the post-industrial city. Whereas the consumption of plot as an easily digestible form of sustenance represents the plowman's lunch that is an inevitable part of his work, the repast of the intellectual is simply another form rendered more palatable by clever disguise. Teleogenic revision, whether at the level of plot actions or at the level of symbolic and semantic units, still involves the same processes and beliefs in effect . It is perhaps a testimony to the subtlety of ideology that it works by segmenting its audience and developing, through its defensive structures, ways of best addressing the defensive needs of those various segments of society. Ideology works in effect by adding to the well-known maxim that 'one man's meat is another man's poison' the postscript that 'nevertheless all men eat meat, assuming that it is the other who eats the poison.'

7

Conclusion: the political novel, or – what is to be done?

The literary work is essentially paradoxical. It represents history and at the same time resists it.

Roland Barthes, *S/Z*

This work is obviously only an outline – a pointer star aimed toward some grander constellation of novelistic theory. In focusing on place, character, plot, and dialogue, I have left out any number of other conventions of the novel as I have left out countless novels that might prove or disprove my arguments. And as for the categories of, say, 'plot' or 'character' it should be obvious that I have spoken only about one or two aspects of those vast concepts. So in no way can I claim to be exhaustive or thorough. What I can claim is a general sense of direction, and a tentative confidence in the soundness of that direction.

In some ways, the main point I have been making is that all novels are inherently ideological and in that sense are about the political and social world. That is, even overtly apolitical novels have embedded in their structure political statements about the world and our organization of our perceptions about that world. Further, the political statement is one that by and large preserves the status quo and defends against radical aspirations. And the reader/text interaction is one that mirrors that larger political orientation.

So the logical question that may follow from politically minded people – particulary those on the left – is that if novels serve to defend us from the ills of the modern world, and encourage resignation and passivity, is the novel a form that can ever be used for progressive purposes? Or what about the overtly political novel that encourages a vision of greater equality or social improvement? What about the feminist vision of *Jane Eyre* or *Villette*? What of the reformist mission of Dickens in *Oliver Twist* or *Hard Times*? Hugo's humanitarian efforts in *Les Misérables* or Zola's exposé of mining conditions in *Germinal*? Chernyshevsky's indictment of middle-class life in Lenin's favorite novel, *What Is To Be Done?* Or what of many recent political novels by black writers like Richard Wright, Ralph Ellison, Toni Morrison, or Alice Walker? Are books like *The Ragged Trousered Philanthropist, Daughter of Earth,* or *Native Son* simply locked into their ideological vices?

The answer to these questions do not fall obviously into black or white categories. The novel must always be thought of as inherently ambivalent. It was so in its origins (Davis, *Factual Fictions* 24) and it continues to be so. One might say that the quality of ambivalence is really one which has permitted the novel to survive by refusing to be assigned one particular meaning or function. Indeed, Marthe Robert claims that the novel is constitutively an 'undefined genre' (3ff.). It being so difficult to assign a predictive meaning, the novel as a form, and novelists as producers, value their in-between function. On the one hand, the novel is a form, a structure. On the other hand it is a story and, after that, a memory. And so it is both formal and without form. It is about the world and yet is fictional. It prescribes behavior and also proscribes the same behavior. It addresses our fantasies and at the same time reins them in.

In its sense of ambivalence, the novel is beyond the control of even its best practitioners. Many authors have described the process of being swept away with their stories – and thus becoming the first readers of stories that evolve elsewhere rather than being their conscious creators. Aside from the demands of the unconscious, writers themselves are subject to the guiding hand of tradition and of the marketplace. These pressures shape the creativity of even the best novelists. Or perhaps these are the best novelists because they can be acute enough to determine those demands and work with them. Marthe Robert claims that the novel is a form whose 'power resides precisely in its total freedom' (7) and as such it can be 'simultaneously democratic or conservative' (19). While she may be right on the level of content, she cannot be correct on the level of form and tradition. Within this apparent freedom of form is a somewhat strictly determined canon that in turn predetermines to a great extent what novelists can write or say.

Wolfgang Iser points out that fictional texts are defined as those which are not about reality but about 'models or concepts of reality' (70). As such, novels must always be part of some thought system or other, some larger social web or paradigm that structures thought and therefore makes it possible. But for Iser literature operates precisely ambivalently both as a representation of that system and also as a challenge to it. He writes that 'the literary text . . . interferes with this structure [inherent in all systems], for generally it takes the prevalent thought system or social system as its context, but does not reproduce the frame of reference which stabilizes these systems' (71). So literature is the product of a system of thought, but also a departure from the limitations of that system. Where my analysis departs from Iser's is in his postulation that literature begins at the end of ideology. As he says

> unlike philosophies or ideologies, literature does not make its selections and its decisions explicit. Instead it questions or recodes the signals of external reality in such a way that the reader himself [or herself] is to find the motives underlying the questions, and in doing so he [or she] participates in producing the meaning. (74)

In this way, Iser participates in a much older tradition that sees literature as escaping from mundane social conditions and attaining a kind of grand universality. What I would like to point in the direction of is an account of the reception of a work that is not universalized, but recognizes the limitation and subjection of the text to its moment. In any case, Iser is helpful in showing us the illusion that the text creates for its own reception which makes it possible to think of fictions as dualistically part of a system of meaning and yet resisting it.

It would be foolish for me to deny the fact that novelists have consciously used their novels to make political statements and to ameliorate intolerable social conditions. It can even be argued that some novels have 'made a difference.' Dickens, along with a lot of other people, did manage to make a dent in the Poor Laws and help improve living conditions among the poor. Sinclair Lewis did bring to public attention the abuses in the meat-packing industry in *The Jungle*. Richard Wright and Ralph Ellison sensitized many readers to the difficulties of being an Afro-American. Sensitive readers can go on from reading a novel to making the connection with the social abuse being openly or covertly opposed within the pages of the book.

Further, there have been novels that have had an impact particularly in revolutionary periods during our own time. In Latin America, novels have galvanized opinion and created solidarity with political movements. In South Africa, novelists like Nadine Gordimer, Elsa Joubert, and John Coetzee continue to raise awareness of social problems. And in America, for example, black women writers like Alice Walker and Toni Morrison are exploring areas of racism and feminism.

But such novels as these represent only the smallest fraction of published novels. Their readers often rank among the convinced and will surely be part of an enlightened middle class – but a middle class nonetheless. Of the million titles that have no doubt been printed since the beginning of the eighteenth century, only a handful come to mind as being capable of fostering social change. The sombre argument rests in the weight of the numbers. The form, by and large, is one that fundamentally resists change. To argue that the novel can defy its defensive function is to argue that horses are born without legs – it happens, but not often, and then in spite of formal requirements.

Yet even such novels, by the nature of the fictional form, are still always dealing not with the social world but with a very particular reshaping of that world. It is a world, as we have shown, based not on the real world but on an explanation of that world. Variables are suppressed, contingencies are limited, complexities are avoided, and the entire armada of literary forms and conventions are shipped in. As Iser notes, 'The repertoire of a literary text does not consist solely of social and cultural norms, it also incorporates elements and indeed, whole traditions of past literature that are mixed together with these norms' (79). Such a representation then, bound as it is to the ideology of literary forms and operating on our consciousness through our defenses, can only in unusual cases be an effective spur to radical change and action.

The political novel is a horse of another color. Those novels that are political are often only so in content. That is, it is entirely possible to think, as an author, that you are making a progressive statement with a novel and, at the same time, to have the form of the novel defeat that statement. As I have tried to show in this study, as soon as an author creates characters, puts them in a place, has them engage in dialogue, and gets embroiled in a plot – as soon as these initial presumptions have been fulfilled – the novelist is stuck with the baggage of ideology, and no porter in the world is going to be able to help alleviate that problem. Susan Suleiman does find strucural features in the overty ideological novel – such as a motif of apprenticeship and of confrontation. But even her work does not negate the ideological tint that permeates the other less obvious forms.

I recently presented this argument when part of a panel made up of academics and novelists. The novelists were not happy with what I have been saying. One black writer got up in outrage and wondered how I dared say that novels were not political. He said that when he read Dickens he grew outraged at social conditions, and when he went to Harlem he had that same anger, and when he wrote he felt the same anger as well. I am the first person to understand his discomfort with my argument, because it is my discomfort as well. I found myself disappointed with the steps that had led me to say that the novel could not do many of the things that my career as a progressive academic made me feel it had to do to justify what I do. But in writing this book I have come to conclusions that I might have objected to earlier. It seems almost impossible to deny the normalizing and regularizing function of novel reading, despite what we all might want, hope, and wish. But hoping is not the same as seeing.

In answer to the writer's anger, I would have to agree that one can become angry at social conditions through reading about them – although novels are not the only or even necessarily the best way to understand social conditions or oppression since they are bound to represent not the real world but some paradigm of it. And even though all our political opinions are based on our formulation of the world – not the world in itself – nevertheless, the ability of the world to change, respond, and transform and therefore to transform our reactions is quite different from the relative fixity of the world presented in fiction. As Iser quotes A. N. Whitehead as saying, 'One all-pervasive fact, inherent in the very character of what is real is the transition of things, the passage one to another' (Iser 68). Although the reading process might amount to an imitation of the way that reality happens, it is always only that. That is, 'reading itself "happens" like an event' (68). But the 'like' in the previous sentence is of the essence.

The quality of anger does not amount to a political response. It is a reading response. Politics by its nature is a group phenomenon tied to action. Academics and writers may think that being convinced of a wrong is the most powerful step, but without the mechanism of carrying that anger into a public arena, anger is a personal defense. As such, it is only one defense handled nicely by the novel. We read, we get angry, and we see the problem solved by the mechanism of plot. We may remember our anger and use it in a politically appropriate situation. And indeed people swept up in major social movements may have had their sensibility shaped by some key novels, but those same novels can convince others to stay at home. And those activists are by and large not there *because* of novels but because of real abuses and oppression. Novels are at best an adjunct to politics, an anaclitic support to some principles. But as a total project, it would be difficult to make the case that novels can have a major radical political effect. Rather, the weight of their political effect is drummed into us through the bulk of novels – which are fantasies that lead us right back to the armchair from which they are enjoyed.

If reception theory teaches us anything, it teaches us that different readers will produce different texts. If readers construct their own readings from the gaps in texts, then obviously they will make a text into a palliative or a cure. But that response, having been observed, must finally be residing somewhere between the reader and the text. That is texts do not spur us into action, we do. The ambivalent structure of novels combined with the weight of ideological defensive structures virtually guarantees that even the dangerous elements within novels will finally only strike the ready iron of the smallest number of readers. For the rest, for the most, the novel will strike, but the iron will not be hot. Or rather, the novel will appear to strike, but having prestructured the blow through the agency of convention and form, the blow will echo with the dead thud of an action whose outcome is comfortably muted.

Further, it has to be said that the novel has totally failed in a political sense as far as the working classes are concerned. Film and television have become the dominant forms of narrative available to the lower classes. At the same time, paradoxically, these media are the most dependent on power and wealth. In order to make a television series or a major film, enormous amounts of money, equipment, and people are required. Novels only need a single author with a pen and access to print, and yet ironically the novel has not lived up to its possibilities for spreading some kind of humanizing and socializing spirit among the most needy groups of people. Only acceptable forms of humanizing need apply – and those are largely the kind meant to civilize and repress through fantasy. Even those novels written by our best minority writers, have little significant effect on the poor and oppressed they often portray, nor are they read by them in any great numbers. This is perhaps the greatest mute indictment against the novel as a political form in America. That is, it mainly preaches to the convinced and in a way that leaves little avenue for practical action. Even *The New York Times* following the lead of *Mother Jones*, the American political magazine, now includes a small inserted box after disaster stories listing organizations accepting donations – but readers of novels must make their own connection to the situation portrayed.

My emphasis has been on the formal arrangements of ideological structures. In viewing the novel as ideological, I see it as political structurally as well as in terms of content. From this perspective, I differ from a writer like Irving Howe whose *Politics and the Novel* sees the political novel as one in which the author focuses on politics. Howe writes: 'By a political novel I mean a novel in which political ideas play a dominant role or in which the political milieu is the dominant setting' (17). Further, for Howe, the political must be actively on the mind of the major characters,

> so that there is to be observed in their behavior, and they are themselves often aware of, some coherent political loyalty or ideological affiliation. They now think in terms of supporting or opposing society as such; they rally to one or another embattled segment of society; and they do so in the name of, and under prompting from, an ideology. (19)

I would rather call this kind of work 'a novel of political content.' And according to my terms, such a novel would be a highly focused sub-example of the way that politics can be in a novel – just as the detective novel is a sub-example of the hermeneutic requirement of the novel as such. Novels of political content can of course affect opinion and 'make a difference' although, as Howe notes, while a political novel 'can complicate and humanize our commitments, it is only very rarely that it will alter those commitments themselves' (22). However, the collective enterprise of the novel, with its in-built ideological defenses, can and does alter our behavior *en masse* – and can do so cumulatively over the years as individual readers and as a society with a novelistic tradition.

This point, that even novels of progressive political content can be derailed by the conservative nature of the literary form, might be best illustrated through example. In Mrs Gaskell's *North and South* the minister's daughter Margaret Hale moves from the south of England to the northern factory town of Milton and meets both the factory owner John Thornton and the impoverished worker Higgins. These two are representatives of a class struggle that reaches a crisis in a violent strike in which Margaret, who opposes Thornton's unsympathetic methods, interposes her body between the strikers and the master and is struck by a rock. The blow and its consequences ends in a marriage between Margaret and Thornton which blends sympathy with power and whose legacy is improved working conditions. The political message of the novel – that factory conditions are bad and are exacerbated by laissez-faire politics – has to be hitched onto a love plot, given the demands of the nineteenth century novel. In turn, the love story requires an erotic solution to a political situation. The symmetry required by having sparring lovers united at the end of the story, takes over the dialectical possibilities in a class struggle. The mediation provided by Margaret triangulates the stand-off between capital and labor. Sexuality then becomes the acceptable substitute for social action, and as Dierdre David has argued, the working classes themselves take on the aura of sexualized or libidinized energies in such novels. So the curtain comes down with the problem resolved, the individual solution of marriage substituting for and replacing the collective solution.

In a novel like *Les Misérables*, the political attack on the penal system that incarcerated and persecuted Jean Valjean becomes dominated by the love story between Cosette and Marius. So the failed revolution in the streets takes on its significance as that event which propels Jean Valjean into the sewers with Marius on his back to complete the union of the star-crossed lovers and which leads to Jean Valjean's deathbed speech in which he upholds that 'there is nothing else that matters in the world except love' (II, 504).

Politics is by definition about the group. The origin of the word is intimately related to the collective *polis* or Greek city-state. The novel on the other hand is weighted toward the individual consciousness. As I have noted, character, identification, dialogue are all strongly marked towards the isolated person – as is the very process of reading itself. The novel does a poor job when it comes to group portraits or group actions. Masses of people tend to be portrayed metaphorically as forces of nature. In reading novels like *North and South*, *Germinal*, or *Les Misérables* we tend to forget the individuals in the large groups and only remember the main characters. When dialogues are between three or more people, the strain on our reading and remembering abilities becomes obvious. In scenes like the one from Flaubert's *Sentimental Education* in which Frédéric Moreau awaits Madame Arnoux while the revolution of 1848 is beginning on the streets of Paris, or the one in which Jean Valjean saves Marius from the barricades in *Les Misérables*, we tend to remember only the foregrounded protagonists and not the numbers involved in collective action.

Thus, it goes without saying that events like revolutions can only be represented poorly in novels. As Lukács has noted in *The Historical Novel*, only the representative individual, set against the background of history, can be accurately portrayed. The novel as a form simply lacks the technology to portray the group as a collective – and why should it not? As an essentially middle-class form it has difficulty serving many other ends than those needed by the majority of its readers. It is worth noting that the most frequent group portrayed in novels of the eighteenth and nineteenth centuries is not the political group but the assembled dancers at a ball. That makes sense, given the priorities I have been describing.

It has become a cliché, but one worth considering, that when novels become political they become boring. This statement clearly recognizes that to a certain extent adding politics to novels changes the nature of novels – almost pushing the limit of what is acceptable. Readers then respond by noticing that the normal mechanism of the novel is not operating in all those defensive ways that keep the reading process going. That does not mean that writers should not try to infuse politics into the novel because novels have a large, relatively captive, audience. But such attempts are preponderantly against the grain of the novel's form.

Very few, if any, novels were produced and widely read during revolutionary periods in Europe. None of the classics – with the exception perhaps of Rousseau's *La Nouvelle Héloïse* – had this origin. Perhaps this is so because the emphasis during such periods is towards action, and the novels of revolution will come at a later date if at all – and often those novels will portray the revolution in a more questioning if not reactionary light. *A Tale of Two Cities* or *Sentimental Education* are two examples that come to mind. One has only to think of the 1960s in America to realize that few novels were popular that were about that period and addressed the political or even social problems of the time. Those accounts – cinematic and otherwise – came fifteen to twenty years after and were suitably apolitical or nostalgic or both.

The theater has been and in certain cases continues to be a much more inherently political form. Of course, theater on Broadway or any of the theatrical productions created by investment banking and geared to a high rate of financial return can only with great difficulty be political in this sense. However, Brecht was able to do to the theater what no novel writer, no matter how great, has been able to do to fiction. This is so because, as Brecht knew quite well, the theater is a social institution. Audiences collectively sit beside each other and experience a spectacle capable of being very private, but also capable of being public and shared in a way that the novel can never be. The novel can never be a public experience because – especially in our own time – so few people read novels compared to experiencing other media. And those who do essentially do so isolated, at different times, and in different places. Ironically, it is probably only in the artificial setting of the classroom that the novel comes closest to being a public and social phenomenon – since all those present have (presumably) read the work recently and have a period of time set aside to discuss the novel and their reaction to it. In non-university life, despite the best of intentions, only the most passing comments are usually shared concerning a novel.

It is hard to imagine a novel being written in our time that could have a political effect. Even if the novel were fantastically popular, it would still reach an incredibly small portion of the population – aside from all the restraints already built into the form. A novel like *The Color Purple* has the possibility of changing people's attitudes (although it was essential that the film version by Stephen Spielberg denied the negative and oppositional quality of the book). But most readers will see it as condemning a way of life that has passed and people who are marginal. Will legislation or social conditions be affected?

The widest selling novels continue to be the romances – in a form that continues all the ideological defenses we have listed. Ann Snitow points this out, saying 'Harlequin romances gloss over and obscure complex social relations: they are a static representation of a quickly changing situation – women's role in late capitalism' (253). It is unlikely that this major genre can have any radical political effect, crippled as it is by the weight of tradition and the demands of the audience.

On the other hand, the only popular media that could have a chance at a political effect now would be film and television. The electronic and celluloid media have become the major form for the conveying of narrative in industrialized countries and most of the modern world. Interestingly, even in fairly underdeveloped countries, film and television have made inroads. The advantage of these forms is that they do not require literacy – so they powerfully expand the scope of the penetration of ideology beyond the still fairly élite reading public in an underdeveloped nation.

In a country like America, I suppose one could argue (although I think somewhat dubiously at this time) that film can be more political than novels. It is true that a film like *Silkwood*, for example, may have had some small effect on the plight of nuclear-industry workers. Certainly the film had a greater political effect than did books on Karen Silkwood's death. And in the case of a television program like 'The Day After' a good deal of discussion of political issues ensued after the broadcast. After all, film has regularly been used as overt propaganda in a way that novels have not. World War Two took place in the celluloid battleground as it did in the skies over Germany. But it would be premature to say that film is the heir to a tradition for which the novel was inappropriately suited.

At least one of the problems is that the film industry is so tightly regulated by those large corporations who produce and distribute films, and the audiences are so conditioned to expect certain elements in a film, that change here will be slow to come. It would take another book to explain the workings of the film industry and how they affect ideology, but in short what one could hope would be possible in

America is the encouragement of independent filmmakers. If films could be made more cheaply and therefore more democratically than they can now be made through the major studios and film distribution networks, then we might have an opportunity to explore new modes of the cinematic experience that Hollywood has been reluctant if not actively loath to sanction. A film like the Chilean *Hour of the Furnaces* which is made to be stopped periodically for discussion between members of the audience is only one small step in the direction. (Usually the film is shown in America without stops at the appropriate points – thus relieving an incipient anxiety on the part of the audience.) However, films by and large are seen by large numbers of people, and then move to video tape for home distribution. Therefore, unlike novels, current films can be discussed by large groups of people. We expect that, regardless of age and class, anyone can discuss the content of widely distributed films. Like the novels of the nineteenth century which appeared serially, films can create an audience of discussants. And discussion is one further step away from the isolation of modern narrative consumption. Such a situation is not always salutory – as we may see in the case of that herald of the 1980s, *Rambo*. The inherent possibility for fascism is the dark side of the faint optimism I am voicing. We should remember that the rise of fascism was concurrent with the rise of the modern mass media, as Adorno and Horkheimer noted at the time.

Another technological advance is beginning through the linking of the computer with the laser video disk. This experimental process involves interaction between the viewer and the film. Interactive video disks do not require the constraints of the consecutive in developing a narrative plot line – each point of information is not linearly related to the other. Thus the plot is free to develop in endless branches of story. For example, if Jane Austen had written *Pride and Prejudice* for interactive video, the viewer would watch the film and then almost immediately be asked whether Elizabeth should go to the dance at which she first meets Darcy. A 'yes' or a 'no' typed into the computer would change the story. So the story will unfold as a joint process of interaction between the author and the reader. While such a system is only now being developed, it clearly avoids the lack of interactivity so characteristic of novel reading which essentially leaves the reader passive and subject to a monolithic unfolding of a tale. Interactive video would at least permit a process closer to that which is involved in story-telling in which the listener can change and influence the outcome of the story.

However, even with video disks, many of the inherent problems of the novel remain. Readers are isolated and alienated – this time with the company of a computer but not with a group. The stories themselves still are subject to the vissicitudes of all novelistic stories, and the permutations of the plot are still limited by the capacity of the video disk and the inventiveness of the 'writers.'

Of course, it goes without saying that video disk or film, like any products of post-industrial leisure culture, are bound to the conditions under which they arise. It will not be possible for the cinema to realize its political potential until a full range of experimentation through decentralization of production and distribution occurs. Until then, the political film will be the anomaly that the political novel remains. The occasional Costa-Gavras, Babenco, Sayles, and so on will make the occasional film – but the form will have to be recognizably un-radical to keep the large audiences coming.

In this climate, the political film will have a rough time, but it is not impossible that the climate will change. European and Latin American filmmakers continue to make political films – partly because their governments provide funds to independent filmmakers and partly because the costs are kept low enough to realize profits for private investors. In America, for a major studio to return a profit on a film, it has to make three times its cost. With the cost of major studio films running at about $15-20 million in 1985, investors need to have blockbusters – so studios are naturally cautious about making political films. Last of all would they consider trying to change the conventions of filmmaking or altering time-honored ideologies.

Well and good for films, but what about novels? One of the things I have tried to highlight in this book is the way in which the novel is an artificial construct as compared to natural narratives which have dominated human life for millennia. People like Mikhail Bahktin have tried to trace a continuous line from the novel back to the folktale, and if such a genealogy exists my point is to stress the discontinuities, the differences, that make the novel quite another type of narrative from the more natural forms of story-telling. Coming out of the folk imagination, refined by time, and honed by interactive response, natural narration is and must be reflective of the people. As Bruno Bettelheim has put it:

> Through the centuries (if not millennia) during which, in their retelling, fairy tales became even more refined, they came to convey at the same time overt and covert meanings – came to speak simultaneously to all levels of the human personality. (5)

By virtue of their pliable nature, such tales evolved in sensuous relation to the conscious and unconscious world of its auditors. The coming of print made it impossible for stories ever to change again. So while print guaranteed the permanence of Shakespeare or Dickens, it destroyed the possibility for stories to move through the collective spine of social life and change sinuously with its reaction. Print helped to turn the story with its collective ownership into individually owned property – which we have come to forget is an odd thing indeed insofar as stories are concerned.[1] The fact that the great novels cannot change may be a comfort to many, but – thought about in another way – this fixity is a sad mark of the novel's lack of connection to the ongoing human community. Like other sacred texts, the only way of accommodating to the control of textuality is through interpretation. So we might say that great novels succeed in being reinterpreted for the needs of different ages. Indeed, the recent growth of interest in interpretation within the literary disciplines at precisely the same time as the waning of the novel as a hegemonic form points to a desire to recreate what is no longer viably being created.

The fairy tale, on the other hand, by virtue of its interconnectedness with the human community is in some sense political. Of course, most folktales arose before the period that we think of as characteristic of mass politics, but scholars like Jack Zipes insist that folktales do reflect the economic and political world of their listeners. In any case, we must recognize the limitations of the novel which can never participate in the pervasiveness and truly interactive aspect of natural narration. The novel as a form, no matter what its political intent, will always live in the gap between natural narrative and artificial commodity.

As Bettelheim says, 'fairy tales suggest images to the child by which he can structure his day dreams and with them give better direction to his life' (7). Few novels can now provide this kind of better direction. Indeed the novel of the twentieth century is geared towards the lower depths. Rather than providing structure and direction to our day dreams, the novel breaks up structure and finds a comfortable route in a minimalistic direction. Despair, angst, ennui, or alternatively the ridiculous and the cynical dominate the effects novelists seek. Bettelheim's definition of a story that can help a listener is instructive: 'to enrich his life, it [the story] must clarify his emotions; be attuned to his anxieties and aspiration; give full recognition to his difficulties, while at the same time suggesting solutions to the problems which perturb him' (5).

Although he is discussing fairy tales, Bettelheim's definition can be applied to the novel – and one might add there the possibility that the novel can suggest political solutions. Some novels can match up to this difficult checklist, and perhaps these are among our best. The fact that the novel can be political, too, is in fact its birthright. Fairy tales and legends are consigned to the world of the universal, even if they do comment on the social lot of the poor. But they can rarely, except by reapplication, comment on the present, the recently past, or the future state of affairs. But the novel, separated as it is from social life, surpasses, paradoxically, natural narrative by being able to comment on the contemporary. The novel has, by and large, failed to live up to this birthright. Perhaps it has been hampered by formal constraints, as I have been arguing, but novelists have not been as inventive in changing those constraints as they have been on the level of content.

It has happened in presenting material from this study that I am asked about the future of the novel and what should be done. I am hardly in a position to advise writers and the public what they should do. Praxis has a life of its own, and I find that rarely does it respond to prescription or proscription. I am not suggesting that novelists cease writing novels because of their inefficacy or because the form will predetermine the effect. Nor am I saying that modern technology will obliterate the novel, in the way that the novel obliterated the romance and the epic. The novel will endure. Having met its match in film and television, it continues to survive. We need our stories and will take them in many forms. But if the novel is to continue being hardy, writers and publishers will have to find ways to resist the proclivity of the novel to feed off the ideological forms of the past. Political resistance begins with awareness. Knowing the function of our collective defenses, we can take strength in setting them up and then wiping them out. Further, there is a sense that reception theory gives us that since the text is only part of the transaction, changing the reader can change the text. Resisting the novel may be thought of as moving from a kind of implied reader to another variety of informed reader – one who is not just competent in literary skills but in the range of affective, political, defensive skills as well. So resisting the novel may in fact be a way of reforming the novel too.

Of course, such a call is utopian but it is not premature. As a culture, we have lived for almost 200 years well adapted to our defenses and relatively harmonious with our literary forms. Is it not yet the time to begin the analysis that will free us from the buffer between margins and the text?

Notes

3 'Known unknown' locations: the ideology of place

[1] There is an argument to be made that during the classical period there were extended descriptions of land. I myself am not a skilled enough scholar in that area to prove or disprove this point. Certainly the colonialist tendencies of Greece or Rome put them in a remotely similar position to the Europe I am describing, but I rather doubt that the literary genres that might be called novelistic used space in the way that novels I am describing did.

[2] The problem I am trying to avoid here is one of the weak points of Terry Eagleton's *The Rape of Clarissa*, which claims that a writer like Richardson was actively attempting to be an ideologist for the new middle classes.

[3] Novels, too, have symbolic uses of terrain. For example, in his book *The Realistic Imagination* George Levine has pointed out that the Victorians tended to see the mountains and the sea as places to be associated with violent emotions and the sublime. But systems are far more intuitive than the highly structured use of space in allegorical works.

[4] Usually the reason given for Defoe's objectomania is his desire to create 'realism.' I have always found this explanation somewhat tautological and based on a kind of hindsight. What is so 'real' about an inventorized object? Would it not have been more 'real' to have taken one object (as Flaubert does with Charles Bovary's hat in the opening of *Madame Bovary*) and described that intricately and fully? Defoe tends toward the list, a form that Rabelais successfully used to defeat any 'real' effect.

4 Characters, narrators, and readers: making friends with signs

1 See for example Paul Delaney, *British Autobiography in the Seventeenth Century*; G. A. Starr, *Defoe and Spiritual Autobiography*; Patricia Meyer Spacks, *Imagining a Self*; Ruth Perry, *Women, Letters, and The Novel*, etc.

2 See my *Factual Fictions* for an extended treatment of this subject.

3 In this regard, Wayne Booth talks in *The Rhetoric of Fiction* a good deal about readers' relations to narrators. He covers this question of universality and proposes that 'although such universals operate to some extent in all successful literature, it is true that most works whose authors have asked the reader to be "objective" have in fact depended strongly on the substitution of unconventional or private values' (143). But Booth's even-handed solution to the problem of universality is virtually ignored in his general discussions of narrators and readers. That is, as he admits in his preface, he had 'to rule out different demands made by different audiences in different times.' His analysis, by not treating specific kinds of narratives as different, eventually runs into the same fallacy as these novels themselves – of universalizing the role of narrator and reader. Booth is excellent at pointing out that narrators manipulate readers and that novels are in effect not universal but rhetorical. But he never moves toward telling us *what* is at stake in such rhetorical control. Historical motivation is absent for him.

4 Critics would have us think otherwise too. Wayne Booth in *The Rhetoric of Fiction* tells us that Tristram's problem of telling his story is entirely of his own making. 'Sterne and the reader are always aware of the existence of a clear, simple chronology of events that could be told in a hundred pages without difficulty' (p. 231). This is a way of saying that both reader and Sterne are aware of a more or less conventional way of telling stories, but Booth does not realize the recentness of the attempt to encapsulate 'life,' place,' and 'character' in the narrative form. The novel attempts things quite different from any 'chronology of events.'

5 Italo Calvino's *If on a winter's night a traveler* . . . and John Barth's *Sabbatical* and *Letters* do this in a comic vein and J. M. Coetzee's *Dusklands* in a surreal one. Elsa Morante's *History: A Novel* does not include the authorial life but does include actual history – not so new a trick if one looks back to *Tom Jones, Les Misérables, Barnaby Rudge*, and *A Tale of Two Cities*, or *Sentimental Education*.

7 Conclusion: the political novel, or – what is to be done?

1 In fact, the difficulty of holding onto stories as property is now becoming a question for the courts since video tapes have made it possible for

cinematic properties to be individually owned. The ease with which a video tape can be duplicated at home calls into question the whole idea that a story can be owned in a total way. Hollywood would like to protect the concept of a story as property, but stories are slipping out of their cassettes and winding up where they do not belong.

Bibliography

Aarsleff, Hans, *The Study of Language in England 1780–1860* (Princeton: Princeton University Press, 1967).

Abercrombie, David, *Studies in Phonetics and Linguistics* (Oxford: Oxford University Press, 1965).

Adams, Percy, *Travel Literature and the Evolution of the Novel* (Lexington: University Press of Kentucky, 1983).

Adorno, Theodor, *Minima Moralia: Reflections From Damaged Life*, trans. E. F. N. Jephcott (London: Verso, 1974).

—— and Horkheimer, Max, *The Dialectic of Enlightenment* (New York: Herder & Herder, 1972; orig. pub. 1947).

Aickins, Joseph, *The English Grammar: Or, The English Tongue* (London, 1693).

Alpers, Svetlana, *The Art of Describing: Dutch Art in the Seventeenth Century* (Chicago: University of Chicago Press, 1983).

Althusser, Louis, *For Marx* (London: New Left Books, 1977).

——, *Lenin and Philosophy* (New York: Monthly Review Press, 1971).

Anon., *A Description of South Carolina* (London: R. & J. Dodsley, 1761), preface in B. R. Carroll (ed.), *Historical Collections of South Carolina* (New York: Harper Brothers, 1836).

Anson, George, *A Voyage Around the World in the Years 1740–44*, ed. Richard Walter and Benjamin Robins (Oxford: Oxford University Press, 1974).

Appleton, Jay, *The Experience of Landscape* (London: John Wiley & Sons, 1982).

Aristotle, *On Poetry and Style*, trans. G. M. A. Grube (Indianapolis: Bobbs-Merrill, 1958).

Auerbach, Erich, *Mimesis*, trans. Willard Trask (New York: Anchor Books, 1957).

Austen, Jane, *Pride and Prejudice* (Harmondsworth: Penguin, 1972; orig. pub. 1813).

Baker, J. H., *An Introduction to English Legal History*, 2nd edn (London: Butterworth, 1979).

Bakhtin, Mikhail, *The Dialogic Imagination*, trans. Caryl Emerson and Michael Holquist (Austin: University of Texas Press, 1981).

Baldick, Chris, *The Social Mission of English Criticism* (Oxford: Oxford University Press, 1984).

Balzac, Honoré de, *Le Père Goriot* (Harmondsworth: Penguin, 1969; orig. pub. 1834–5).

Banfield, Ann, *Unspeakable Sentences: Narration and Representation in the Language of Fiction* (Boston: Routledge & Kegan Paul, 1982).

Barrell, John, *The Dark Side of the Landscape* (Cambridge: Cambridge University Press, 1980).

Barthes, Roland, *Empire of Signs*, trans. Richard Howard (New York: Hill & Wang, 1982).

———, *Roland Barthes*, trans. Richard Howard (New York: Hill & Wang, 1977).

———, *S/Z*, trans. R. Miller (New York: Hill & Wang, 1974).

Becker, Carl L., *The Heavenly City of the Eighteenth-Century Philosophers* (New Haven: Yale University Press, 1932; repr. 1965).

Bell, Daniel, *The End of Ideology: On The Exhaustion of Political Ideas in the Fifties* (New York: Free Press, 1962).

Benjamin, Walter, *Illuminations* (New York: Schocken, 1969).

Berger, John, *About Looking* (New York: Pantheon, 1980).

———, *Ways of Seeing* (Harmondsworth: Penguin, 1972).

Bernstein, J. M., *The Philosophy of the Novel: Lukács, Marxism, and the Dialectics of Form* (Minneapolis: University of Minnesota Press, 1984).

Bettelheim, Bruno, *The Uses of Enchantment: The Meaning and Importance of Fairy Tales* (New York: Knopf, 1976).

Booth, Wayne, *The Rhetoric of Fiction* (Chicago: University of Chicago Press, 1961).

Boswell, James, *Life of Johnson* (Oxford: Oxford University Press, 1982; orig. pub. 1791, 1793, 1799).

Braudel, Fernand, *The Structures of Everyday Life* (New York: Harper & Row, 1981).

Brenner, Charles, *An Elementary Textbook of Psychoanalysis* (New York: Doubleday, 1974).

Bibliography

Brontë, Charlotte, *Jane Eyre* (Harmondsworth: Penguin, 1983; orig. pub. 1847).

Brooks, Cleanth (and Wimsatt, William K.), *Literary Criticism* (New York: Knopf, 1957).

Brooks, Peter, *Reading for the Plot* (New York: Knopf, 1984).

Brown, Homer, 'The displaced self in the novels of Daniel Defoe,' *English Literary History* 38, 4 (December 1971): 55–90.

Brownstein, Rachel, *Becoming a Heroine: Reading About Women in Novels* (New York: Viking, 1964).

Bunyan, John, *The Life and Death of Mr Badman* (Oxford: Oxford University Press, 1929; orig. pub. 1680).

———, *Pilgrim's Progress* (Oxford: Oxford University Press, 1960; orig. pub. 1678).

Burke, Edmund, *Reflections on the Revolution in France* (Harmondsworth: Penguin, 1968; orig. pub. 1790).

Burney, Fanny, *Evelina* (Oxford: Oxford University Press, 1984; orig. pub. 1778).

Calvino, Italo, *If on a winter's night a traveler . . .*, trans. William Weaver (New York: Harcourt Brace Jovanovich, 1981).

———, *Invisible Cities* (New York: Harcourt Brace Jovanovich, 1979).

———, *Italian Folktales* (New York: Harcourt Brace Jovanovich, 1980).

Carrol, Peter, *Puritanism and the Wilderness: The Intellectual Significance of the New England Frontier 1629–1700* (New York: Columbia University Press, 1969).

Caserio, Robert, *Plot, Story, and the Novel: From Dickens and Poe to the Modern Period* (Princeton: Princeton University Press, 1979).

Cassirer, Ernst, *The Philosophy of Symbolic Forms*, trans. Ralph Manheim (New Haven: Yale University Press, 1953).

Cebik, L. B., *Fictional Narrative and Truth: An Epistemic Analysis* (Lanham: University Press of America, 1984).

Chambers, Ross, *Story and Situation: Narrative Seduction and the Power of Fiction* (Minneapolis: University of Minnesota Press, 1984).

Chatman, Seymour, *Story and Discourse: Narrative Structure in Fiction and Film* (Ithaca: Cornell University Press, 1978).

Chernyshevsky, Nikolai, *What is to be Done?* (New York: Ardis, 1985).

Clark, Kenneth, *Landscape Into Art* (Boston: Beacon Press, 1961; orig. pub. 1949).

Clark, T. J., *The Painting of Modern Life: Paris in the Art of Manet and His Followers* (Princeton: Princeton University Press, 1984).

Cohen, Murray, *Sensible Words: Linguistic Practice in England 1640–1785* (Baltimore: Johns Hopkins University Press, 1977).

Condon, W. S. and Ogston, W. D., 'Sound film analysis of normal and pathological behavior patterns,' *Journal of Nervous and Mental Diseases* 143 (December 1973): 338–47.

Conrad, Joseph, *Heart of Darkness* (New York: Norton, 1972).

Cooper, James Fenimore, *The Pioneers* (Albany: State University of New York Press, 1980; orig. pub. 1823).

Crane, R. S., 'The concept of plot and the plot in *Tom Jones*,' in Martin Battestin (ed.), *Twentieth Century Interpretations of Tom Jones* (Englewood, NJ: Prentice-Hall, 1968).

Dampier, William, *New Voyage Round the World* (London, 1697).

David, Dierdre, *Fictions of Resolution in Three Victorian Novels* (New York: Columbia University Press, 1982).

Davies, Robertson, *Unfinished Business* (Harmondsworth: Penguin, 1970).

Davis, Lennard J., *Factual Fictions: Origins of the English Novel* (New York: Columbia University Press, 1983).

——, 'Flaubert,' in Jacques Barzun and George Stade (eds), *European Writers: The Romantic Century* (New York: Scribner, 1985).

Davis, Natalie Zemon, 'Beyond the market: books as gifts in sixteenth-century France,' *Transactions of the Royal Historical Society*, 5th ser., 33 (1983).

Day, Angel, *The English Secretarie* (London, 1595).

Defoe, Daniel, *Moll Flanders* (New York: Norton, 1973; orig. pub. 1722).

——, *Robinson Crusoe* (New York: Norton, 1975; orig. pub. 1719).

——, *The Further Adventures of Robinson Crusoe* (Oxford: Blackwell, 1928; orig. pub. 1719).

——, *The History of Colonel Jack* (Oxford: Oxford University Press, 1965; orig. pub. 1722).

——, *A Tour Thro' the Whole Island of Great Britain* (London: Frank Cass, 1968; orig. pub. 1724–6).

Delaney, Paul, *British Autobiography in the Seventeenth Century* (London: Routledge & Kegan Paul, 1969).

Denton, Daniel, *A Brief Description of New York formerly called New Netherlands* (London, 1670).

Dickens, Charles, *Bleak House* (Harmondsworth: Penguin, 1985; orig. pub. 1853).

——, *David Copperfield* (Harmondsworth: Penguin, 1969; orig. pub. 1850).

——, *Dombey and Son* (Harmondsworth: Penguin, 1970; orig. pub. 1848).

——, *Hard Times* (Harmondsworth: Penguin, 1970; orig. pub. 1854).

——, *Oliver Twist* (Harmondsworth: Penguin, 1970; orig. pub. 1838).

——, *A Tale of Two Cities* (Harmondsworth: Penguin, 1970; orig. pub. 1859).

Doyle, Arthur Conan, *The Adventures of Sherlock Holmes* (New York: Harper, 1892).

Bibliography

Dunlop, John, *A History of Fiction* (London: Longman, 1814).

Eagleton, Terry, *Criticism and Ideology* (London: Verso, 1978).

———, *Literary Theory: An Introduction* (Minneapolis: University of Minnesota Press, 1983).

———, *The Rape of Clarissa* (Minneapolis: University of Minnesota Press, 1982).

Fabian, Johannes, *Time and the Other: How Anthropology Makes Its Object* (New York: Columbia University Press, 1983).

Faulkner, William, *The Sound and the Fury* (New York: Vintage, 1946; orig. pub. 1929).

Fell, John, *An Essay Towards an English Grammar* (London: C. Dilly, 1784).

Fielding, Henry, 'An essay on conversation,' in *Miscellanies*, vol. I, ed. Henry Knight Miller (Middletown: Wesleyan University Press, 1972).

———, *Shamela* (Boston: Houghton Mifflin, 1961).

———, *Tom Jones* (Harmondsworth: Penguin, 1970; orig. pub. 1749).

Fish, Stanley, *Surprised by Sin: The Reader in Paradise Lost* (Berkeley: University of California Press, 1971).

Fitzgerald, F. Scott, *The Great Gatsby* (New York: Scribner, 1953; orig. pub. 1925).

Flaubert, Gustav, *Bouvard and Pécuchet* (Harmondsworth: Penguin, 1976; orig. pub. 1881).

———, *Madame Bovary* (New York: Norton, 1965; orig. pub. 1856–7).

———, *Sentimental Education* (Harmondsworth: Penguin, 1970; orig. pub. 1869).

Forster, E. M., *Aspects of the Novel* (Harmondsworth: Penguin, 1968; orig. pub. 1927).

Foster, William, (ed.), *Letters Received by the East India Company* (London: Sampson Low, Marston & Co., 1899).

Foucault, Michel, *The Archeology of Knowledge* (New York: Harper & Row, 1972).

———, *Foucault Reader*, ed. Paul Rabinow (New York: Pantheon, 1984).

———, *Power/Knowledge: Selected Interviews and Other Writings, 1972–1977* (New York: Pantheon, 1980).

———, 'What is an author?', trans. Josué V. Harari, in Josué V. Harari (ed.), *Textual Strategies: Perspectives in Post-Structuralist Criticism* (Ithaca: Cornell University Press, 1979).

Franklin, Wayne, *Discoverers, Explorers, Settlers: The Diligent Writers of Early America* (Chicago: Chicago University Press, 1979).

Freud, Sigmund, *Civilization and its Discontents* (Chicago: Chicago University Press, 1979).

———, *Complete Psychological Works: Standard Edition*, trans. and ed. J. Strachey (New York: Norton, 1976).

——, 'A difficulty in the path of psychoanalysis,' S.E. 17:137, in *Complete Psychological Works* (orig. pub. 1917).

——, *The Ego and the Id* (New York: Norton, 1960; orig. pub. 1923).

——, *The Future of an Illusion* (New York: Norton, 1961; orig. pub. 1927).

——, *General Psychological Theory* (New York: Macmillan, 1963).

——, *Group Psychology and the Analysis of the Ego*, S.E. 18:67 (1921).

——, *The Interpretation of Dreams* (New York: Avon, 1980; orig. pub. 1900).

——, *Introductory Lectures on Psychoanalysis* (New York: Norton, 1966; orig. pub. 1916–17).

——, 'Instincts and their vicissitudes,' S.E. 14:111, in *General Psychological Theory* (New York: Macmillan, 1963).

——, 'Mourning and melancholia,' in *Complete Psychological Works* 14: 237–59 (orig. pub. 1917).

——, 'Remembering, repeating, and working through,' in *Complete Psychological Works* 12: 145–56 (orig. pub. 1914).

——, 'The resistance to psychoanalysis,' in *Complete Psychological Works* 19: 213–22 (orig. pub. 1925).

——, *Totem and Taboo*, trans. J. Strachey (New York: Norton, 1963).

——, 'Why war?', in *Complete Psychological Works* 22: 203–18 (orig. pub. 1933).

Gaskell, Elizabeth, *North and South* (Harmondsworth: Penguin, 1970; orig. pub. 1855).

Genette, Gérard, *Figures of Literary Discourse* (New York: Columbia University Press, 1982).

Gilmore, Michael T., 'Property and the Early American Novel' (unpublished paper).

Glacken, Clarence J., *Traces on the Rhodian Shore: Nature and Culture in Western Thought from Ancient Times to the End of the Eighteenth Century* (Berkeley: University of California Press, 1967).

Goethe, Johann Wolfgang von, *The Sorrows of Young Werther* (New York: Signet, 1962; orig. pub. 1774).

Goffman, Erving, *The Presentation of Self in Everyday Life* (New York: Doubleday, 1959).

Goldknopf, David, 'The failure of plot in *Tom Jones*,' in M. Battestin (ed.). *Twentieth-Century Views of Tom Jones* (Englewood Cliffs, NJ: Prentice-Hall, 1968).

Goldsmith, Oliver, *The Vicar of Wakefield* (Harmondsworth: Penguin, 1982; orig. pub. 1766).

Gramsci, Antonio, *The Modern Prince and Other Writings* (New York: International Publishers, 1980).

Greenburg, Joanne, *In This Sign* (New York: Aron, 1972).

Bibliography

Greenson, Ralph R., *Techniques and Practice of Psychoanalysis* (New York: International University Press, 1967).

Greimas, A. J., *Du Sens* (Paris: du Seuil, 1970).

Hall, Stuart, 'Rediscovery of ideology' in *Culture, Media, Language: Working Papers in Cultural Studies 1972–7* (London: Hutchinson, 1980).

Hardy, Thomas, *Far From the Madding Crowd* (New York: Norton, 1985).

Harris, Richard and Rubinstein, David, 'Paralanguage, communication, and cognition,' in Adam Kendon, Richard M. Harris, and Mary Ritchie Key (eds), *Organization of Behavior in Face-to-Face Interactions* (The Hague: Mouton, 1975).

Hart, Adrian Liddle (ed.), *The Sword and the Pen: Selections From the World's Greatest Military Writings* (New York: Crowell, 1976).

Herodotus, *The Histories* (Harmondsworth: Penguin, 1971).

Hilles, Frederick, 'Art and artifice in *Tom Jones,*' in Maynard Mack and Ian Gregor (eds), *Imagined Worlds: Essays on Some English Novels and Novelists in Honour of John Butt* (London: Methuen, 1968).

Hochman, Baruch, *Character in Literature* (Ithaca: Cornell University Press, 1985).

Holder, William, *Elements of Speech: An Inquiry into the Natural Production of Letters* (London: J. Martin, 1669).

Holland, Norman, *The Dynamics of Literary Response* (New York: Norton, 1975).

Howe, Irving, *Politics and the Novel* (New York: Horizon, 1957).

Hugo, Victor, *Les Misérables*, trans. Norman Denny (Harmondsworth: Penguin, 1980; orig. pub. 1862).

Hyde, Louis, *The Gift: Imagination and the Erotic Life of Property* (New York: Random House, 1983).

Ingram, Bruce S. (ed.), *Three Sea Journals of Stuart Times* (London: Constable, 1936).

Iser, Wolfgang, *The Act of Reading: A Theory of Aesthetic Response* (Baltimore: Johns Hopkins University Press, 1978).

James, Henry, 'The novels of George Eliot,' *Atlantic Monthly* (October 1866).

Jameson, Fredric, *The Political Unconscious: Narrative as a Socially Symbolic Act* (Ithaca: Cornell University Press, 1981).

——, *The Prisonhouse of Language* (Princeton: Princeton University Press, 1972).

Jauss, Hans R., *Aesthetic Experience and Literary Hermeneutics*, trans. Michael Shaw (Minneapolis: University of Minnesota Press, 1982).

Keegan, John, *The Face of Battle* (New York: Viking, 1976).

Joyce, James, *Ulysses* (Harmondsworth: Penguin, 1969; orig. pub. 1922).

Kennedy, William, *Ironweed* (New York: Penguin, 1983).

Kermode, Frank, 'Novel and narrative,' in John Halperin (ed.), *The Theory of the Novel: New Essays* (Oxford: Oxford University Press, 1974).

————, *The Sense of An Ending* (Oxford: Oxford University Press, 1967).

Kohut, Heinz, *The Search for the Self: Selected Writings of Heinz Kohut, 1950–1978*, ed. P. Ornstein (New York: International Universities Press, 1978).

Labov, William, *Language in the Inner City: Studies in Black English Vernacular* (Philadelphia: Pennsylvania Press, 1972).

Lasch, Christopher, *The Culture of Narcissism* (New York: Norton, 1979).

————, *The Minimal Self* (New York: Norton, 1984).

Laver, John, 'Communicative functions of phatic conversation,' in Adam Kendon, Richard M. Harris, and Mary Ritchie Key (eds), *Organization of Behavior in Face-to-Face Interactions* (The Hague: Mouton, 1975).

Lawrence, D. H., *Reflections on the Death of a Porcupine* (Bloomington: Indiana University Press, 1963, repr. 1969).

Levine, George, *The Realistic Imagination: English Fiction from Frankenstein to Lady Chatterly* (Chicago: University of Chicago Press, 1981).

Lichtheim, George, *The Concept of Ideology and Other Essays* (New York: Vintage, 1967).

Lieberman, Philip, 'Linguistic and paralinguistic interchange,' in Adam Kendon, Richard M. Harris, and Mary Ritchie Key (eds), *Organization of Behavior in Face-to-Face Interactions* (The Hague: Mouton, 1975).

Locke, John, *Some Thoughts Concerning Education* (London: A. & J. Churchill, 1709).

Lukács, Georg, *Essays on Realism*, ed. Rodney Livingstone, trans. David Fernbach (Cambridge, Mass.: MIT Press, 1980).

————, *The Historical Novel*, trans. H. and S. Mitchell (Lincoln: University of Nebraska Press, 1983).

————, *History and Class Consciousness*, trans. Rodney Livingstone (Cambridge, Mass.: MIT Press, 1971).

————, *Soul and Form*, trans. Anna Bostock (Cambridge, Mass.: MIT Press, 1974).

————, *The Theory of the Novel*, trans. Anna Bostock (Cambridge, Mass.: MIT Press, 1971).

McCullers, Carson, *The Heart is A Lonely Hunter* (Harmondsworth: Penguin, 1981).

Macherey, Pierre, *A Theory of Literary Production*, trans. G. Wall (London: Routledge & Kegan Paul, 1978).

McKendrick, Neil, Brewer, John and Plumb, J. H., *The Birth of A Consumer Society: The Commercialization of Eighteenth-Century England* (London: Europa, 1982).

Macpherson, C. B., *The Rise of Possessive Individualism: Hobbes to Locke* (Oxford: Oxford University Press, 1962).

Bibliography

Malory, Sir Thomas, *Le Morte D'Arthur* (London: Dutton, 1967).

Mannheim, Karl, *Ideology and Utopia* (New York: Harcourt Brace Jovanovich, 1936).

Marcus, Steven, *Freud and the Culture of Psychoanalysis* (Boston: Allen & Unwin, 1984).

———, *Representations* (New York: Random House, 1975).

Margolis, J., *Philosophy of Psychology* (Englewood Cliffs, NJ: Prentice-Hall, 1984).

Martin, Wallace, *Recent Theories of Narrative* (Ithaca: Cornell University Press, 1986).

Marx, Karl, *Theories of Surplus Value; Selections* (New York: International Publishers, 1952).

———, *Capital* (New York: International Publishers, 1968).

———, *A Contribution to the Critique of Political Economy* (repr. New York: International Publishers, 1971).

———, *Grundrisse* (Harmondsworth: Penguin, 1973).

——— and Engels, Friedrich, *The German Ideology*, ed. R. Pascal (New York: International Publishers, 1960).

Maynard, John, *Charlotte Brontë and Sexuality* (Cambridge, Mass.: Harvard University Press, 1984).

Meisner, W. W., 'Notes on identification,' *Psychoanalytic Quarterly* 41 (1972): 224–59.

Miller, Nancy, 'The "I" in drag,' *The Eighteenth Century* (Winter 1981).

Milligan, Jacob, *A Short Description of the Province of South Carolina* (London: John Hinton, 1763), in B. R. Carroll (ed.), *Historical Collections of South Carolina* (New York: Harper Brothers, 1836).

Moerman, Michael and Sacks, Harvey, 'On understanding in the analysis of natural conversation,' in Kinkade, M. D. (ed.), *Linguistics and Anthropology* (Lisse, Holland: Peter de Ridder Press, 1975).

Monboddo, James Burnett, *Of the Origins and Progress of Language* (Menston: English Scholar Press, 1967; orig. pub. 1773).

Mylne, Vivienne, 'The punctuation of dialogue in eighteenth-century French and English fiction,' *The Library: A Quarterly Journal of Bibliography*, 1: 43–61 (1979).

Nadeau, Maurice, *The Greatness of Flaubert*, trans. B. Bray (New York: Open Court, 1972).

Ollman, Bertell, *Alienation: Marx's Conception of Man in Capitalist Society* (Cambridge: Cambridge University Press, 1977).

Patey, Douglas Lance, *Probability and Literary Form: Philosophic Theory and Literary Practice in the Augustan Age* (Cambridge: Cambridge University Press, 1984).

Paulson, Ronald, *Literary Landscape: Turner and Constable* (New Haven: Yale University Press, 1982).

Pavel, Thomas G., *The Poetics of Plot: The Case of English Renaissance Drama* (Minneapolis: University of Minnesota Press, 1985).

Perry, Ruth, *Women, Letters, and the Novel* (New York: AMS Press, 1980).

Petrarch, *Letters*, ed. Morris Bishop (Bloomington: Indiana University Press, 1966).

Piaget, Jean, *The Construction of Reality in the Child* (New York: Basic Books, 1954).

Plato, *The Republic* (Harmondsworth: Penguin, 1970).

Propp, Vladimir V., *Morphology of the Folktale* (Washington: American Folklore Society, 1968).

Ralegh, Sir Walter, *The Discovery of the Large, Rich, and Beautiful Empire of Guiana, with a Relation of the Great and Golden City of Manoa (which the Spaniards call El Dorado)*, ed. Robert H. Schomburgh (New York: Franklin, 1848).

Rank, Otto, *Das Inzest-Motif in Dictung und Sage* (Leipzig and Vienna, 1912).

Richardson, Samuel, *Clarissa* (New York: Houghton Mifflin, 1962; orig. pub. 1748).

———, *Pamela* (Harmondsworth: Penguin, 1980; orig. pub. 1740).

———, *Selected Letters*, ed. John Carroll (Oxford: Oxford University Press, 1963).

Ricoeur, Paul, *Time and Narrative* (Chicago: University of Chicago Press, 1964).

Rimmon-Kenan, Shlomith, *Narrative Fiction: Contemporary Poetics* (London: Methuen, 1983).

Robert, Marthe, *Origins of the Novel*, trans. Sacha Rabinovitch (Bloomington: Indiana University Press, 1980).

Rousseau, Jean-Jacques, *Julie ou la nouvelle Héloïse* (Paris: French & European, 1967; orig. pub. 1765).

Sacks, Harvey, Schegloff, Emanuel A., and Jefferson, Gail, 'A simplest systematic for the organization of turn taking for conversation,' in J. Schenkein (ed.), *Studies in the Organization of Conversational Interaction* (New York: Academic Press, 1978).

Said, Edward W., *Beginnings: Intention and Method* (New York: Basic, 1975).

———, *Orientalism* (New York: Pantheon, 1978).

Salinger, J. D., *The Catcher in the Rye* (Harmondsworth: Penguin, 1969; orig. pub. 1951).

Salzman, Paul, *English Prose Fiction 1558–1700: A Critical History* (Oxford: Clarendon Press, 1985).

Sartre, Jean-Paul, *Nausea* (Harmondsworth: Penguin, 1970; orig. pub. 1935).

Bibliography

Schegloff, Emanuel, and Sacks, Harvey, 'Opening up closings,' in Roy Turner (ed.), *Ethnomethodology: Selected Readings* (Harmondsworth: Penguin, 1974).

Scholes, Robert, and Kellogg, Robert, *The Nature of Narrative* (Oxford: Oxford University Press, 1966).

Shakespeare, William, *The Tempest* (New York: Dutton, 1954).

Shelley, Mary, *Frankenstein* (Berkeley: University of California Press, 1984; orig. pub. 1818).

Sill, Geoffrey, *Defoe and the Idea of Fiction* (New Brunswick: Rutgers University Press, 1983).

Sitter, John, *Literary Loneliness in Mid Eighteenth-Century England* (Ithaca: Cornell University Press, 1982).

Slater, Phillip, *The Glory of Hera: Greek Mythology and the Greek Family* (Boston: Beacon Press, 1968).

Smith, Barbara Herrnstein, *On the Margins of Discourse* (Chicago: University of Chicago Press, 1978).

Smollett, Tobias, *Humphrey Clinker* (Harmondsworth: Penguin, 1971; orig. pub. 1771).

Snitow, Ann, 'Mass market romance: pornography for women is different,' in Ann Snitow, Christine Stansell, and Sharon Thompson (eds), *Powers of Desire: The Politics of Sexuality* (New York: Monthly Review Press, 1983).

Southall, Raymond, *Literature, The Individual, and Society* (London: Lawrence & Wishart, 1977).

Spacks, Patricia Meyer, *Imagining a Self: Autobiography and the Novel in Eighteenth-Century England* (Cambridge, Mass.: Harvard University Press, 1976).

Stafford, Barbara Maria, *Voyage Into Substance: Art, Science, Nature, and the Illustrated Travel Account 1760–1840* (Cambridge, Mass.: MIT Press, 1984).

Starr, G. A., *Defoe and Spiritual Autobiography* (Princeton: Princeton University Press, 1965).

Steele, Joshua, *Prosodia Rationalis* (English Scholar Press, 1969; orig. pub. 1779).

Sterne, Lawrence, *The Life and Opinions of Tristram Shandy* (Harmondsworth: Penguin, 1970; orig. pub. 1760–7).

Stierle, Karlheinz, 'The reading of fictional texts,' in Susan R. Suleiman and Inge Crosman (eds), *The Reader in the Text: Essays on Audience and Interpretation* (Princeton: Princeton University Press, 1980).

Stone, Lawrence, *The Family, Sex, and Marriage in England 1500–1800* (New York: Harper & Row, 1977).

Suleiman, Susan R., *Authoritarian Fictions: The Ideological Novel as a Literary Genre* (New York: Columbia University Press, 1983).

————— and Crosman, Inge (eds), *The Reader in the Text: Essays on Audience and Interpretation* (Princeton: Princeton University Press, 1980).

Swift, Jonathan, *Poetical Works*, ed. Herbert Davis (Oxford: Oxford University Press, 1967).

—————, *Gulliver's Travels* (New York: Norton, 1970; orig. pub. 1726).

Thackeray, William Makepeace, *Vanity Fair* (Harmondsworth: Penguin, 1968; orig. pub. 1848).

Thompson, James, 'Jane Austen and the limits of language,' *Journal of English and German Philology* (forthcoming).

Thomson, George, *Aeschylus and Athens* (London: Lawrence & Wishart, 1973).

Todorov, Tzvetan, *The Conquest of America* (New York: Harper & Row, 1984).

Trilling, Lionel, *The Opposing Self: Nine Essays in Criticism* (New York: Harcourt Brace Jovanovich, 1950).

Tuan, Yu-Fu, *Topophilia: A Study of Environmental Perception, Attitude, and Values* (Englewood Cliffs, NJ: Prentice-Hall, 1974).

Turner, A. Richard, *The Vision of Landscape in Renaissance Italy* (Princeton: Princeton University Press, 1966).

Van der Donck, Adriaen, *A Description of the New Netherlands* (Amsterdam: Evert Nieuwenhof, 1656), trans. Jeremiah Johnson in Thomas F. O'Donnel (ed.), *Collections of the New York Historical Society* 2nd ser., vol. I (Syracuse: Syracuse University Press, 1968).

Van Zandt, Roland, *The Catskill Mountain House* (New Brunswick: Rutgers University Press, 1966).

Vico, Giambattista, *The New Science* (Cambridge: Cambridge University Press, 1975).

Walker, Alice, *The Color Purple* (London: The Women's Press, 1983).

Warren, Leland, 'Turning reality round together: guides to conversation in eighteenth-century England,' *Eighteenth Century Life*, new ser., vol. VIII, (May 1983): 65–87.

Watt, Ian, *The Rise of the Novel* (Berkeley: University of California Press, 1964).

Watts, Cedric, *The Deceptive Text: An Introduction to Covert Plots* (Brighton: Harvester, 1984).

Webb, Igor, *From Custom to Capital: The English Novel and the Industrial Revolution* (Ithaca: Cornell University Press, 1981).

Weimann, Robert, *Structure and Society in Literary History* (Baltimore: Johns Hopkins University Press, 1976, rev. edn 1984).

Wein, Cathy, 'The interplay of affect and cognition in the development of identity as revealed in children's figure drawings' (unpublished Ph.D. thesis; City University of New York, 1983).

Welsch, Alexander, *The Hero of the Waverly Novels* (rev. edn New Haven: Yale University Press, 1968).

White, Hayden, *Metahistory: The Historical Imagination in Nineteenth-Century Europe* (Baltimore: Johns Hopkins University Press, 1974).

Williams, Raymond, *Marxism and Literature* (Oxford: Oxford University Press, 1977).

——, *The Sociology of Culture* (New York: Schocken, 1982).

Winnicott, D. W., *The Child, the Family and the Outside World* (Harmondsworth: Penguin, 1964).

Xenophon, *The Persian Expedition (Anabasis)*, trans. Rex Warner (Harmondsworth: Penguin, 1972).

Zipes, Jack, *Breaking the Magic Spell: Radical Theories of Folk and Fairy Tales* (London: Heinemann, 1979).

Zola, Emile, *Germinal*, trans. L. W. Tancock (Harmondsworth: Penguin, 1969).

Index

Index

Index

Index

novelists 137–49

Oedipal conflict 126, 129–30, 132, 145
Ollman, Bertell 30
'omnipotence of thought' 121

painting: Indian, views on 81; landscape 73–7, 78, 79–80, 101; as property 101; representation of objects in 71
Paris 64–5; Balzac's 89; Hugo's 92
Paulson, Ronald 74
Pavel, Thomas 206
Perry, Ruth 140, 241n
personality 111f
Petrarch
    Ascent of Mount Ventoux 59
photographs 156
physical description 121–4
Piaget, Jean 127–8
place *see* location
Plato
    The Republic 133
plot: Aristotelian view 197–9; centrality of self 202; and chaos 222; and character 196; choice 219; as commodity 202–4, 211–12, 218; compared with epic 200–1, 205; concept of 194f; 'consecutive' form 205–6; derivation of word 201; distinctness of structure in novel 192f; and folktales 199, 200–1, 236–8; and idea of history 212–21; and modernism 220–2; and probability 203; reader-response critique 197, 200, 219; repetition in 18–19; and Russian Formalists 195, 197, 199–200; and Structuralists 195–6; teleological 206–12, 220–2; and time 218
Plumb, J. H. 204
Poe, Edgar Alan 210
professionalization of novelist 142–9
property 62–3, 87–101 *see also* commodity
Propp, Vladimir 192, 196, 197, 199, 206

psychoanalysis 13–14, 18, 19, 112, 121
Puritans 11–12, 16–17, 66, 121, 219

Ralegh, Sir Walter 72–3
Rambo 235
Rank, Otto 129
reader *see* novel reader
recognition 118–21
reification 133–4, 174
repetition 18–19, 205
resistance: to novel reading 15–19; political and psychic differentiated 12–13
Richardson, Samuel 203, 218–19, 240n
    Clarissa 116, 135, 141, 171, 173
    Pamela 119, 124, 135, 141, 173, 188, 189, 208
Ricoeur, Paul 199, 212, 213
Rimmon-Kenan, Shlomith 192, 206, 218
Robbe-Grillet, Alain 222
Robert, Marthe 129, 225–6
Rogers, Francis 76
Rousseau, Jean-Jacques 186
    La Nouvelle Héloïse 233
Rowson, Susanna 18
Rubenstein, David 175
Russian Formalists 195, 197, 199–200

Said, Edward 63, 137, 152
Salinger, J. D.
    The Catcher in the Rye 141
Salzman, Paul 207
Sartre, Jean-Paul
    La Nausée 208–9
Saussure, Ferdinand de 42
Scholes, Robert 205
Scott, Sir Walter 141
self and other 3–5, 21
Shakespeare, William
    The Tempest 59
    Twelfth Night 211
Shelley, Mary
    Frankenstein 144, 148
Sherlock Holmes stories 209–10
shorthand 171
Silkwood 234
Sill, Geoffrey 62